the difference
더 디퍼런스
더 좋은 책을 만들기 위한 남다른 열정

빠르고 정확한 독해를 위한

Just
READING

1

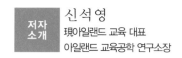

신석영
現아일랜드 교육 대표
아일랜드 교육공학 연구소장

주요저서
Just Reading 1, 2, 3 (전 3권)
Just Grammar Starter 1, 2, 3 (전 3권)
I can Reading 1, 2, 3, 4 (전 4권)
I can Grammar 1, 2, 3, 4 (전 4권 / 메가스터디 Mbest 인터넷 강의교재)
Easy I can Grammar 1, 2, 3, 4 (전 4권)
한국에서 유일한 중학 영문법 (전 6권)
한국에서 유일한 고교 영문법 (전 2권)
Easy I'm your grammar (원서 전 3권 / 대만 수출 / 메가스터디 Mjunior 인터넷 강의교재)
Easy I'm your grammar Workbook (전 3권)
You're my grammar (원서 전 3권)
You're my grammar Workbook (전 3권)

Just Reading HR●**1**

지은이　신석영
발행인　조상현
발행처　더디퍼런스

등록번호　제2015-000237호
주소　서울시 마포구 마포대로 127, 304호
문의　02-725-9988
팩스　02-6974-1237
이메일　thedibooks@naver.com
홈페이지　www.thedifference.co.kr

ISBN 979-11-86217-19-1 (53740)

빠르고 정확한 독해를 위한

Just READING

1

신석영 지음

더디퍼런스

PROLOGUE

"꿈에 젖은 수년보다 강렬한 한 시간이 더 많은 것을 이룬다"라는 말이 생각납니다. 지금 누구보다도 강렬한 인생을 살고 있는 학생들이 아닌가 싶습니다. 대학을 목표로 열심히 공부하는 학습자들에게는 공부를 잘하는 방법과 어떻게 준비하고 대처를 해야 좋은 점수를 받을 수 있을까? 하는 의문과 절실함은 항상 변함이 없습니다. 똑같은 노력과 주어진 시간이 같다면 좀 더 효과적으로 공부할 수 있도록 도움을 줄 수 있는 안내자와 같은 좋은 책과 선생님들이 절실히 필요할 때입니다. "한 권의 책이 사람의 인생을 바꿀 수도 있다"는 말이 있습니다.

이 책은 저자들이 직접 현장에서 오랜 세월동안 직접 가르치며 만들었습니다. 아이들과 함께 울고, 웃고, 기뻐하며 힘들고 행복했던 시간들을 함께 하면서 조금씩 다듬어 나갔습니다.

힘든 곳과 아픈 곳을 직접 어루만지며 또한 학생들에게서 더 많은 가르침을 받은 저자들이 그것을 해소할 수 있도록 심혈을 기울였습니다.

영어를 잘 듣고, 말하고, 쓰기 위해서는 많이 읽어야 합니다. 영어는 읽어 이해할 수 있는 속도와 정확도의 범위만큼만 들리며, 읽은 내용이 숙지되면 회화가 이루어지고, 글로 표현하면 영작이 따라오게 됩니다. 독해영역이 상당히 별개의 분야처럼 이해되어 회화와 영작도 별도의 훈련이 필요한 것처럼 여겨져 왔는데, 이와 같은 고정관념을 깨는 대수술이 필요합니다. 크라센(Crashen)이라는 언어학자는 '많이 읽을 것'을 강조합니다. 그는 배경지식을 알고, 읽어서 이해할 수 있는 영문을 많이 읽는 것이 영어 정복의 지름길임을 지적합니다. 오늘날 싱가포르의 영어 실력이 이를 증명하는데, 싱가포르의 리콴유 전 총리는 학교 교실 뒤에 영문서적을 수십, 수백 권을 비치해 두고 읽기 교육을 시켰습니다. 우리나라는 우선 말해야 한다는 강박관념에 사로잡혀 읽기 교육이 안 되고 있는 현실입니다.

대학 수학능력 시험과 토플, 토익과 같은 시험에서의 관건은 다양한 지문을 얼마나 많이 접하고 또 얼마나 빨리 이해하느냐에 달려 있습니다. 가장 좋은 방법은 쉬운 지문부터 단계별로 공부하면서 영어 독해와 영작 그리고 듣기에 대한 자신감을 가지도록 하는 것입니다. 그런데 현재 영어 교육은 학습자 중심이 아닌 현실과 동떨어져 있고 학습자에 대한 세심한 배려나 사랑이 없어 보입니다. 학습자들은 처음부터 어려운 지문을 접하게 되거나, 흥미없는 소재를 바탕으로 단계학습을 하게 되는데, 그런 이유로 영어를 몇 년을 배워도 투자한 시간과 노력에 비하여 드러나는 학습효과가 실로 미미합니다. 이에 따라, 학생들은 영어가 주는 재미를 느낄 수 없을 뿐 아니라, 오히려 스트레스만 늘어갈 뿐입니다. 당연히 학교시험과 '영어 자체'에는 늘 자신 없어합니다.

Just Reading 시리즈는 이런 학생들을 위해 정밀하게 제작된 Reading 교재입니다. 수능과 TOEFL, TOEIC에 맞춘 지문과 문제는 학생들에게 실제적인 도움을 줄 것입니다.

사실, 저자들의 목표와 이상은 더 높은 곳에 있습니다. 우리가 안고 있는 근본적인 문제는 학습분위기 저변에 깔린 비판적 성향과, 고정된 사고방식 그리고 검증되지 않은 낡은 선입견들입니다. 한 언어가 자리 잡기 위해서는 다양한 과정이 요구되는데 그 중 가장 중요한 부분은 실제 많은 훈련을 할 수 있는 기회와 학습자의 자신감입니다.

언어는 말이요, 말은 정신이요, 정신은 사상입니다. 사상은 인격을 만듭니다. 생소한 언어체계가 우리의 뇌에 자리 잡기까지는 많은 양의 독서를 필요로 합니다. 이 교재는 학습자들이 다양한 범교과서적인 소재를 읽고 즐기는 동시에 많은 도움 장치들로 구성되어 있음을 밝혀 둡니다. 단순한 대학입시가 목적이 아닌 하나의 과정으로 더 큰 꿈과 미래를 향해 나아갈 대한민국 모든 학생들에게 응원을 보냅니다.

마지막으로 이 책의 문법 설명 중 상당수는 김성은 님의 저서 '브릿지 베이직'에서 우수한 해석 원리 기법을 허락 하에 인용하였습니다. 현재도 영어교육을 위해 헌신을 하고 계시고 더 좋은 영어교육을 위해 해석 원리 기법 사용을 허락해 주셔서 다시 한번 깊은 감사를 드립니다.

대표저자 신 석 영

About **Reading** I
독해를 위한 공부 방법

독해력 이란? 독해력은 Reading Power, 즉 '읽어 이해할 수 있는 능력'을 말한다. 많은 학생들이 '독해'가 무엇인지를 물어보면 십중팔구 읽고 해석하는 것, 읽고 번역하는 것이라 한다. 지금까지 수능, 토익, 토플 같은 시험에서는 한번도 '읽고 해석'하는 시험을 낸 적이 없다. Reading Comprehension, 즉 읽고 이해하는 것이 독해이다. reading의 첫 출발은 '글을 쓴 작가의 의도'를 파악하는 것, 글을 통하여 작가의 중요한 생각(main idea)을 알아내는 것이다. 고난도 독해력 측정이라는 것은 이러한 글의 중요성을 파악하고 추론해내는 능력이 있는지를 측정하는 것을 가리킨다. 왜 main idea를 통해 독해력을 측정하는 것일까? 이는 이러한 정도의 수준 높은 문제를 풀 줄 아는 학생이 대학의 학문을 이해할 수 있을 것으로 판단하기 때문이다.

독해에 필요한 필수 요소는 무엇인가?

독해도 요령이 있어야 글 속에서 헤매지 않고 주제를 파악할 수 있다. 유명한 그리스 신화에서 테세우스는 동굴의 괴물을 죽이려고 들어갔다가 살아온 유일한 사람인데, 그는 연인이 준 실을 가지고 갔다가 나중에 그 실을 따라 나옴으로써 죽음의 미로에서 살아나왔다고 한다. 학생들이 지문을 대하면 미로와 같고 문장들은 복잡한 통로와 같을 것이다. 이때 실과 같은 요령을 터득한다면 미로와 같은 지문 속에서 명쾌한 해답을 찾을 수 있을 것이다.

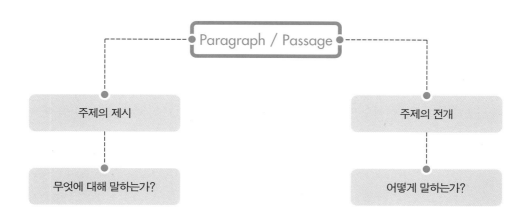

1 이 글은 무엇에 관한 것인가?

주제 문장(Topic Sentence/Main idea)이란, 주제(Topic)가 포함된 문장으로, 그 글이나 단락의 내용이 무엇에 관한 것인가를 함축적으로 대변하는 문장이다. 따라서, 이 주제 문장을 통해 글을 읽는 독자는 그 글이 어떤 내용인가를 예상할 수 있고, 글을 쓰는 작가는 하나의 생각(idea)에 충실한 글을 쓸 수 있게 된다.

또한, 주제 문장은 사실(fact)보다는 대개 글쓴이의 견해(opinion)가 들어 있는 문장으로, 주제(topic)와 이에 대한 제한 진술(controlling statement)로 구성된다.

주제를 더욱 짧게 요약하면 그것이 제목(Title)이 된다. 그 외에 Topic/Key Point 등으로 표현할 수 있다. 제목은 어떠한 글에서든지 지문을 중요한 하나의 요소로 통합시키는 것이 된다. 따라서 제목은 간단한 몇 단어로 나타내야 한다.

2 작가는 제목에 대해서 어떤 생각을 말하려고 하는가?

제목, 즉 글쓴이가 어떠한 것에 대해 말하려고 할 때, 그 말하려는 자신의 생각이 곧 주제(Main idea)가 된다. 이것은 주제문으로 표현이 되는데, 제목을 문장으로 나타내는 것이 주제문이다. '무엇이 어떠하다'라고 표현한다. 제목을 묻는 문제가 중요한 이유는 제목을 옳게 파악할 수 있다면 글의 중요한 요소를 파악하고 있는 것으로 볼 수 있기 때문이다.

3 자신의 생각을 어떻게 표현하는가?

글쓴이는 주로 글의 첫머리 부분에 '화젯거리'를 제시한다. '화젯거리(Controlling Statement)'는 마찬가지로 주제에 해당되는데 자신의 주장을 화젯거리로 제시하고 이를 논리적으로 납득할 수 있는 다양한 설명으로 주제를 뒷받침해 주는 문장들로 구성된다. 이러한 문장 구성 요소들을 Supporting Sentences라고 한다. 주제를 뒷받침해 주는 보충, 부연 설명이 연이어 나오는데, 흔히 독해 문제에서 본문의 내용과 일치/불일치를 물어보는 문제는 이러한 세부적인 보충설명을 올바로 이해하는지를 측정하는 문제이다.

전체 Supporting details(보충·부연 설명 문장)가 글의 주제와 논리적으로 잘 구성되어 하나의 흐름으로 연결이 잘 되었다면 이것을 우리는 '통일성'을 잘 갖춘 글이라고 한다. 문단은 하나의 주제문(Topic sentence)을 중심으로 하여 각 문장들이 주제문을 뒷받침하도록 관련성 있게 구성되어 있어야 한다. 비약을 하거나 논지에 어긋나는 문장이 나오는 경우가 있다. 이러한 문장은 제거하거나 수정해야 한다. 글쓰기와 교정 능력을 간접 평가하기 위해 자주 출제되고 있다.

4 내가 읽은 내용을 통해 어떤 결론을 추론해낼 수 있는가?

글의 도입부분에서 화젯거리, 즉 작가의 main idea를 파악하고 이것을 뒷받침해 주는 보충·부연 설명글을 모두 이해했다면 그 글에 대한 결론(Concluding Sentence)을 내릴 수 있어야 한다. 이때 결론은 글속에 제시되어 있을 수도 있고, 결론을 추론해내야 하는 경우도 있다. 결론을 묻는 문제는 파악했던 주제와 내용과 의미가 같아야 한다. 내가 읽은 내용과 거리가 멀다면 주제에서도, 결론에서도 벗어나 있다고 판단해야 한다. 함정 문제에서는 일반적인 타당성 있는 결론을 제시하기도 하는데, 반드시 글의 주제와 관련된 결론을 유추해내는 것이 중요하다.

About **Reading** II

독해 원리 정리

Paragraph 구성 원리

Main Idea / Controlling Statement 주제문

Support sentence

Support sentence

Support sentence

Support sentence

Support sentence

Concluding Sentence 결론 문장

❶ 하나의 단락(문단)은 몇 개의 문장이 모여 하나의 주제(핵심사상)를 다룬다.

❷ 단락은 일관된 하나의 주제와 그것을 보충 설명하는 문장들로 구성된다.

❸ 보충 설명하는 문장을 다시 세부적으로 보충하거나, 예를 드는 문장이 있다.

●●● 어떤 글에서, 글쓴이가 말하거나 설명하려는 것이 그 글의 주제(main idea) 가 된다. 이것은 글을 쓰는 사람의 입장에서 보면 글쓴이가 말하고자 하는 것이 무엇 인지를 전달하고 독자의 입장에서 보면 이 글이 무엇에 관한 것인지를 알게 한다.

About **Just Reading Series** ┃

시리즈의 특징

1 **각 Level별 65개의 실생활과 관련된 재미있는 독해 지문**

각 Level별로 65개의 지문으로 구성되어 있으며, 5개의 지문이 하나의 Chapter로 이루어져 있다. 재미있는 주제와 다소 딱딱한 역사, 인물에 대한 지문까지 세밀화 된 단계에 맞는 수준의 지문을 실었다. 유익한 지문을 통해 학생들은 다양한 시사, 문화, 역사, 인물, 사회, 과학 분야를 모두 배울 수 있도록 균형 있게 배치되어 있어, 어떠한 유형의 독해 문제라도 당황하지 않고 대처할 수 있는 자기훈련의 기회를 제공하여 재미있게 공부할 수 있다.

2 **수능 기출 문제 수록**

각 Chapter 별로 수능 기출 문제와 응용 문제가 수록되어 있다. 특히 독해력을 측정하는 문제가 큰 비중을 차지하면서, 문제 출제도 사고력을 배양할 수 있도록 응용문제를 실어 원하는 대학 진학을 희망하는 학생들에게 도전정신과 자신감을 심어 줄 수 있도록 구성되었다.

3 **종합적 사고력, 분석력, 이해력을 획기적으로 길러 줄 참신한 문제**

화제와 주제 파악에 중점을 두되, 본문 내의 빈칸 추론하기, 요약하기, 어법(어휘) 문제, 논술형 문제, 결론 문제의 출제의도를 밝혀 놓아 독해력 측정의 여러 문제 유형에 자신있게 대처할 수 있도록 하였다. 수능에 출제되는 모든 영역과 영어 제시문을 통해 각종 영어 시험에 대비할 수 있도록 구성되었다.

4 **지문을 난이도에 따라 적절히 배열**

각 Level을 세밀하게 나누어 영어에 대한 두려움을 쉽게 극복하도록 하였다. 각 Chapter 별 마지막 지문은 200자 이상의 장문으로 구성하여 지문에 대한 종합적인 분석이 가능하게 하였고, HR • 3에서는 장문이 2개씩 구성되어 풍부한 읽을 거리를 통해 단계적인 실력 향상에 도움이 될 것이다.

5 **선생님 · 학생 · 학부모 모두가 참여할 수 있는 교재**

기존의 교재들은 항상 집필자가 이끌어가는 단방향적인 교재였으나 본 교재는 위 삼자가 교재 중심으로 들어와서 서로 대화할 수 있도록 Check Box를 Chapter 별로 두어 학습의 효과를 높이도록 하였다.

About **Just Reading Series** ll

구성의 특징

Preview's Word

단어도 모르면서 영어한다 하지 마!

각 Chapter에 필요한 단어를 미리 공부하고 스스로 테스트할 수
있도록 구성. 단순한 암기보다는 collocation으로 의미 단위 어휘
확인이 가능하도록 하였다. 학생들은 단어를 지루하고 어려운 것
이 아닌 '살아 있는 말'로 인식하게 될 것이며, 이러한 과정은 사
고력 증진에 상당한 도움이 될 것이다.

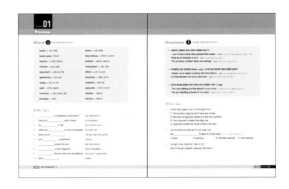

Preview's Grammar

기본 문법도 모르면서 독해한다 하지 마!

다양한 지문을 접하기 전에 핵심 문법을 미리 예문을 통해 익힌 후
간단한 문제를 통해 점검할 수 있도록 하였다. 제시된 문제는 수능
어법 유형으로 간단히 확인 테스트를 할 수 있게 구성하였다.

본문 속 단어

단어 조사해 오셔!

보통의 책은 지문 밑에 단어 해설을 정리해놓은 것이 보통이나,
핵심 단어를 학생들이 스스로 조사해올 수 있도록 하였으며 이는
실제 수업에서 선생님이 숙제를 내주실 부분이다. 이렇게 하는 목
적은 어휘는 한두 가지의 의미만을 내포하고 있는 것이 아닌 다양
한 지문과, 상황에 따라 그 의미가 결정되므로 독해 속 지문을 통
해 학습자가 어휘의 뜻을 추론해보는 것 또한 사고력 향상을 위해
반드시 필요한 부분이다.

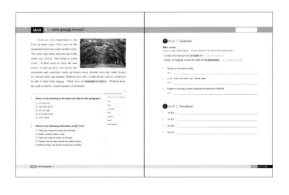

Drill 1 • Grammar

〈구문 독해 + 어휘 + 영작 + 해석 연습〉이 통합적으로 이루어지
도록 구성하였다. 독해 해석 후 문제 풀이만 하면 끝나는 것이 아
니라, 각 Unit마다 자가 학습 및 숙제를 내주어 학부형에게 확인
을 받아 오는 시스템이다. 전통적인 문법이 아닌 현대식 영어로
영어와 한국어의 유사점을 비교·설명하여 우리나라 학습자들이
가장 난감해 하는 영문 구조들을 확실하게 연습할 수 있다.

Drill 2 • Translation

본문 속에 있는 핵심 문장을 미리 한글로 해석 연습을 하는 코너
이다. 번역가가 될 필요는 없지만, 고민하면서 해석해보는 연습이
정확한 독해에 상당한 도움이 될 것이다.

Review Test

각 Chapter에서 배운 어휘와 구문, 문법을 복습, 확인하는 코너
이다. 현장수업에서는 Weekly 테스트 또는 Daily 테스트로 활용
하여 학생들의 실력과 복습 정도를 확인, 점검할 수 있다.

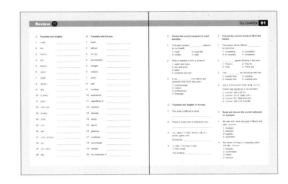

Check Box

부모의 학습 참여가 학생들의 학습에 상당한 긍정적 영향이 있다
는 연구 결과가 있었듯이, 본 교재에서는 숙제 및 학습 과정 이수
를 반드시 학부형 사인을 받아 선생님께 확인 받도록 하여 학생들
의 학습 효과를 극대화하도록 하였다.

CHAPTER

01

Word 🏠 단어도 모르면서 영어 한다 하지 마!

☐ **harsh** *a.* 거친, 가혹한

☐ **wash away** 씻어내다

☐ **various** *a.* 다양한, 다방면의

☐ **mixture** *n.* 혼합, 혼합물

☐ **argument** *n.* 논쟁, 논의, 주장

☐ **agreement** *n.* 동의, 합의

☐ **range** *n.* 범위, 열, 연속

☐ **split** *v.* 쪼개다, 분할하다

☐ **common** *a.* 공통의, 평범한, 흔한

☐ **broaden** *v.* 넓히다

☐ **press** *n.* 신문, 출판물

☐ **discontinue** *v.* 중지하다, 그만하다

☐ **publish** *v.* 출판하다, 발표하다

☐ **newspaper** *n.* 신문, 신문사

☐ **effort** *n.* 노력, 수고, 분투

☐ **heavenly** *a.* 하늘의, 천국의

☐ **material** *n.* 물질, 재료

☐ **separate** *v.* 가르다, 분리하다

☐ **release** *v.* 방출하다

☐ **revolve** *v.* 회전하다

⠿ Mini Quiz

1 _____ a newspaper subscription　　신문 구독을 중단하다

2 have a(n) _____ with a friend　　친구와 말다툼하다

3 be _____ in half　　반으로 쪼개지다(나뉘다)

4 within the _____ of one's knowledge　　지식의 범위 안에

5 take a lot of _____　　(어떤 일이) 많은 노력이 필요하다

6 a(n) _____ punishment　　가혹한 벌

7 _____ around the sun　　태양 주위를 공전하다

8 _____ a new magazine　　새로운 잡지를 발행하다

9 _____ the two boys who are fighting　　싸우고 있는 두 소년을 떼어놓다

10 labor _____　　노동협약

Grammar 👨 기본 문법도 모르면서 독해한다 하지 마!

★ 다양하게 사용되는 **that** 어떻게 이해해야 하는가?

I *can't believe* **that she passed the exam**. 〈목적어〉 나는 그녀가 시험을 통과했다는 것을 믿을 수 없다.

That he is honest *is* true. 〈주어〉 그가 정직하다는 것은 사실이다.

The problem *is* **that I have no money**. 〈보어〉 문제는 내가 돈이 없다는 것이다.

★ 우리말에는 없는 현재완료 〈**have + p.p.**〉, 과거의 일이 현재에 어떻게 영향을 미칠까?

I **have** never **seen** anything like that before. 〈경험〉 나는 저렇게 생긴 것은 전에 본 적이 없다.

He **has known** her since last year. 〈계속〉 그는 그녀를 작년부터 알고 지냈다.

★ 명사의 동작을 설명할 때 명사 뒤에 쓰이는 현재분사 〈명사 + **-ing**〉

The man **sitting on the bench** *is* my uncle. 그 벤치에 앉아 있는 사람은 우리 삼촌이다.

The girl **reading a book** *is* my sister. 책을 읽고 있는 소녀가 나의 여동생이다.

∷ Mini Quiz

1   다음 중 밑줄 친 <u>that</u>의 쓰임이 나머지와 <u>다른</u> 하나는?

① The trouble is <u>that</u> we don't have any money.

② She told me <u>that</u> she wanted to meet her boyfriend.

③ This computer is better than <u>that</u> one.

④ <u>That</u> God created the whole world is not clear.

2   다음 우리말에 맞게 빈칸을 채울 때 가장 적절한 것은?

We _____ English for three years. 우리는 3년 동안 영어를 배우고 있다.

① learn   ② learning   ③ had been learned   ④ have learned

3   다음 괄호 안에서 어법에 맞는 것을 고르시오.

Who is the girl [played / playing] the piano?

[1] Trees are very important to our lives in many ways. First, trees in the mountains keep rain water in their roots. The water stays there and runs out of the earth very slowly. This helps to form rivers. [2] If there were no trees, the rain water would quickly run down the mountains and sometimes wash our houses away. Second, trees also make homes for various birds and animals. Without trees, they would all die, and we would not be able to hear birds singing. [3] Third, trees are beautiful to look at. [4] Without them, the earth would be a much harsher environment.

1 **Which of the following is the best main idea for this paragraph?**

① 강의 생성 과정
② 산림 보호의 중요성
③ 조류 보호 방법
④ 홍수의 원인과 결과
⑤ 나무의 유용성

2 **Which of the following information is NOT true?**

① Trees are homes for birds and animals.
② Water is kept in trees' roots.
③ Trees can help us wash our houses.
④ People and animals cannot live without trees.
⑤ Without trees, we would not see any animals.

단어 조사해 오세요~ **Word**

root
stay
run down
form
various
harsh
environment

Drill 1 Grammar

형용사 + to do

to부정사가 형용사 뒤에 위치할 때 '~하기에' 로 해석한다. 이를 부정사의 부사적 용법이라 한다.

- Is this river *dangerous* to swim in? 이 강은 수영하기에 위험합니까?
- Some of English words are *difficult* to pronounce. 몇몇 영어단어들은 발음하기 어렵다.

---

1   Gimchi is not hard to make.

해석 ◎ _____

2   이 차는 운전하기에 안전하지 않다. (drive, safe)

영작 ◎ _____

3   English is not easy to learn because the grammar is difficult.

해석 ◎ _____

Drill 2 Translation

1   1번 문장 ◎ _____

2   2번 문장 ◎ _____

3   3번 문장 ◎ _____

4   4번 문장 ◎ _____

Unit 2 빛의 숨은 비밀

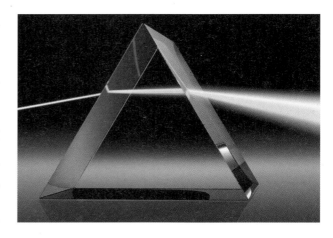

The light that we get from the sun is white. But white has a lot of colors. [1] In 1666, Newton used a glass prism to split sunlight into a range of colors. This is called a spectrum. [2] By doing this, he was able to show that white light is a mixture of all the colors of the rainbow. Raindrops can act like natural prisms, so if there is sunshine and rain, a rainbow may be formed. There have always been _____ about how many colors there are in a rainbow. Often people say there are seven: red, orange, yellow, green, blue, indigo, and violet. [3] In fact, there are millions of colors in a rainbow. [4] But we only have names for some of them.

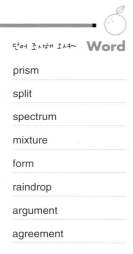

1 What is the best word for the blank?

① arguments
② agreements
③ stories
④ contracts
⑤ legends

2 Write T if the statement is true or F if it's false.

(1) _____ The light that we get from the sun is white. It has only one color.

(2) _____ Newton showed that light is a mixture of all the colors of the rainbow.

단어 조사해 오셔~ **Word**

prism

split

spectrum

mixture

form

raindrop

argument

agreement

Drill 1 Grammar

there is[are] + N(주어)

〈There + be동사〉의 be동사는 대표적인 1형식 동사로, '있다 ~가' 라는 의미를 표현하는 대표적인 구문이다.

- There is *a man* who wears only one sock. 한 쪽 양말만 신는 남자가 있다.

- There are *many magazines* for you to read in the train. 당신이 기차에서 읽을 많은 잡지가 있다.

1   There are some books to read.

    해석 ◎ _____

2   There are seven days in a week.

    해석 ◎ _____

3   버스를 기다리는 많은 사람들이 있었다. (lots of, waiting, people, bus)

    영작 ◎ _____

Drill 2 Translation

1   1번 문장 ◎ _____

2   2번 문장 ◎ _____

3   3번 문장 ◎ _____

4   4번 문장 ◎ _____

[1] While you are traveling outside of your country, you may find that there are universal common values regardless of cultural differences. For example, honor, love, justice, and courtesy, all of which are valued highly in our society, are also regarded as valuable in other countries. [2] But some people in one country cannot understand that people in another country have the same value systems because the way those values are shaped and handled is different. If you travel to another country, however, you will be able to better understand its culture, and to learn that the people in that country _____. This will be the greatest gain of travel. [3] Travel always broadens and expands our minds because new experiences allow us to view things differently.

1 이 글의 빈칸에 가장 적절한 것은?

① learn how to speak other languages
② experience the culture or customs in that country
③ have the same value systems you have
④ understand a variety of languages
⑤ have the same summer vacation

2 What is the greatest benefit of travel in the paragraph?

① learning about general values
② learning the ability to solve problems
③ learning about different food
④ learning the importance of understanding and cooperation
⑤ understanding the value of culture

단어 조사해 오셔~ **Word**

honor

universal

common

valuable

regardless of

justice

courtesy

broaden

expand

experience

🍴 Drill 1 Grammar

명사절 접속사 that

접속사 that이 이끄는 절이 문장에서 주어, 목적어, 보어 자리에 들어갈 수 있다. 즉, 문장 맨 앞에 또는 동사 뒤에 위치하게 된다. that절 안에 있는 주어, 동사를 해석해서 '주어 + 동사 라는 것', '주어 + 동사 라고' 의 뜻으로 해석해 주면 된다.

> [That ... V2 ...] + V1 + [that ... V3 ...] - that 앞에 명사가 없다.
> '~것, ~라는 것'   '~것, ~라는 것'

- **That she is honest** *is* true.   그녀가 정직하다는 것은 사실이다.

- The doctor *advised* **that the patient should exercise**.   의사는 그 환자가 운동을 해야만 한다고 충고했다.

1 I believe that you will do better next time.

   해석 ◎ _____

2 The problem is that he is sick.

   해석 ◎ _____

3 그녀가 미래에 좋은 대학에 들어가리라는 것은 가능하다. (enter, college, possible, in the future)

   영작 ◎ _____

🍷 Drill 2 Translation

1 1번 문장 ◎ _____

2 2번 문장 ◎ _____

3 3번 문장 ◎ _____

[1] Few people are aware that 1883 is an important year in the history of the Korean press. [2] In that year the newspaper was first published in Korea in an effort to educate the people and bring necessary changes to the country. Three times a month it brought the readers news about the country and the rest of the world. A year later the newspaper was discontinued for a while due to a fire. It had to close in 1888 because of lack of money. [3] In spite of its short life, it changed forever how people got their news in Korea. 기출

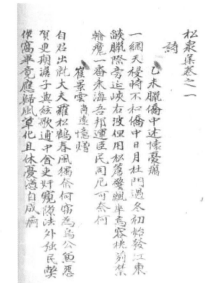

1 What is the best title for this paragraph?

① How to Read Korean Newspapers
② The Beginning of Newspapers in Korea
③ A Big Fire in the Newspaper Printing House
④ International News in Korean Newspapers
⑤ How Newspapers Changed Korean History

2 What was the purpose of publishing a newspaper in Korea? Write the answer in English.

단어 조사해 오세요~ **Word**

aware

press

publish

in an effort to do

educate

necessary

for a while

due to

lack

in spite of

 **Drill 1** Grammar

수동태의 한계

'행위를 하는 주체에 초점을 두느냐' 아니면 '행위 대상의 중심이 되느냐'에 따라 문장의 형태가 달라진다. 능동태는 행위가 중심이며, 수동태는 대상에 더 중점을 두고 표현하게 된다. 수동태는 '~가 …되다 / …지다 / …당하다 / …를 받다' 정도로 해석하면 된다.

- The magazine **is read** by a lot of people. 그 잡지는 많은 사람들에 의해 읽혀진다.
- The museum **was built** in 1998. 그 박물관은 1998년에 지어졌다.

1 Movie stars are loved by teenagers.

해석 ◎ _____

2 My homework will be finished soon (by me).

해석 ◎ _____

3 이 드레스는 앙드레 김에 의해 디자인되었다. (This dress, design, Andre Kim)

영작 ◎ _____

4 다음 주어진 단어를 바르게 배열하여 문장을 완성하시오. (read, many, by, is, teenagers)

영작 ◎ The book _____

Drill 2 Translation

1 1번 문장 ◎ _____

2 2번 문장 ◎ _____

3 3번 문장 ◎ _____

Including the earth, there are eight planets in the solar system. In the center of the solar system, there is the sun. It holds the planets together by the force of its gravity, and all the planets revolve around the sun. As well as the eight planets, there (A) are / is thousands of other smaller heavenly bodies, such as asteroids, comets, and meteors, which circle the sun. Some scientists believe that the planets and the sun were formed at the same time. However, others believe that the sun (B) was formed / formed first, and that a large thread of gaseous materials was drawn from another star when it approached the sun closely. Then this thread of materials separated into several pieces and they began to revolve around the sun. They are the planets.

The earth we are living on is one of a family of planets circling the sun. The earth, the largest rocky planet, was formed about 4.5 billion years ago. Scientists say that the earth was formed from condensed gaseous materials. The surface of the earth is usually made of rocks, and radioactive materials accumulate in these rocks. When these radioactive materials release heat, pockets of molten rock or magma are produced. Also the earth's surface is unique from the other planets because it is the only one with liquid water. Water helps to make surface features such as rivers, lakes and oceans.

The earth's interior is divided into four layers which is typical of rocky planets. It is cool on the surface but very hot deep inside the planet. The center, or core, is as hot as 9000 degrees F. There is a layer (C) called / calling the crust. Beneath the crust, there is the mantle. The mantle is 18,000 miles thick with rock. In addition, there are two cores. The outer core is about 1,350 miles thick, whereas the inner core is about 1,700 miles thick.

1 **What is the article mainly about?**

① information about the number of planets in the universe
② arguments between scientists about the earth's formation
③ size of the universe and other planets
④ description of the solar system and the earth's structure
⑤ estimated measurements of the earth

2 **What is the position of the sun in the solar system? Write the answer in English.**

3 **Beneath the crust, there is a layer called the** _____ .

① mantle   ② asteroids   ③ comets
④ volcano   ⑤ iron

4 (A), (B), (C)의 각 네모 안에서 어법에 맞는 표현을 골라 짝지은 것은?

	(A)		(B)		(C)
①	is	......	formed	......	called
②	is	......	was formed	......	calling
③	are	......	formed	......	called
④	are	......	was formed	......	calling
⑤	are	......	was formed	......	called

planet

gravity

revolve

asteroid

comet

meteor

form

gaseous

approach

separate

condense

accumulate

radioactive

release

unique

feature

typical

crust

Review ☺

A **Translate into English.**

1 다양한 _____

2 뿌리 _____

3 머무르다 _____

4 환경 _____

5 형성하다 _____

6 빗방울 _____

7 혼합물 _____

8 제공하다 _____

9 명예 _____

10 전 세계의 _____

11 넓히다 _____

12 가치가 있는 _____

13 잠시동안 _____

14 부족한 _____

15 노력 _____

16 중력 _____

17 가르다, 분리하다 _____

18 잡다 _____

19 안의, 안쪽의 _____

20 행성 _____

B **Translate into Korean.**

1 harsh _____

2 without _____

3 run out _____

4 environment _____

5 sunlight _____

6 rainbow _____

7 prism _____

8 split _____

9 courtesy _____

10 experience _____

11 regardless of _____

12 common _____

13 educate _____

14 aware _____

15 due to _____

16 gaseous _____

17 condense _____

18 accumulate _____

19 release _____

20 be composed of _____

C **Choose the correct answers to each question.**

1 Fruit peel contains _____ vitamins for our health.

① harsh ② essential
③ conflict ④ fulfill

2 What is needed to form a rainbow?

① water and cloud
② rain and torch
③ glass
④ sunshine and rain

3 In our _____, it is rude to ask someone how much they earn.

① communicate
② culture
③ professional
④ language

D **Translate into English or Korean.**

1 This book is difficult to study.

_____

2 There is a man who is looking for you.

_____

3 모든 사람들이 이 게임이 재미있는 것을 안다.
(know, game, fun)

Everybody _____.

4 이 건물은 1700년대에 지어졌다.
(1700s, build)

This building _____.

E **Choose the correct words to fill in the blanks.**

1 The essays will be difficult _____ by tomorrow.

① completing ② completed
③ to complete ④ completion

2 _____ geese drinking in the park.

① There is ② They're
③ Their ④ There are

3 Tom _____ we should go with him.

① insisted that ② insisting
③ insisted who ④ insisting who

4 밑줄 친 부분에 유의하여 적절한 해석을 고르시오.

Sophia was injured by a car accident.

① Sophia는 교통사고를 냈다.
② Sophia는 운전 중 사람을 치었다.
③ Sophia는 본인 차량을 폐차시켰다.
④ Sophia는 교통사고로 부상당했다.

F **Read and choose the correct antonym or synonym.**

1 My wife and I were divorced in March last year. <synonym>

① changed
② released
③ together
④ separated

2 We dream of living in a heavenly place one day. <antonym>

① fantastic
② comfortable
③ hellish
④ luscious

CHAPTER 1	DATE	SELF CHECK	TEACHER	PARENTS	CONFIRM
Preview					
Unit 1					
Unit 2					
Unit 3					
Unit 4					
Unit 5					
Review					

What's In Trade Names?
회사이름 어떻게 지었을까? 그냥 아무렇게 만들었을까?

아디다스라는 브랜드는 우리나라에서도 매우 친근한 브랜드입니다. 10대 청소년들은 집에 한두 가지 정도는 이 제품이 있을 정도로 한국에서도 매우 인기가 많은 제품이죠. Adidas는 Nike, Reebok과 함께 세계 3대 스포츠 브랜드인데, 1920년대 독일의 작은 마을 Adolf Dassler가 가족들과 함께 수제화를 만들기 시작하던 것이 그 시초가 되었습니다. Adidas라는 명칭은 Adolf의 애칭인 Adi와 '성'인 Dassler 의 앞 세 글자인 'Das'를 따서 만든 것입니다. 처음에는 트레이닝 전용화로 시작하였지만 점점 축구화나 테니스화 같은 신발까지 생산하기 시작했습니다. 아돌프는 당시 최고의 육상 스타인 제시 오웬즈를 찾아가 오웬즈에게 스파이크 달린 경기화를 경기 때 착용해 주길 요청했죠. 그의 성의에 감복한 오웬즈는 결국 승낙했고, 올림픽에서 4관왕이라는 대기록을 이루어냈습니다. 오웬즈가 신은 경기화 '다슬러 슈즈'는 전 세계의 이목을 집중시켰고, 이 상품은 불티나게 팔리기 시작했습니다. 1998년 프랑스 월드컵 공식후원사가 되면서 축구 이미지를 강화하여 열성적인 축구팬들을 공략했던 아디다스는 오늘날 유럽에서 가장 인기있는 athletic shoes 공급업체가 되었습니다. 하지만 이에 만족하지 않고 Nike가 주도하는 미국 시장을 본격적으로 공략하는 등 아디다스는 이제 탈유럽 마케팅에 전력을 기울이고 있습니다.

CHAPTER 02

Word 🏠 단어도 모르면서 영어 한다 하지 마!

- **complex** *a.* 복잡한 *n.* 집합체
- **interaction** *n.* 상호작용
- **occupy** *v.* 차지하다, 종사하다
- **community** *n.* 공동사회, 지역사회
- **supply** *v.* 공급하다, 보충하다
- **crash** *v.* 충돌, 파괴, 무너짐
- **increase** *v.* 증가하다
- **development** *n.* 발달, 개발, 성장
- **between A and B** A와 B 사이에
- **such as** 예컨대, 이를테면

- **in addition** 게다가, 더하여
- **likewise** *ad.* 이와 마찬가지로
- **helpful** *a.* 유익한, 유용한
- **necessity** *n.* 필수품, 필요성
- **at least** 적어도
- **culture** *n.* 문화, 교양
- **exchange** *n.* 교환, 환전 *v.* 교환하다
- **daily life** 일상생활
- **spin** *v.* 돌리다, (실을) 잣다
- **certain** *a.* 확실한, 일정한, 어떤

:: Mini Quiz

1	a hospital _____	종합병원
2	_____ the needed of food	식량의 필요를 공급하다
3	_____ in power	힘이 증가하다
4	_____ of the Third World	제3세계의 성장
5	relations _____ Korea _____ Japan	한국과 일본 간의 관계
6	_____ information about courses	강좌에 대한 유용한 정보
7	a basic _____ of life	생활의 기본 필수품
8	the rate of _____	환율
9	popular _____	대중문화
10	at a(n) _____ place	일정한 장소에

Grammar 기본 문법도 모르면서 독해한다 하지 마!

★ 주어 역할을 하는 동명사, 동사는 단수

Riding a bicycle *is* my hobby. 자전거를 타는 것이 내 취미이다.

Using chopsticks *is* very difficult for foreigners. 젓가락을 사용하는 것은 외국인에게 매우 어렵다.

★ 사람이 주어일 때 감정을 나타내는 과거분사

I **was** very **embarrassed** when I fell down on the street. 길에서 넘어졌을 때 나는 매우 창피했다.

She **was excited** to see her favorite singers. 그녀는 그녀가 좋아하는 가수들을 보게 되어 흥분되었다.

★ 강한 추측을 의미하는 조동사 must

must는 have to와 ought to와 같은 뜻으로 사용되며 모두 95% certainty, necessity, prohibition을 나타낸다.

The man in front of the door **must** be my blind date today.

문 앞에 있는 남자가 분명 오늘 소개팅할 남자임에 틀림없어.

Jane **must** be late today because she went to sleep late last night.

Jane은 어제 늦게 자서 분명 오늘 늦을거야.

:: Mini Quiz

1   다음 괄호 안에서 어법에 맞는 형태를 고르시오.

Talking with friends always [make / makes] me relaxed.

2   다음 중 어법에 <u>틀린</u> 부분을 골라 바르게 고치시오.

I am <u>interesting</u> in <u>movies</u> so I want to <u>be</u> a <u>filmmaker</u>.
   ①   ②   ③ ④

3   다음 밑줄 친 <u>must</u>의 쓰임 중 <u>다른</u> 하나는?

① I <u>must</u> study hard.

② You <u>must</u> run because you are late.

③ Tom <u>must</u> finish his homework.

④ She <u>must</u> be a doctor.

[1] You are a member of your family, a player on the community baseball team, and a student in your school. You are also a citizen of your country. In short, you occupy several different positions in the complex structure of society. This means you should play many roles in different situations. [2] Generally, you have little difficulty performing each of your roles because you know <u>what is expected</u> of you. This knowledge guides you through your daily interactions. But sometimes you will get caught in a conflict. Each of your roles makes demands on you, and you may be asked to play two or more roles at the same time. [3] When many roles make conflicting demands on you, you may feel quite uncomfortable and at times frustrated. For example, your family is going on a picnic this coming Sunday. But your best friend wants you to join his or her birthday party on the same day. When such role conflicts occur, you need to do the more important things first. Thus, the ability to decide what to do in what order is an essential skill and can help you fulfill multiple social roles.

1 **Choose the best main idea of this paragraph.**

① 다양한 역할 수행에는 갈등이 있을 수 있다.
② 학교 교육은 풍부한 교육을 제공한다.
③ 지역사회 발전을 위한 많은 노력이 요구된다.
④ 시민정신은 국가발전의 원동력이다.
⑤ 화목한 가정은 건강한 사회의 기초이다.

2 밑줄 친 **what is expected**의 의미로 알맞은 것을 본문에서 찾을 때, 적절한 것은?

① demands   ② knowledge   ③ conflicts
④ family   ⑤ community

단어 조사해 오세요~ **Word**

in short

occupy

play a role

interaction

conflict

frustrate

occur

essential

fulfill

multiple

🍴 Drill 1 Grammar

help 동사의 특징

〈help + X〉는 'X를 돕다'의 뜻이 된다. 하지만 〈help + X + Y〉의 형태가 오면 'X를 Y하게 돕다'의 뜻이 된다. 즉 〈주어 + 동사 + 목적어 + 목적격보어〉의 5형식 문장에서만 발생하는데, 이러한 문법적인 용어보다는 Y자리에 '행동'이 필요하다는 것을 아는 것이 중요하다.

$$\underset{\text{돕다}}{\text{help}} \quad + \quad \underset{\text{X가}}{\text{X}} \quad + \quad \underset{\text{Y하는 것을}}{\text{Y}} \left\langle \begin{array}{c} \text{원형부사} \\ \text{to부정사} \end{array} \right\rangle \text{둘 다 사용가능}$$

- Our teacher helped *us write* an essay. 우리 선생님은 우리가 수필 쓰는 것을 도와주셨다.
  Our teacher helped *us to write* an essay.
- Yoga helps *me relieve* stress. 요가는 내가 스트레스 푸는 것에 도움이 된다.
  Yoga helps *me to relieve* stress.

---

1   Taking a bath in warm water helps you calm down.

   해석 ◎ _____

2   그녀는 내가 그 프로젝트를 끝내는 것을 도와주었다. (the project)

   영작 ◎ _____

3   Your goals will help you keep you motivated.

   해석 ◎ _____

🍴 Drill 2 Translation

1   1번 문장 ◎ _____

2   2번 문장 ◎ _____

3   3번 문장 ◎ _____

People are happy with developments in medicine. Then they worry about the increased number of births. [1] Scientists make great advances in agricultural chemistry, greatly increasing our food supply. [2] Then our rivers become so polluted that we cannot even swim in them. We are happy with the developments in air transportation and impressed by the great airplanes. Then we are frightened by the horrors of air crash or air war. [3] We are excited by the fact that space can now be entered. [4] But we will undoubtedly see the other side there, too.

기출

1 **What is this paragraph mainly about?**

① 의학 연구의 역사
② 우주 탐사의 불가피성
③ 최신 무기의 폐해
④ 기술 개발의 저해 요인
⑤ 과학 발전의 양면성

2 **Which problem is NOT mentioned in the paragraph?**

① car accidents
② air crash
③ polluted rivers
④ the number of births
⑤ seeing the bad side of things

단어 조사해 오세요~ **Word**

medicine

advance

agricultural

chemistry

food supply

pollute

air transportation

impress

frighten

air crash

undoubtedly

🍴 Drill 1 Grammar

so〔such〕~ that

so〔such〕는 that과 천생연분이어서, 언제나 함께 쓰인다. so〔such〕는 기호적인 역할로 보고 해석에 큰 의미를 두지 않는다. 뒤에 나오는 that은 'that 이하'라고 해석하면 된다.

- He worked so *hard* that his boss would give him a very important job.
  그는 열심히 일했다 (그래서 that 이하다) 그의 사장님이 그에게 아주 중요한 일을 주었다.

- I was so *tired* that I went to bed early last night.
  나는 피곤했다 (그래서 that 이하다) 나는 지난밤에 일찍 자러 갔다.

1　The stone was so heavy that I could not move it.

　　해석 ◐ _____

2　민수는 좋은 학생이다, 그래서 모든 선생님들은 그를 특별하다고 생각한다.
　　(all the teachers, special, think, that, such)

　　영작 ◐ _____

3　He is such a genius that his friends believe he is able to solve the problem.

　　해석 ◐ _____

🍴 Drill 2 Translation

1　1번 문장 ◐ _____

2　2번 문장 ◐ _____

3　3번 문장 ◐ _____

4　4번 문장 ◐ _____

[1] In 300 B.C., Egyptians had to pay a lot of tax to the ancient Roman government. [2] The Romans kept records of all taxpayers' information, such as birth dates and genders, in order to make sure that no future taxpayer escaped. [3] The taxpayers had to pay for everything they had, including land, crops, animals and goods. In addition, men between fourteen and sixty paid a tax just for being male. _____ , [4] when people complain about taxes today, you can tell them that they're lucky they were not born in ancient Egypt.

1 **Choose the best word(s) to fill in the blank.**

① Besides
② At first
③ Likewise
④ For example
⑤ Therefore

2 **What is this paragraph mainly about?**

① History of Ancient Rome
② Calculation of Roman tax
③ How Egyptians paid tax in 300 B.C.
④ Knowing that we are lucky today
⑤ We should stop paying tax.

단어 조사해 오서~ **Word**

Egyptian

pay

tax

ancient

Roman

government

include

gender

escape

in addition

Drill 1 Grammar

to부정사의 이해

to부정사가 이동을 나타내는 동사 다음에 올 경우와 이를 더 강조하기 위해 in order to 또는 so as to를 쓸 수 있다. 이 때는 '~하기 위하여' 로 해석한다.

• **In order to keep** the promise, I started early in the morning.

  약속을 지키기 위하여 나는 아침 일찍 출발했다.

• Sam and John went to New York **to attend** university.

  Sam과 John은 대학에 가기 위해 뉴욕으로 갔다.

1 The thief covered his head with a big black hat in order not to be recognized.

  해석 ◯ _____

2 I hurried to the subway station in order not to be late for school.

  해석 ◯ _____

3 그는 버스를 잡기 위하여 아침을 먹고 급히 버스 정류장으로 갔다. (hurry, catch, bus stop, in order to)

  영작 ◯ He ate his breakfast and _____

Drill 2 Translation

1 1번 문장 ◯ _____

2 2번 문장 ◯ _____

3 3번 문장 ◯ _____

4 4번 문장 ◯ _____

There are three main reasons why people learn foreign languages. [1] First, some people who are interested in other cultures and histories *want* to learn foreign languages. They can better understand the cultures and customs of the people who speak that language. [2] Second, some people who *want* to travel to other countries may *want* to learn foreign languages in order to communicate with the people living in those countries. [3] It is much easier to make friends with the local people if travelers can speak in the local language. Finally, there are professional reasons why people learn foreign languages. [4] For instance, some international companies want their workers to speak in at least two foreign languages so that the workers can communicate with each other better. Other than these reasons, there are also many reasons why people think that learning a different language is helpful. [5] However, the most important reason why people learn foreign languages is it will help them understand other people and their cultures better.

1 **What is the best title for this paragraph?**

① Three Reasons to Understand Other Cultures
② New Methods of Learning Foreign Languages
③ Necessity of Understanding Other Cultures
④ Purposes of Learning Foreign Languages
⑤ Three Ways of Having Cultural Exchanges

2 **Why do people want to learn foreign languages?**

① in order to get high scores on exams
② to make pen-pal friends
③ to watch TV programs from other countries
④ to communicate internationally
⑤ to improve communication and understand other cultures better

단어 조사해 오셔~ **Word**

be interested in

make friends

custom

communicate

local

professional

for instance

international

culture

reason

Drill 1 Grammar

부정사의 이해

부정사가 동사 앞이나 동사 뒤의 순서로 오는 경우, '~하는 것, ~하기' 로 해석한다. 이를 전통영문법에서는 '명사적 용법' 이라 한다.

- **To get** rich information *was* very expensive.   풍부한 정보를 얻는 것은 비용이 아주 많이 들었다.
- She *wanted* **to visit** his house again.   그녀는 그의 집을 다시 방문하기를 원했다.

---

1   Not to do your homework is bad for your grades.

해석 ◉ _____

2   텔레비전을 보는 것은 시간을 낭비하는 것이다. (to watch, to waste)

영작 ◉ _____

3   To eat with your mouth open is considered rude in some cultures.

해석 ◉ _____

Drill 2 Translation

1   1번 문장 ◉ _____

2   2번 문장 ◉ _____

3   3번 문장 ◉ _____

4   4번 문장 ◉ _____

5   5번 문장 ◉ _____

It is really very interesting to find that many things which we use in our daily life have taken their names from certain persons. For example, many of us use things like sandwiches, blankets, cardigans and many other articles and items are used by us without knowing about the people after whom these products have been named.

Let's start with the sandwich. It got its name from John Montague, the Earl of Sandwich, the first naval chief of Great Britain. He was very fond of gambling. He was  so fond of it that he did not want anyone to _____ him during his gambling sessions. So, he ordered his servant to bring sliced meat between two slices of bread regularly for his lunch and dinner. Later on, his unique meal came to be known as the sandwich.

Like 'sandwich,' the word 'blanket' also came from the name of a person called Thomas Blanket. He was an English weaver in the 14th century. He is said to have spun the first blanket on a loom.

Likewise, the horsemen under the Earl of Cardigan who led the Charge of the Light Brigade, wore knitted woolen waistcoats. After the Earl of Cardigan, these waistcoats were later called cardigans.

단어 조사해 오세요~ **Word**

article

item

naval

chief

be fond of

session

regularly

weaver

loom

knit

waistcoat

1　**What is the purpose of the passage?**

① to convince

② to explain

③ to advertise

④ to associate

⑤ to support

2　**How were the items in the article named?**

① After the people who used them first.

② John Montague and Thomas Blanket named them.

③ According to how they were used.

④ They were named by the leaders of England.

⑤ They were named by the companies.

3　**Write T if the statement is true or F if it's false.**

(1) _____　The Earl of Sandwich liked to gamble very much.

(2) _____　Sandwich contained many ingredients.

(3) _____　The Earl of Cardigan used to knit woolen waistcoats.

4　**Choose the best word(s) to fill in the blank.**

① teach

② win

③ play with

④ eat with

⑤ disturb

A   Translate into English.

1   구조 _____

2   대립, 분쟁 _____

3   지도하다 _____

4   본질적인 _____

5   진보, 발전 _____

6   화학 _____

7   오염시키다 _____

8   감동시키다 _____

9   이집트 사람 _____

10   고대의 _____

11   정부 _____

12   벗어나다, 탈출하다 _____

13   프로의, 전문가의 _____

14   풍습 _____

15   국제의 _____

16   지역의 _____

17   짜다, 뜨다 _____

18   책임, 의무 _____

19   규칙적으로 _____

20   방해하다 _____

B   Translate into Korean.

1   interaction _____

2   frustrate _____

3   occur _____

4   perform _____

5   air crash _____

6   undoubtedly _____

7   agricultural _____

8   frighten _____

9   pay _____

10   include _____

11   gender _____

12   in addition _____

13   for instance _____

14   culture _____

15   make friends _____

16   be interested in _____

17   article _____

18   naval _____

19   session _____

20   chief _____

C **Choose the correct answers to each question.**

1. When many roles make conflicting demands on you, you may feel uncomfortable and _____ .
① professional
② interested
③ frustrated
④ satisfied

2 His speech was calculated for good _____ .
① difference
② effect
③ affect
④ belief

3 There are important _____ why people learn foreign languages.
① regions
② reasons
③ friends
④ learners

D **Translate into English or Korean.**

1 She helped her mom do the laundry.

_____

2 He bought his girlfriend a necklace in order to surprise her.

_____

3 그녀는 피아니스트가 되기 위해 열심히 피아노 연습을 했다. (practice, a pianist, in order to, hard)

_____

E **Choose the correct words to fill in the blanks.**

1 I will help you _____ the project
① finishing
② finished
③ to finish
④ will finish

2 She was _____ strong that she could move the stone.
① but
② however
③ so
④ such

3 _____ his promise, he started early in the morning.
① Keeping
② To be kept
③ If he will keep
④ In order to keep

4 They promised to go skiing together.
(해석 찾기)
① 그들은 스키장에 같이 가기로 약속했다.
② 그들은 함께 스키장에 가서 약속을 했다.
③ 그들은 약속을 하고 스키장에 같이 갔다.
④ 그들은 약속을 하기 위해 스키장에 갔다.

F **Match the words and the meanings.**

essential	local	regularly	advance

1 _____ relating to an area near you

2 _____ at the same time each day, week, month, etc.

3 _____ absolutely necessary to a particular situation

4 _____ new discoveries and inventions

CHAPTER 2	DATE	SELF CHECK	TEACHER	PARENTS	CONFIRM
Preview					
Unit 1					
Unit 2					
Unit 3					
Unit 4					
Unit 5					
Review					

Why Do Doughnuts Have Holes?
도넛에는 누가 구멍을 뚫어 났나요?

요즘 던킨 도넛이 대유행을 하고 있는데, 여러분은 혹시 도넛을 먹으면서 왜? 가운데에 구멍을 뚫어 놓았는지 생각해 본 적이 있나요? 그냥 맛있게 보이게 하려고? 구멍만 없으면 한 입 정도 더 먹을 수 있을 것 같은데... 도넛에 구멍이 난 사연이라도 있는지 그 궁금증을 해결해 보자구요.

도넛에 왜 구멍이 있는가에 대해서는 여러 가지 무성한 얘기들이 많이 있답니다. 네덜란드인들이 미국에 도넛을 처음 소개한 것으로 알려져 있는데, 그 때는 도넛이 아닌 기름에 그냥 튀긴 오일케이크(oily cakes)라 불리었답니다. 달콤하게 설탕을 뿌린 오일케이크는 1600년대 초에 네덜란드에서 살았던 미국 이민자 필 그림에 의해 아메리카 대륙에 전해졌습니다. 1차 세계대전 때 군인들에게 음식을 나누어 주던 구세군은, 군인들이 이 케이크를 가지고 다니기가 쉽지 않다는 것을 깨닫고, 그래서 한 가운데에 구멍을 뚫어 도넛이 총부리에 들어가게 해서 군인들이 두 손을 자유롭게 쓸 수 있도록 한 것은 머리를 잘 쓴 일이었습니다. 해군대좌 출신인 핸슨 그레고리가 1847년 어머니가 만든 도넛에 구멍을 낸 것은 가운데는 불이 통하지 않아 덜 익어 소화가 안 되는 것을 해결하기 위해 만들었다는 설과 그가 군함을 조종하면서 조타기에 끼워놓고 먹기 위해 뚫었다는 설도 있습니다.

CHAPTER 03

Word 🏠 단어도 모르면서 영어 한다 하지 마!

□ **survive** *v.* 살아남다, 견디다		□ **broaden** *v.* 넓히다, 넓게 하다	
□ **notice** *n.* 통지 *v.* 주의하다		□ **experience** *n.* 경험 *v.* 경험하다	
□ **comprise** *v.* ~로 구성되다		□ **means** *n.* 방법, 수단	
□ **traditional** *a.* 전통의, 고풍의		□ **tempt** *v.* 유혹하다, 부추기다	
□ **whole** *a.* 전체의, 전원의		□ **appearance** *n.* 외모, 출현	
□ **own** *a.* 자기 자신의, 고유한		□ **deal** *v.* 다루다 *n.* 거래	
□ **commercial** *a.* 상업상의 *n.* 광고		□ **housing** *n.* 주거, 주택	
□ **throughout** *ad.* 도처에, ~동안 내내		□ **sudden** *a.* 돌연한, 갑작스러운	
□ **value** *n.* 가치, 가격		□ **require** *v.* 요구하다, 필요로 하다	
□ **honor** *n.* 명예, 영광, 체면		□ **concentrate** *v.* 집중하다, 모으다	

∷ Mini Quiz

1 _____ the plane crash   비행기 추락 사고에서 살아남다

2 _____ his new hair style   그의 새 머리 스타일을 알아채다

3 a cultural _____   문화적 가치

4 TV _____   텔레비전 광고

5 make up your _____ mind   너 자신의 마음을 결정하다

6 a deep mystical _____   매우 신비한 경험

7 The offer _____ me.   그 제안에 마음이 끌렸다.

8 judge by _____   외모로 판단하다

9 make a(n) _____ with the company 그 회사와 거래를 성사시키다

10 _____ in class   수업 시간에 집중하다

Grammar

기본 문법도 모르면서 독해한다 하지 마!

★ 명사 역할을 하는 〈**what + to**부정사〉는 동사 '앞, 뒤'에 위치하여 명사구 역할만을 한다.

I can't decide **what to wear** today.   나는 오늘 무엇을 입을지 결정하지 못했다.

I don't know **what to do**.   무엇을 해야 할지 나는 잘 모르겠다.

★ 관계대명사 **which**절은 앞에 나온 명사(선행사) 즉, '사물, 동물, 식물'을 수식한다.

I like cars **which are made in Italy**.   나는 이탈리아에서 만들어진 차를 좋아한다.

The house **which was built by my grandfather** is very old.

할아버지가 지으신 그 집은 매우 낡았다.

★ 관계대명사 **who**절은 앞에 나온 명사(선행사) 즉 '사람'을 수식한다.

The girl **who is wearing pink shoes** is my little sister.

분홍색 신을 신고 있는 소녀가 내 어린 여동생이다.

This is my aunt **who took care of me** when I was young.

이분이 내가 어렸을 때 나를 돌봐주셨던 이모다.

:: Mini Quiz

1   다음 괄호 안에서 어법에 맞는 것을 고르시오.

My mom always worries about [what to eat / to eat] for dinner.

2   다음 중 어법에 틀린 부분을 찾아 바르게 고치시오.

<u>Is</u> that the girl <u>which</u> <u>likes</u> you?
① ②   ③   ④

3   다음 밑줄 친 <u>which</u>의 쓰임 중 <u>다른</u> 하나는?

① I like doughnuts <u>which</u> are very sweet.

② <u>Which</u> is your book?

③ The book <u>which</u> was written by him is very popular.

④ Look at the book <u>which</u> is on the table.

Approximately forty years ago, two naked men were seen in a dense forest in the southern Philippine Islands. [1] The only thing each man was wearing was a small leaf. A hunter who came upon these two men noticed that they were looking for food without any tools except wooden sticks. These men were members of a small tribe, which was comprised of only twenty-five people. Who were these people? They called themselves the Tasaday. [2] The caves they were living in were completely protected by the jungle, so those caves could not be noticed even from a few yards away. The Tasaday knew nothing about the world outside of their jungle. [3] They did not even know how to hunt or plant crops. [4] How could have they survived for so long without being discovered? They had wild berries, bananas, small fish and frogs for food. However, they could make fire and use it to cook food. The Tasaday had survived 50 thousand years with their traditional way of life.

1 **Choose the best title for this paragraph.**

① The Tasaday's Food and Shelter
② Changing Customs of the Tasaday
③ A Hunter in the Philippine Islands
④ Stone-age People in the 21st Century
⑤ Reasons for the Tasaday's Disappearance

2 **Choose the sentence that best explains the Tasaday in this paragraph.**

① They farmed.
② They didn't know anything about the outside world.
③ They didn't know how to use fire.
④ They ate mostly vegetables.
⑤ They were good hunters.

단어 조사해 오셔~ **Word**

approximately

look for

dense

protect

notice

tribe

comprise of

Tasaday

completely

crop

protect

discover

traditional

 **Drill 1** Grammar

관계사 생략

문장 안에서 관계사의 생략 빈도는 아주 높으므로 확실히 이해해 두지 않으면 정확한 독해를 할 수가 없게 된다. 문장에서 〈명사 + 명사〉가 쉼표도 없이 연이어서 나오는 경우 거의 관계사가 생략된다.

> 명사 + (관계사) + [명사 ~~~] : 앞의 명사를 꾸며 주며 우리말 '하는, 했던' 을 붙여 해석

- These are the comic books [my friend gave me.] 이것들은 내 친구가 나에게 준 만화책이다.
  명사   명사

- The movie [I saw yesterday] was not worth the money. 내가 어제 본 영화는 돈이 아까웠다.
  명사   명사

---

1   Anything you donate will be very helpful for the poor people.

해석 ◎ _____

2   She is not the woman I wanted to meet.

해석 ◎ _____

3   지난밤에 읽은 그 이야기는 매우 무서웠다. (last night, horrible, the story)

영작 ◎ _____

 **Drill 2** Translation

1   1번 문장 ◎ _____

2   2번 문장 ◎ _____

3   3번 문장 ◎ _____

4   4번 문장 ◎ _____

¹Greenhouses, of which roofs and walls are built with glass or plastic, are often called hothouses or, in Europe, glasshouses. ²Because the temperature, light, and moisture can be controlled in greenhouses, many different kinds of plants or vegetables can grow in there throughout the whole year. In the outdoors, it is impossible to control these things. Nowadays you may see greenhouses all around the world. ³The reason why people build greenhouses is because they can grow vegetables or plants any time of the year. Many large greenhouses, which grow vegetables, are commercial ones. ⁴However, there are also small greenhouses which people build to grow their own vegetables.

1 **What is another name for a greenhouse?**

① vinyl house
② plastic house
③ hothouse
④ home garden
⑤ castle

2 **Which details are NOT included in the underlined words 'these things'? (two answers)**

① temperature
② light
③ moisture
④ the roof and walls
⑤ plants

단어 조사해 오세~ **Word**

greenhouse

temperature

moisture

control

throughout

outdoor

nowadays

commercial

Drill 1 Grammar

주어가 길어 문장 뒤로 보내는 경우

주어가 to 부정사(구)로 길어질 때, 그 주어를 문장의 뒤로 보내는 것이 일반적이다. 이 때 비어있는 주어 자리에는 가주어 It을 대신 쓰고, 뒤로 보낸 부정사는 우리말 '~하는 것, ~하기' 와 같이 주어처럼 해석해 주면 된다. 'it은 주어가 아니기 때문에 해석하지 않는다' 는 것은 잘못된 설명이다. 문장의 주인인 주어자리에 들어왔으므로 '그것' 이라는 말을 붙여 해석해 주는 연습이 필요하다.

> [To finish the work] is not easy. 주어가 길면 무조건 it을 쓰고 뒤로 보낼 수 있다.
> 　　　주어가 길다
> It is not easy to finish the work. 더 효율적이고 자연스러운 문장이 된다.

- To love and to be loved is the greatest happiness.
  = It is the greatest happiness to love and to be loved. 그것은 가장 큰 행복이다. 사랑하는 것과 사랑받는 것.

- It is difficult to live without a computer nowadays. 요즘 컴퓨터 없이 사는 것은 어렵다.

1　It is not easy to make a speech in English.

　　해석 ◯ _____

2　It is necessary for you to listen to other people's advice.

　　해석 ◯ _____

3　그것은 중요하다, 여행하는 것, 다른 나라들로. (다른 나라들로 여행하는 것은 중요하다.)
　　(to other countries, to travel, it)

　　영작 ◯ _____

 Drill 2 Translation

1　1번 문장 ◯ _____

2　2번 문장 ◯ _____

3　3번 문장 ◯ _____

4　4번 문장 ◯ _____

Everyone knows that the first telephone was invented by Alexander Graham Bell. [1] But not many people know that the telephone was not his only invention. Four years after inventing the telephone, he invented the photophone. [2] Whereas the telephone used electricity to carry sound through wires, the photophone used a beam of light that traveled through the air to carry sound waves. [3] To operate the photophone, Bell spoke close to a mirror that was built to reflect sunlight. The vibrations of his voice vibrated the mirror, and the vibrating mirror caused the reflected light to vibrate. [4] The receiver was made to change the vibrations of the light into electrical signals, and the earphone changed the electrical signals back into _____ .

1 **Choose the best word to fill in the blank.**

① letters
② music
③ memory
④ sounds
⑤ numbers

2 **Which phrase expresses the paragraph best?**

① The invention of the telephone and the operation of the photophone
② Biography of phones and how to operate electrical signals
③ How to operate the telephone or photophone
④ Discovery of sunlight reflection
⑤ The speed of sound waves

단어 조사해 오세요~ **Word**

invent

photophone

beam

operate

reflect

vibration

receiver

signal

Drill 1 Grammar

문장 맨 앞에 오는 to부정사

문장 맨 앞에 나오는 to부정사가 '~위하여'로 해석되는 경우가 있다. 주어로 사용되어 '~것, ~기' 해석되는 경우와 잘 구분해야 한다. 많은 독서를 통해 확실히 이해해야 한다.

> To v₁ ~~~~, S (명사) + v₂   ~하기 위하여, S는···
>
> 주로 쉼표로 분리하여 명사가 나온다, 쉼표 옆에 있는 명사(주어)를 꾸며 주면서 우리말 '~위하여'로 해석한다.

- **To make good friends**, you must first be a good friend.
  좋은 친구를 사귀기 위하여, 너는 먼저 좋은 친구가 되어야 한다.

- **To travel all over the world**, you need to understand English.
  전 세계를 여행하기 위하여 너는 영어를 이해해야 한다.

---

1 To learn a language well, you have to make the best use of the Internet.

해석 ◎ _____

2 To understand philosophy, you must have an open and abstract mind.

해석 ◎ _____

3 여자친구를 위한 선물을 사기 위하여, Dennis는 백화점에 갔다. (buy, the department store, gift, girlfriend)

영작 ◎ _____

Drill 2 Translation

1   1번 문장 ◎ _____

2   2번 문장 ◎ _____

3   3번 문장 ◎ _____

4   4번 문장 ◎ _____

[1] People in the advertising business are always trying every means to tempt consumers to buy products. In some commercials, famous actors appear as doctors to sell cold medicines. [2] Some other commercials employ charts or graphs to convince us that their products are better than others. In addition, there are some ads which make us think that our lives will be improved if we have the products they advertise. [3] For instance, some commercials that advertise mattresses say that we will feel happier the next day if we sleep on a certain kind of mattress. Some other ads say that we will regret it if we don't buy their products immediately. They say, "Don't miss this chance! You won't have this deal tomorrow."

1 **Choose the best title for this paragraph.**

① The History of Advertisements
② Positive Effects of Advertisements
③ Some Advice for Smart Shopping
④ The Importance of Advertisements
⑤ Various Techniques of Advertisements

2 **What is the goal of advertising?**

① to make us think that their products will improve our lives
② to criticize other products by comparing
③ to explain their products and tempt consumers to buy them
④ to make consumers regret it if they don't purchase the products quickly
⑤ to sell products to a select few individuals

단어 조사해 오세요~ **Word**

consumer

commercial

medicine

employ

in addition

product

advertise

regret

immediately

deal

 **Drill 1** Grammar

전명구란?

〈전치사 + 명사〉의 덩어리를 '전명구' 라 한다.

전치사는 언제나 뒤에 명사를 데리고 다닌다. 〈전치사 + 명사〉의 덩어리가 명사 뒤에서 앞에 있는 명사를 꾸며주는 형용사(구)와 같은 역할을 하거나 문장 맨 앞 또는 맨 뒤에 위치하여 부사구 역할을 하는 2가지 형태가 있다. 영어에서 유일하게 중요한 역할을 하지 않는 명사가 바로 전치사와 함께 쓰인 명사이다. 이 명사는 문장에서 주어도, 목적어도, 보어도 될 수 없다는 것을 명심해 두자.

- **In a little town**, there lived a ghost. (작은 마을에,) 귀신이 살았었다.
- A dead body was found **in the basement of their house**. (그들 집의) (지하실에서) 시체가 발견되었다.
- The word 'impossible' is not **in my dictionary**. '불가능' 이라는 단어는 (내 사전에) 없다.

1 The prisoners on the bus are very dangerous criminals.

해석 ◎ _____

2 There was not a star in the sky.

해석 ◎ _____

3 내가 어렸을 때, (시골에) 살았다. (the country, young, when)

영작 ◎ _____

Drill 2 Translation

1 1번 문장 ◎ _____

2 2번 문장 ◎ _____

3 3번 문장 ◎ _____

(A)

Some people who graduate from high school go to colleges which are far from their houses. Since most of them are still very young, they may have a hard time if they have to live apart from their families all of sudden. _____, their parents are sometimes worried about housing and traffic expenses. However, students who

decide to go to a community college can live with or near their families and save a lot of money, since almost every county has more than one community college.

(B)

University students are offered many kinds of events and parties at school. Therefore, students sometimes have difficulty to concentrate on their studies. Meanwhile, community colleges usually do not offer as many extracurricular activities as universities do, so community colleges may be a better environment for serious study. _____, libraries at community colleges may be more adequate for specialized fields of studies, which are required in our society, even though they are often not as large as those at universities.

1 **Choose a title that is appropriate for both of the paragraphs.**

① Variety in University Life
② The Importance of Higher Education
③ Advantages of Community Colleges
④ Difficulties of Choosing a Good Job
⑤ Differences between High School and College

2 **Choose the best expression to fill in the two blanks.**

① In addition
② As a result
③ For example
④ In other words
⑤ On the contrary

3 **Write T if the statement is true or F if it's false.**

(1) _____ Community college students get better results than university students.

(2) _____ There are many advantages of going a community college.

(3) _____ Universities have an excellent environment in which to study.

4 **Write the advantages of going to a community college. Write in English.**

단어 조사해 오셔~ **Word**

graduate from

sudden

expense

community college

concentrate

meanwhile

extracurricular

adequate

specialize

require

society

university

Review ☺

A Translate into English.

1 알아차리다 _____

2 완전히, 완벽하게 _____

3 발견하다 _____

4 구성되다 _____

5 온실 _____

6 온도 _____

7 조절(관리)하다 _____

8 야외의 _____

9 넓히다 _____

10 정의 _____

11 확장하다 _____

12 공통의 _____

13 사용하다, 쓰다 _____

14 광고하다 _____

15 즉시, 즉각 _____

16 확신시키다 _____

17 갑작스러운 _____

18 알맞은 _____

19 전문화하다 _____

20 집중하다 _____

B Translate into Korean.

1 dense _____

2 traditional _____

3 look for _____

4 approximately _____

5 commercial _____

6 moisture _____

7 throughout _____

8 nowadays _____

9 courtesy _____

10 valuable _____

11 regardless _____

12 universal _____

13 consumer _____

14 product _____

15 in addition _____

16 commercial _____

17 extracurricular _____

18 require _____

19 expense _____

20 meanwhile _____

C **Choose the correct answers to each question.**

1 Two naked men were seen in a _____ forest in the southern Philippine Islands.

① sparse   ② dense
③ traditional   ④ common

2 The reason why people build greenhouses is because _____.

① greenhouses are very cold inside
② greenhouses are very big inside
③ people can live in greenhouses any time of the year
④ people can grow vegetables in greenhouses any time of the year

3 What is not a benefit of going to a community college?

① You can save money on housing.
② You can save money on traffic expenses.
③ You can go to many kinds of events and parties at school.
④ You can concentrate on your studies.

D **Translate into English or Korean.**

1 The students in this classroom are very smart.

_____

2 This is the book she talked about.

_____

3 네가 읽었던 그 책은 나의 할아버지가 쓰신 책이다.
(that, read, was written, the book)

_____

E **Choose the correct words to fill in the blanks.**

1 It is impossible _____ him again.

① to see   ② saw
③ will see   ④ have seen

2 I will buy you anything you want. (해석 찾기)

① 나는 네가 원하는 무엇이든 사줄게.
② 네가 원하면 무엇이든 살 수 있어.
③ 나는 네가 원하는 무엇이든 사줄 수 없어.
④ 내가 사주는 것은 네가 원하던 것이야.

3 The man _____ is my father.

① wears glasses
② wore glasses
③ glasses
④ that is wearing glasses

4 A teacher went _____.

① classroom
② into the classroom
③ the classroom
④ into

F **Write the proper words in the blanks.**

1 consume : consumer
= _____ : advertiser

2 complete: completely
= approximate : _____

3 vibrate : vibration
= _____ : operation

4 indoor : outdoor
= dryness : _____

CHECK
BOX

CHAPTER 3	DATE	SELF CHECK	TEACHER	PARENTS	CONFIRM
Preview					
Unit 1					
Unit 2					
Unit 3					
Unit 4					
Unit 5					
Review					

Why Is Garlic Believed to Repel Vampires?
왜 사람들은 마늘이 흡혈귀를 물리친다고 생각하죠?

매년 여름에는 항상 끊임없이 등장하는 귀신 얘기와 공포영화, 더위를 잊기 위해 공포영화만큼 인기 있는 것도 없는 듯합니다. 하지만 여러분들이 가끔 드라큘라가 나오는 서양영화를 볼 때면 절대 죽지 않는 용감한 주인공이 흡혈귀와 싸울 때 마늘과 십자가를 사용하는 것을 본 적이 있을 겁니다. 정말로 흡혈귀가 마늘을 무서워하기는 하는 건가요?

영화에서 보면 뱀파이어가 햇빛, 십자가, 그리고 특히 마늘을 무서워하는데, 마늘이 흡혈귀를 물리친다는 생각은 마늘 상인들 때문에 시작된 듯해 보입니다. 이 상인들은 전 유럽을 휩쓸어버린 흑사병에 걸리지 않는 것 같았기 때문이었습니다. 흑사병은 무차별적으로, 아이든, 어른이든, 여자든, 돈이 많든 적든지 간에 모두 휩쓸어갔지만 이상하게도 어떤 이유에서인지 마늘 상인들의 발병률은 낮았다고 합니다. 그 당시에는 지금처럼 의술이 발달하지 않아, 왜 이런 병에 걸려 사망하는지 설명할 길이 없었기 때문에 사람들은 흡혈귀 같은 귀신에다가 그 발병 원인을 돌리곤 했었습니다. 마늘 상인은 일반인들보다 흑사병에 잘 감염되지 않았기 때문에, 사람들은 마늘이 흡혈귀를 물리치는 게 틀림없다고 추론했던 것입니다. 그리고 나서 19세기말 파스퇴르에 의해 최초로 페스트(흑사병)균이 발견되기까지 유럽인들이 페스트의 발병 원인과 치료법을 알 수가 없었고 20세기에 들어서야 벼룩과 쥐가 사람에게 페스트균을 옮긴다는 사실을 발견하게 되었습니다.

CHAPTER 04

Word 🏠 단어도 모르면서 영어 한다 하지 마!

☐ **put on** 입다, 신다, 켜다, 틀다	☐ **resource** *n.* 자원, 물자, 수단
☐ **Greek** *a.* 그리스의, 그리스 사람의	☐ **increase** *v.* 늘다, 증가하다, 불리다
☐ **role** *n.* 배역, 역할, 임무	☐ **arms** *n.* 팔, 무기, 병사
☐ **various** *a.* 가지각색의, 여러 가지의	☐ **outer** *a.* 밖의, 멀리 떨어진
☐ **come up with** ~에 따라잡다, 생각해내다	☐ **demand** *v.* 요구하다, 청구하다
☐ **stroke** *n.* 타격, 울림, 발작	☐ **threaten** *v.* 위협하다, 협박하다
☐ **injury** *n.* 상해, 손상, 피해	☐ **against** *prep.* ~에 저항하여, 반대하여
☐ **recover** *v.* 되찾다, 회복하다	☐ **defend** *v.* 방어하다, 변호하다
☐ **endless** *a.* 끝이 없는, 무한의	☐ **reluctant** *a.* 마음 내키지 않은
☐ **emerge** *v.* 나오다, 나타나다	☐ **eventually** *ad.* 결국, 드디어, 마침내

⠿ Mini Quiz

1 _____ my hat   모자를 쓰다

2 fill the _____ of   ~의 임무를 다하다

3 a collection of short stories by _____ authors   여러 작가들이 쓴 단편집

4 _____ a plan   계획을 생각해내다

5 _____ from an illness   병에서 회복하다

6 the problem _____   문제가 나타났다

7 natural _____   천연자원

8 _____ an apology   사과를 요구하다

9 _____ his opinion   그의 의견을 변호하다

10 _____ to kill him   그를 죽이겠다고 협박하다

Grammar 🧑 기본 문법도 모르면서 독해한다 하지 마!

★ 조동사 **used to**는 과거의 규칙적인 습관을 나타낼 때 쓰인다. '했(었)다' 로 해석한다.

I **used to** drink coffee after every meal. 매 식사 후에 나는 커피를 마시곤 했다.

I didn't **used to** go shopping before I met you. 너를 만나기 전에는 쇼핑을 다니지 않았었어.

★ 종속접속사 **as**는 시간, 이유를 의미하는 부사절을 이끈다.

She was talking on the phone **as I entered the room**.

내가 방에 들어갔을 때 그녀는 통화 중이었다.

I didn't have dessert **as I was full**. 나는 배가 불렀기 때문에 나는 디저트를 먹지 않았다.

★ 열등비교를 할 때 〈**less** + 형용사/부사 원급 + **than**〉을 쓴다.

This is **less expensive than** that. 저것보다는 이것이 덜 비싸다.

Your explanation is **less difficult than** his. 너의 설명이 그의 설명보다 덜 어렵다.

⠿ Mini Quiz

1 다음 괄호 안에서 어법에 맞는 형태를 고르시오.

She used to [cleaned / clean / cleaning] her room by herself.

2 다음 중 어법에 틀린 부분을 골라 바르게 고치시오.

She speaks less fluency than he does.
　　　①　　　 ②　　 ③　　 ④

3 다음 밑줄 친 <u>as</u>의 쓰임 중 <u>다른</u> 하나는?

① I can do my homework <u>as</u> I listen to music.

② This box can be used <u>as</u> a chair.

③ I like this book <u>as</u> it is easy to read.

④ Clean your room <u>as</u> you watch TV.

For thousands years, people have used these for various purposes. [1] If you wear these, you may feel like becoming another person. [2] In early times, hunters *put* these *on* to deceive animals. The hunters believed that animals let them come closer when they were wearing these. In addition, these were used for religious reasons. All over the world, people have worn these to represent gods or demons. [3] Also, ancient Greek and Roman actors used to wear these to show the audience what kind of roles they were playing. These days, actors do not wear these so often. However, children love to wear these on special occasions, such as on Halloween.

1 **What does the underlined these mean?**

① wigs
② gloves
③ masks
④ name tags
⑤ handkerchiefs

2 **What is NOT true about 'these?'**

① They represent certain gods or demons.
② They were useful for hunters.
③ They are loved by children.
④ Many actors these days have to wear them to show their character.
⑤ People sometimes wear them at the parties.

단어 조사해 오세요~ **Word**

various

purpose

deceive

religious

represent

demon

ancient

audience

occasion

Halloween

🍴 Drill 1 Grammar

to부정사의 부사적 용법

to부정사의 앞에 쓰인 동사의 뜻이 움직임을 나타낼 때 to부정사는 우리말 '~위하여' 로 해석한다.

> **V** + **to do:** ~하기 위하여
> (이동이나, 움직임)

- He *went* to Beijing **to learn** Chinese. 그는 중국어를 배우기 위하여 베이징에 갔다.
- Justin *used* his computer **to find** some information. Justin은 정보를 찾기 위해 컴퓨터를 사용했다.

---

1   He went to the bookstore to buy some books.

해석 ◎ _____

2   Yoon-sun stayed up late to finish her homework.

해석 ◎ _____

3   He went to the restaurant to meet his first love from high school.

해석 ◎ _____

4   많은 학생들이 좋은 직업을 갖기 위해 대학에 들어간다. (attend, get, a good job)

영작 ◎ _____

🍴 Drill 2 Translation

1   1번 문장 ◎ _____

2   2번 문장 ◎ _____

3   3번 문장 ◎ _____

[1] Some scientists argue that females tend to _____ when they use languages, whereas males use only the left hemisphere. [2] As a result, according to the scientists, females tend to show better linguistic abilities. [3] In their findings, females tend to make use of a larger number of words when they speak and to come up with more proper words more quickly compared to males. Moreover, female stroke or brain injury patients take less time to recover than male patients. [4] In addition, females are less likely to be permanently injured because they utilize a larger network of cells in the brain compared to males.

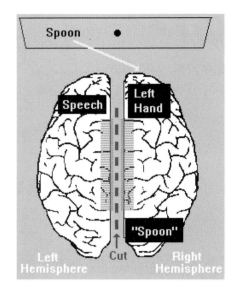

1 **Choose the best title for this paragraph.**

① Words Often Used by Men
② The Structure of the Human Brain
③ Ways of Successful Language Learning
④ People Who Are Likely to Get a Stroke
⑤ Benefits of Women Using Both Sides of the Brain

2 **Choose the best answer to fill in the blank.**

① use body language more
② hesitate with expression
③ be kind to a listener
④ use both sides of their brain
⑤ speak louder than males

단어 조사해 오세요~ **Word**

argue

hemisphere

according to

tend to

linguistic

ability

injury

compare to

recover

permanently

utilize

cell

Drill 1 Grammar

시간의 부사절 접속사 when

시간의 부사절 〈when + S + V〉는 '주어가 ~할 때' 라고 해석한다.

- **When** *I was studying*, the phone rang. 내가 공부하고 있었을 때, 전화가 울렸다.
- **When** *the well's dry*, we know the worth of water. 우물이 마를 때, 우리는 물의 가치를 알게 된다.

---

1 When I was driving down a rural road, I saw a strange woman.

해석 ○ _____

2 When it rains, they usually wear rubber boots.

해석 ○ _____

3 나는 어렸을 때, 스페인어를 공부했다. (a child, Spanish, study)

영작 ○ _____

Drill 2 Translation

1 1번 문장 ○ _____

2 2번 문장 ○ _____

3 3번 문장 ○ _____

4 4번 문장 ○ _____

[1] As human activity increases in Antarctica, new problems have emerged. [2] Even though the number of people who have visited Antarctica is not very large, the few people that did have caused a large impact. [3] Tourists often leave their garbage behind, and they

sometimes threaten wild creatures by making too much noise. [4] But the worst part is that the endless human need for natural resources is threatening the whole continent.

1 **What does this paragraph describe about Antarctica?**

① Recovery of the Ecological System
② Capture of Wild Animals
③ Problems Caused by the Humans
④ Disputes Caused by the Right of Ownership
⑤ Rapid Increase in the Number of Wild Animals

2 **이 글의 내용과 일치하는 것은?**

① All the problems in Antarctica are almost solved.
② All the people who visit Antarctica pollute the place.
③ Animals are not affected by the noise pollution.
④ Human activity in Antarctica is decreasing.
⑤ The human has the most effect on Antarctica.

단어 조사해 오세요~ **Word**

activity

increase

Antarctica

emerge

impact

tourist

threaten

wild creature

natural

resource

continent

Drill 1 Grammar

우리말에는 없는 현재완료 〈have + p.p.〉

현재완료는 여러 가지 용법이 있다고 배우면서 거기에 맞는 해석을 하다가 더욱 이상하게 꼬이는 경험을 했을 것이다. 그것은 우리말에 없어서 억지로 끼워 맞출 수 없기 때문이다. 따라서 〈have + p.p.〉 형태를 만날 때 우리말 '했다, 했었다' 로 해석 하는 게 더 정확하다. 즉, '과거에서 시작하여 현재도 하고 있거나 막 끝났다' 는 의미를 내포하고 있다.

- I have learned English since I was an elementary school student.

  나는 초등학생 때부터 영어를 공부했다.

- Rowling has written five books in the Harry Potter series.

  Rowling은 해리포터 시리즈 다섯 권을 썼다.

1   Karen has lost her MP3 player.

   해석 ◯ _____

2   Jason and Emma got married in 1999. They have been happily married for 9 years.

   해석 ◯ _____

3   I started to study English five years ago and I'm still studying it. 〈현재완료를 사용한 문장으로〉

   영작 ◯ _____

Drill 2 Translation

1   1번 문장 ◯ _____

2   2번 문장 ◯ _____

3   3번 문장 ◯ _____

4   4번 문장 ◯ _____

In the 1950's, the United States was concerned about national defense and space technology. The Communists took over China in 1949 and in the early 1950's, the Soviet Union developed nuclear weapons. [1] To make the situation worse, the Soviet Union launched Sputnik 1, the world's first satellite, into outer space in 1957. Thus, the United States government worried about losing its place as the world's most powerful nation. [2] Americans felt threatened and, therefore, asked *their government* to spend more money on national defense and space technology. As a consequence, the U.S. increased its budget on arms and outer space exploration. [3] A decade later, the United States finally came from behind and sent the first man to the moon in 1969. As a result, the United States became stronger in national defense and in space technology than ever before.

1   **Which of the following statements is <u>NOT</u> true according to the paragraph? (two answers)**

① The U.S. communized China in 1949.
② The U.S. sent up the first satellite before the Soviet Union did.
③ The U.S. invested more money in defense.
④ The U.S. sent the first man to the moon in 1969.
⑤ The U.S. became more powerful in defense and technology.

2   **Why was the U.S. threatened by the Soviet Union?**

① The U.S. was financially behind the Soviet Union.
② The Soviet Union had more soldiers than the U.S.
③ The Soviet Union warned the U.S.
④ The Soviet Union developed nuclear weapons and launched Sputnik 1.
⑤ The Soviet Union was the richest country in the world.

단어 조사해 오셔~ **Word**

concern

defense

communist

Soviet Union

nuclear weapon

launch

satellite

threaten

as a consequence

budget

exploration

decade

Drill 1 Grammar

5형식 문장의 이해

5형식은 영작과 회화에 사용 빈도가 가장 높은 형식이다. 따라서 실제 문장 속에서 우리말로 바로 이해가 될 수 있도록 많은 독서가 필요하다. 그 중 명령의 의미를 지니는 동사는 order, command, ask, advise, require, permit, tell, want, force 등이 있는데, 이러한 동사들은 '~에게 …하라고' 로 해석한다.

> V + X(한테) + Y (하라고) – Y자리에는 예외 없이 거의 to do 형태가 온다. 즉 'X가 Y하다' 라는 동작, 행동이 필요하기 때문이다.

- The manager **commanded** *his clients* **to leave** the hotel immediately.
  V(명령했다)　　　　　X(가)　　　　Y(하라고)

  매니저는 그의 고객들에게 즉시 호텔을 벗어나라고 요구했다.

- He **ordered** *Tell's little son* **to stand** up in the square.

  그는 텔의 어린 아들에게 광장에 서있으라고 명령했다.

1　You can lead a horse to water, but you can't force it to drink.

　　해석 ◎ _____

2　The general commanded his soldiers to fight bravely for their country.

　　해석 ◎ _____

3　선생님은 학생들에게 많은 책을 읽으라고 요구했다. (asked, a lot of books, to read)

　　영작 ◎ _____

 Drill 2 Translation

1　1번 문장 ◎ _____

2　2번 문장 ◎ _____

3　3번 문장 ◎ _____

Copernicus must be one of the most famous astronomers in history. He was born in Poland in 1473. When he was born, he was named "Niklas Koppernick." In the 15th century, people believed that the earth was in the center of the universe. They believed that the sun and all the other stars circled the earth. Copernicus _____. He proposed three theories: the earth goes around the sun; the earth spins as it travels; and the earth is only a member of the solar system.

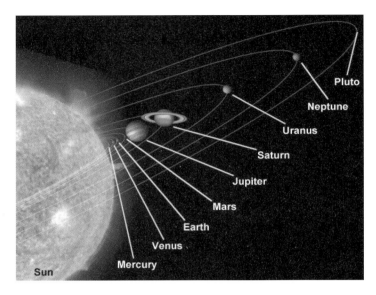

Many of his students asked Copernicus to write a book about those ideas. However, he was reluctant to do so, since those ideas were against the common beliefs of that time. Also he thought that the church would not allow him to publish such a book. But eventually, in 1543, he finished writing his book. On the day of the same year he died, he received a copy of it. His book created a sensation. The public found it very controversial. Unfortunately, Copernicus did not have a chance to defend his theory.

1 **What is the best main idea of the passage?**

① the truth about Copernicus

② controversy of the earth by public

③ theories of Copernicus

④ personality of Copernicus

⑤ timidness of Copernicus

단어 조사해 오세요~ **Word**

Copernicus

astronomer

propose

reluctant

belief

eventually

sensation

controversial

unfortunately

theory

2 **Why was Copernicus reluctant to write a book at first?**

① He didn't want to tell others his top secret theory.

② Because no one would believe him at that time.

③ He didn't have enough money to write the book.

④ Because many people didn't know the heliocentric theory.

⑤ It was against the law for him to write the book.

* heliocentric theory 지동설

3 **Choose the best answer to fill in the blank.**

① thought this idea was wrong

② tried to publish his own book

③ was not a very intelligent astronomer

④ was assure of his assertion

⑤ kept his theories as a top secret

4 이 글의 내용을 한 문장으로 요약하고자 한다. 빈칸 (A)와 (B)에 들어갈 말로 가장 적절한 것은?

> Copernicus was the first person who proposed that the sun was
> _____(A)_____ of the universe and all the planets
> _____(B)_____ around it.

① famous ··· acknowledged ② common beliefs ··· recognized

③ the center ··· revolved ④ heliocentricism ··· orbited

⑤ the universe ··· revolved

Review ☺

A Translate into English.

1 나타내다, 상징하다 _____

2 관중 _____

3 속이다 _____

4 목적 _____

5 주장하다, 논의하다 _____

6 능력 _____

7 회복하다 _____

8 이용하다, 활용하다 _____

9 증가하다 _____

10 나타나다, 일어나다 _____

11 자원 _____

12 위협하다 _____

13 방어, 방위, 수비 _____

14 인공위성 _____

15 요구하다 _____

16 발사하다 _____

17 마침내, 결국 _____

18 이론 _____

19 제안하다 _____

20 믿음, 의견, 생각 _____

B Translate into Korean.

1 various _____

2 demon _____

3 religious _____

4 occasion _____

5 compare to _____

6 permanently _____

7 linguistic _____

8 tend to _____

9 impact _____

10 activity _____

11 wild creature _____

12 continent _____

13 communist _____

14 budget _____

15 decade _____

16 concern _____

17 astronomer _____

18 reluctant _____

19 sensation _____

20 controversial _____

C **Choose the correct answers to each question.**

1   All over the world, people have worn masks to _____ gods or demons.
　① represent　② various
　③ ancient　④ occasion

2   According to scientists, females tend to show better linguistic _____ .
　① injury　② recover
　③ cell　④ ability

3   People sometimes _____ wild creatures by making too much noise.
　① increase　② threaten
　③ activity　④ tourist

D **Translate into English or Korean.**

1   I went to the library to find the book.

　_____

2   My family has lived in this apartment since I was 10 years old.

　_____

3   사장은 그에게 그 프로젝트를 다음 주까지 끝내라고 지시했다. (ordered, finish, the project, the boos, by next week)

　_____

4   내가 어렸을 때, 엄마가 이 모자를 사주셨다. (young)

　_____,

　my mother bought me this hat.

E **Choose the correct words to fill in the blanks.**

1   When you were on the bus, I called out your name. (해석 찾기)
　① 네가 버스에 탔고 나는 너의 이름을 불렀다.
　② 네가 버스에 있을 때 내가 너의 이름을 불렀다.
　③ 네가 버스에서 내리고 내가 너의 이름을 불렀다.
　④ 네가 버스에서 내렸기 때문에 내가 너의 이름을 불렀다.

2   I _____ Chinese characters for 11 years.
　① have studied　② has studied
　③ was studied　④ will be studied

3   My teacher told me _____ .
　① to study　② studying
　③ have to study　④ has to study

F **Choose the same word for both sentences.**

recover	ability	various

1   There were _____ questions on the test.
　My mother likes _____ flowers.

2   My dog _____ed from an injury.
　I hope you _____ your health soon.

3   You have a special _____ to solve math problems.
　He had a natural _____ to survive hard times.

CHAPTER 4	DATE	SELF CHECK	TEACHER	PARENTS	CONFIRM
Preview					
Unit 1					
Unit 2					
Unit 3					
Unit 4					
Unit 5					
Review					

Who Discovered Cheese?
치즈는 누가 발견했나요?

요즘 세대는 치즈를 밥에 비벼먹는, 한국인으로서는 다소 엽기적인(?) 식문화 형태로 변하였습니다. 맛있는 치즈 케이크와 치즈 피자, 치즈에 빵을 찍어먹는 퐁듀, 치즈 안주를 곁들인 포도주까지, 그리고 보면 어느새 치즈가 우리 식생활 문화에 상당수 많은 부분을 차지하고 있습니다. 그런데 이렇게 맛있는 치즈는 대체 누가 만들었을까요? 아니면 우연히 누군가 발견하게 된 건가요?

치즈는 4,000년 이상 된 음식이랍니다. 처음에는 우연히 발견되었답니다. 여기저기 돌아다니며 물건을 파는 아랍 상인인 Kanana가 송아지 위를 말려서 만든 가죽 주머니에 우유를 넣고 낙타 등에 얹어 놓고 긴 여행 중에 사막 위를 걷고 있는 동안 갈증이 나서 우유를 마시려고 주머니를 열어 보았을 때 놀랍게도 우유는 온데간데 없고 걸죽하고 단단한 물체가 보였다고 합니다. 태양열을 쬐고 낙타가 걸어가면서 움직여서 우유는 놀랍게도 유장(whey: 응유와 분리된 액체)만 나오고 우유는 흰 덩어리로 변화되어 있는 것을 발견했습니다. 그 이유는 물통으로 사용된 송아지의 위주머니 안에 렌넷(rennet)이라는 효소가 남아 있어서 그것이 우유에 작용하여 하얀 덩어리를 만들고 낙타의 진동과 사막의 뜨거운 열기에 의하여 치즈가 만들어지게 되었습니다. 이렇게 해서 우유를 마시려다가 대신 치즈를 발견하게 된 그 상인은 상당히 운이 좋았던 거죠. 맛이 좋고 장기간 보존이 가능하여 계속적으로 발전되어 그리스, 로마를 거쳐 유럽지역에 전파되었다고 합니다. 오늘날에는 가공하지 않은 우유나 저온 살균한 우유에서 나오는 박테리아로 치즈를 만든다고 합니다.

CHAPTER

05

Word 🏠 단어도 모르면서 영어 한다 하지 마!

- while *conj.* ~하는 동안, 하지만
- wrist *n.* 손목, 손재주
- introduce *v.* 소개하다, 도입하다
- invention *n.* 발명, 발명품
- unfair *a.* 불공평한, 교활한
- public *a.* 공공의, 공립의
- deserve *v.* ~할 만하다, 값어치가 있다
- pile (up) *v.* 쌓이다, 모으다
- reasonable *a.* 논리적인, 적당한
- heal *v.* 고치다, 깨끗이 하다

- recently *ad.* 요즈음, 근래에
- tendency *n.* 경향, 풍조, 추세
- research *n.* 연구, 탐구, 조사
- organic *a.* 유기체의, 기관의
- tune *n.* 곡조, 가락, 조화
- record *v.* 기록하다, 녹음하다
- second thought 재고, 숙고
- inspire *v.* 격려하다, 영감을 주다
- waste *v.* 낭비하다, 놓치다
- succeed *v.* 성공하다, 뒤를 잇다

∷ Mini Quiz

1	_____ oneself	자기소개를 하다
2	_____ treatment	불평등한 대우
3	in _____	공공연히, 공중 앞에서
4	_____ attention	주목할 만하다
5	at a(n) _____ price	적당한 가격으로
6	a general _____	일반적인 추세
7	_____ fertilizer	유기비료
8	out of _____	음조가 맞지 않는, 비협조적인
9	on _____	다시 생각해 보니
10	_____ in solving a problem	문제를 해결하는 데 성공하다

Grammar 👤 기본 문법도 모르면서 독해한다 하지 마!

★ **to**부정사의 의미상 주어는 〈**for** + 목적격〉으로, **to**부정사 앞에 쓰면 된다.

It is unusual **for me** *to get up* early in the morning. 내가 아침에 일찍 일어나는 것은 드문 일이다.

To make it easy **for her** *to get* there, we drew a map.

그녀가 그곳에 쉽게 갈 수 있게 하려고 우리는 지도를 그려 주었다.

★ 재귀대명사 관용표현 중 〈**by oneself**〉는 '혼자서' 라는 뜻이다. '혼자 힘으로' 를 뜻하는 〈**for oneself**〉와는 구별해야 한다.

She did her homework **by herself** because her friend didn't come.

그녀는 그녀의 친구가 오지 않아서 혼자 숙제를 했다.

I went to grandmother's house **by myself**. 나는 혼자서 할머니 댁에 갔다.

★ **to**부정사의 부사적 용법 중 많이 쓰이는 '~하기 위하여' 라는 목적을 나타내는 예문을 살펴보자.

I went to a department store **to meet** my friend. 나는 친구를 만나기 위해 백화점에 갔다.

I want to go abroad **to study** English. 나는 영어를 공부하기 위해 외국에 가고 싶다.

:: Mini Quiz

1 다음 주어진 표현이 들어갈 알맞은 곳은?

[for us]

It is (①) important (②) to check (③) the time (④) when we take the test.

2 다음 to부정사의 쓰임 중 <u>다른</u> 하나는?

① I slept for 10 hours <u>to get rid</u> of fatigue.

② He threw a party <u>to surprise</u> his girlfriend.

③ I didn't mean <u>to hurt</u> you.

④ We went to the store <u>to buy</u> a jar of jam.

3 다음 밑줄 친 <u>myself</u>의 쓰임 중 <u>다른</u> 하나는?

① I have to do it by <u>myself</u>.　　② I love <u>myself</u>.

③ I ate dinner by <u>myself</u>.　　④ I cleaned my room by <u>myself</u>.

[1] The first wristwatch was invented in 1790 by a watchmaker in Geneva, Switzerland. (a) He had gotten the idea while taking a walk in a park near his shop. (b) [2] He saw *a young woman holding* her infant child with both her arms. (c) [3] To make it easy for her to check the time, she had tied her pocket watch around her wrist. (d) Soon, he had made the first wristwatch in history. (e) [4] The invention of the first wristwatch was inspired by the smart young mother.

1 Choose the best place for the sentence given below.

> The watchmaker ran back to his store and began working.

① (a)　　　　② (b)　　　　③ (c)
④ (d)　　　　⑤ (e)

단어 조사해 오셔~ **Word**

wristwatch

watchmaker

take a walk

infant

invention

inspire

2 If the sentence is true, write T, if the sentence is false, write F.

(1) _____　The child tied her watch around her wrist.
(2) _____　The watchmaker's shop was far from the park.
(3) _____　The watchmaker got his idea from a young mother.

Drill 1 Grammar

감각동사의 특징

감각동사는 5형식 동사가 될 수 있다. 목적어의 '동작', 즉 행동을 표현할 경우 목적격 보어 자리에 '-ing' 형태를 쓴다. 특히 목적어의 진행 중인 동작을 나타낼 때 사용한다.

> **V** + **X** + **Y** (행동하는 순간, 진행 중인 행위를 표현해야 하므로 –ing형태)
> (감각동사)　X(목적어)가　Y(동작)를 한다

- We watched *the sun* rising over the sea.　우리는 해가 바다위로 떠오르는 것을 지켜보았다.
  　　지켜보았다　　　X가　　Y하는 것을

- I saw *a man* crossing the bridge.　나는 한 남자가 다리를 건너는 것을 봤다.

1　She felt her face turning red.

　　해석 ◎ _____

2　I saw some children swimming in the river.

　　해석 ◎ _____

3　사람들은 발밑에서 지진이 땅을 흔드는 것을 느꼈다.
　　(feel, the ground, beneath their feet, an earthquake, shaking)

　　영작 ◎ _____

 Drill 2 Translation

1　1번 문장 ◎ _____

2　2번 문장 ◎ _____

3　3번 문장 ◎ _____

4　4번 문장 ◎ _____

[1] Do you agree that people doing dirty work should get wages higher than now?

Cindy: Everybody hates to do other people's dirty work. And dirty work can be physically challenging and dangerous. [2] It is unfair that the people who clean public bathrooms, other people's houses, offices or streets are not paid well.

Michael: The more difficult it is to be trained for a job, the more money you deserve. [3] For instance, you should invest a lot of money and time until you become a medical doctor, not to mention that you should make an enormous effort. Therefore, it is reasonable that you make a lot of money once you finish your studies and become a doctor. But you don't need any real training to become a maid or a janitor.

Tom: Suppose how smelly it will be if garbage piles up on the streets for a week. [4] Then you will realize how important those workers are and why they should be paid higher.

---

1 **Who answered the question in a positive way?**

① Cindy
② Michael
③ Michael, Cindy
④ Cindy, Tom
⑤ Cindy, Michael, Tom

2 **Choose the sentence that best summarizes this paragraph.**

① Michael wants to become a doctor but Cindy and Tom disagree with it.
② Each person has a different job and they're proud of it.
③ It is not so easy to earn money.
④ People should study harder to get fine jobs.
⑤ People are having a debate whether workers who do dirty jobs should be paid.

단어 조사해 오셔~ **Word**

wage

physically

deserve

for instance

invest

medical

mention

enormous

reasonable

maid

janitor

suppose

Drill 1 Grammar

It is + 형용사 + that ~

It은 우리말 무조건 '그것' 으로 해석하고 that은 우리말 '것, 라고' 를 붙여 해석한다. 영어는 주어와 동사가 가까워야 핵심 말을 먼저 설명할 수 있다. 주어가 조금만 길어도 무조건 가주어 it을 먼저 쓰고 진주어는 뒤로 보낸다.

- **It is true that** health is above wealth. 그것은 진실이다, 건강이 재산에 앞선다는 것은.

- **It is clear that** we should find other alternative energy sources.
그것은 확실하다, 우리가 다른 대체 에너지 자원을 찾아야 한다는 것이.

1 It is strange that she has come home so late at night.

해석 ◐ _____

2 It is strange that people should be afraid to die, for death is a necessary end and it will come when it comes.

해석 ◐ _____

3 사람들이 예전보다 더 오래 사는 것은 확실하다. (live longer, before, certain, than)

영작 ◐ _____

Drill 2 Translation

1 1번 문장 ◑ _____

2 2번 문장 ◑ _____

3 3번 문장 ◑ _____

4 4번 문장 ◑ _____

[1] For centuries, there has been a tendency for us to think of health only in terms of physical bodies. [2] The medical community did not look seriously at the possibility that our mind could play an important role in illness and healing. Recently, _____, there has been a lot of research that proves our mind affects illness and healing. [3] A medical center reported that a larger portion of their patients were people who did not have an organic disease but were seeking psychological help.

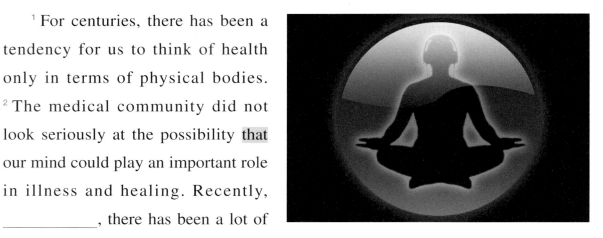

기출

1 이 글의 요지로 가장 적절한 것은?

① 환자는 의사의 처방을 잘 따라야 한다.
② 의사는 병을 치료하는 데 보람을 느낀다.
③ 규칙적인 검진은 질병 예방에 필요하다.
　발병과 치유에는 환자의 심리적 영향이 크다.
⑤ 의학이 발달해도 언제나 새로운 질병이 나타난다.

2 Choose a phrase to fill in the blank.

① in addition
② in the end
③ as a result
④ however
⑤ for example

단어 조사해 오셔~ **Word**

tendency

in terms of

medical community

seriously

play a role in

illness

seek

research

prove

affect

a large portion of

organic

psychological

 **Drill 1** Grammar

관계대명사 that

관계사는 같은 말의 반복을 피하기 위해 두 문장의 공통된 부분을 하나로 연결시키는 역할을 한다. 〈명사 + that〉일 때, '~하는, ~할, ~했던'로 앞에 있는 명사를 꾸며 주며 해석한다.

> The man [that *will sing tonight*] is Mir. 오늘밤 노래를 부를 사람이 Mir이다.
>   V₁   V₂

- Egypt is a country [**that** *has many interesting histories.*] 이집트는 재미있는 역사가 많은 나라이다.

---

1 The Beatles that changed music forever were the most famous rock'n'roll band in the world.

해석 ◎ _____

2 John Pemberton was the first man that invented Coca-Cola.

해석 ◎ _____

3 The woman that I saw yesterday was a ghost.

해석 ◎ _____

4 미선이는 그 비밀을 아는 유일한 소녀이다. (the only girl, know, the secret)

영작 ◎ _____

 **Drill 2** Translation

1 1번 문장 ◎ _____

2 2번 문장 ◎ _____

3 3번 문장 ◎ _____

A long time ago, there was no _____. [1] At that time, the songs people sang were what they made by themselves or what they had learned from other people. [2] Once a song was made, it was passed along from one person to another. The song

changed a lot after a while as people sang it in different ways. [3] However, about nine hundred years ago, some Italian monks came up with an idea to write a tune or melody. [4] They recorded the musical sounds simply by using lines and dots. These monks, thus, became the first known music composers.

1 **Choose the best phrase to fill in the blank.**

① folk songs
② music halls
③ written music
④ singing groups
⑤ instruments

2 **What is NOT mentioned in the paragraph?**

① Music was passed straight to the monks to record.
② Italian monks were the first to begin to write tunes or melodies.
③ In the beginning, people only sang and learned from each other.
④ Dots and lines were used by the monks to record music.
⑤ Italian monks were the first formal composers.

단어 조사해 오세욤~ **Word**

once

pass along

monk

tune

record

simply

dot

composer

Drill 1 Grammar

관계대명사 what

what은 명사절로 사용되어 문장에서 '주어, 목적어, 보어 역할' 을 한다. 선행사 없이 단독으로 다니는 '왕따' what은 거의 '~것' 으로 해석하면 되므로, 정확히 해석하는 연습이 필요하다.

- **What** history teaches us *is* very important.　역사가 우리에게 가르쳐 주는 것은 매우 중요하다.

- **What** is important *is* to bring a painting back to an artist's original intent.
  중요한 것은 그림을 예술가의 원래 의도로 되돌리는 것이다.

1　When doing anything, just focus on what you are doing.

　　해석 ◎ _____

2　Poetry provides us with what is missing in our own lives.

　　해석 ◎ _____

3　Kelly는 그녀가 배우는 것을 절대 잊어버리지 않는다. (what, learns, she, forgets, never)

　　영작 ◎ _____

Drill 2 Translation

1　1번 문장 ◎ _____

2　2번 문장 ◎ _____

3　3번 문장 ◎ _____

4　4번 문장 ◎ _____

(A)

To be successful in your life, all you have to do is to get started. You cannot win anything unless you begin something! And in order to begin, you must do something now. <u>Many people have negative images about themselves</u>: they don't think that they can succeed. However, don't wait until you're ready to make big decisions. If you do nothing and just wait, you'll never accomplish anything. For example, if you want to write a novel, don't waste your time and hope to get inspired someday. Simply open a notebook and hold a pencil. You may not have anything to write when you start, but pretty soon the inspiration will come.

(B)

(a) I want to describe the classical concert yesterday, which was one of the most intense experiences of my life. It was very enjoyable. (b) Especially the violinist was excellent! (c) I made up my mind to practice the violin until I can play like the violinist. (d) Actually, I first thought I would not be good at playing the violin no matter how hard I practiced. (e) However, on second thought, I decided to give myself a chance to learn to play the violin.

1 **What is the moral in the passages (A) and (B)?**

① Bad news travels fast.

② Beginning is half done.

③ Too many cooks spoil the broth.

④ Where there is smoke, there is fire.

⑤ When in Rome, do as the Romans do.

2 **Choose the sentence in the paragraph (B) that corresponds to the underlined <u>Many people have negative image about themselves</u> in paragraph (A).**

① (a)

② (b)

③ (c)

④ (d)

⑤ (e)

3 **According to the passages, what is the most important thing to have success in life?**

① Always practice hard.

② Read lots of novels.

③ Wait for a big opportunity.

④ Study hard at school.

⑤ Initiate something without hesitation.

단어 조사해 오세요~ **Word**

successful

unless

negative

decision

accomplish

inspiration

enjoyable

especially

make up

actually

no matter how

moral

correspond

A Translate into English.

1 유아 _____

2 소개하다 _____

3 손목 _____

4 시계 제조업자 _____

5 투자하다 _____

6 의학의 _____

7 합당한, 정당한 _____

8 큰, 거대한 _____

9 진지하게 _____

10 증명하다 _____

11 ～에 영향을 주다 _____

12 찾다, 추구하다 _____

13 일단 ～하면 _____

14 곡, 가락 _____

15 작은 점 _____

16 기록하다 _____

17 부정적인 _____

18 이루다, 성취하다 _____

19 ～을 결심하다 _____

20 영감 _____

B Translate into Korean.

1 inspire _____

2 invention _____

3 while _____

4 tie _____

5 mention _____

6 suppose _____

7 deserve _____

8 janitor _____

9 medical community _____

10 play a role in _____

11 organic _____

12 psychological _____

13 pass along _____

14 monk _____

15 composer _____

16 instrument _____

17 enjoyable _____

18 moral _____

19 correspond _____

20 unless _____

C Choose the correct answers to each question.

1 The first _____ was invented in 1790 by a watchmaker in Geneva, Switzerland.

① wrist   ② clock
③ wristwatch   ④ infant

2 It is _____ to expect you to make a lot of money once you finish your studies and become a doctor.

① seriously
② enormous
③ medical
④ reasonable

3 Our minds can play an important role in _____ and healing.

① illness   ② seek
③ organic   ④ affect

D Translate into English or Korean.

1 I heard you calling my name.

_____

2 It is terrific that you got a job.

_____

3 그가 약속을 어긴 남자다.
(that, broke, promise)

He is _____.

4 네가 지금 듣고 있는 것이 내가 제일 좋아하는 노래다. (what, hear)

_____ is my favorite song.

E Choose the correct words to fill in the blanks.

1 It is _____ that you have to work on Christmas day.

① awful   ② wonderful
③ inspire   ④ surprise

2 I felt somebody tapping my shoulder.
(해석 찾기)

① 나는 누군가가 내 어깨를 두드리는 것을 느꼈다.
② 누군가는 내가 어깨를 두드리는 것을 느꼈다.
③ 누군가가 자기 어깨를 두드리는 것을 느꼈다.
④ 나는 누군가의 어깨를 두드려 주었다.

3 The baby _____ was crying at the concert is John's baby.

① this   ② these
③ that   ④ those

4 _____ is a dress made by Designer Andre Kim.

① What
② You wear
③ What you are wearing
④ Wearing

F Match the meanings for each word.

1 tune   ① a feeling which gives you new and creative ideas

2 inspiration   ② a series of musical notes that is pleasant and easy to remember

3 moral   ③ to have a close similarity or connection

4 correspond   ④ principles and beliefs concerning right and wrong behavior

CHAPTER 5	DATE	SELF CHECK	TEACHER	PARENTS	CONFIRM
Preview					
Unit 1					
Unit 2					
Unit 3					
Unit 4					
Unit 5					
Review					

Why Do Small Paper Cuts Hurt More Than Bigger Cuts?
왜 종이에 벤 작은 상처가 큰 상처보다 더 아픈 걸까요?

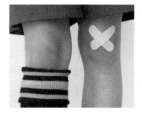

가끔 새 책을 사서 뿌듯한 마음으로 무심코 책일 읽다가, 또는 열심히 일을 하다가 나도 모르게 종이에 손을 베는 경험을 누구나 한번 씩 해보았을 것입니다. 특히 종이가 너무 빳빳해서 손을 베는 경우가 많은데, 상식적으로 칼로 벤 상처가 더 아파야 하는데, 연필을 잡아도 아프고, 물만 조금 닿아도 쓰라리고, 도대체 요 쪼그만 상처가 왜 이렇게 아프고 쑤시는 걸까요?

아마도 종이에 벤 작은 상처가 큰 상처보다 더 신경 쓰이고 짜증이 나기 때문일 것입니다. 왜 피도 나지 않는 그런 하찮고 가벼운 상처가 그리도 통증이 큰 걸까요? 우리 손가락에는 신경 말단 부분이 피부 표면 가까이에 있기 때문이라고 합니다. 우리의 손에는 거의 어떤 신체 부위보다 더 신경 말단 부분이 많이 있습니다. 종이에 벤 상처는 이 신경 말단 부분을 자극하여 손상을 주지만, 그리 큰 상처를 내지는 않습니다. 그래서 사람들은 대부분 더 깊이 베였을 때만큼 종이에 벤 상처를 치료하지 않아도 된다고 생각하고 경향이 있습니다. 종이에 벤 상처에 밴드에이드를 붙인다고 해서 상처가 더 빨리 아물지는 않겠지만, 상처 부위를 촉촉하게 유지시키면 통증을 덜 수 있다고 합니다.

CHAPTER

06

Word 🏠 단어도 모르면서 영어 한다 하지 마!

- **break** *v.* 고장내다, 부수다   *n.* 중단
- **symbolize** *v.* 상징하다, 기호화하다
- **escape** *v.* 달아나다, 벗어나다
- **origin** *n.* 기원, 원인, 유래
- **whole** *a.* 전체의, 완전한
- **memory** *n.* 기억, 추억, 기념품
- **form** *n.* 형태, 모습   *v.* 형성하다
- **last** *v.* 지속하다   *a.* 마지막의
- **business** *n.* 업무, 장사, 회사
- **convenient** *a.* 편리한, 형편이 좋은

- **communicate** *v.* 의사소통하다
- **present** *a.* 참석한, 현재의   *v.* 나타내다
- **accept** *v.* 인정하다, 수락하다
- **matter** *n.* 물질, 문제, 사정
- **theorize** *v.* 이론을 세우다
- **state** *v.* 진술하다   *n.* 상태, 정부
- **useful** *a.* 쓸모 있는, 유용한
- **misunderstand** *v.* 오해하다
- **indicate** *v.* 가리키다, 나타내다
- **universal** *a.* 보편적인, 우주의

∷ Mini Quiz

1	_____ from the burning house	불타는 집에서 도망쳐 나오다
2	the _____ of civilization	문명의 기원
3	have a poor _____	기억력이 나쁘다
4	in the _____ of	~의 형태로
5	a(n) _____ tool	편리한 도구
6	_____ by e-mail	이메일로 의사소통하다
7	a(n) _____ of	~에 관한 문제
8	a(n) _____ of war	전쟁상태
9	_____ a place on a map	지도에서 어느 장소를 가리키다
10	_____ trend	일반적인 경향

Grammar 🎓 기본 문법도 모르면서 독해한다 하지마!

★ 현재 사실과 반대되는 상황을 가정할 때 〈If + 주어 + 과거형동사, 주어 + **would** + 동사원형〉을 쓴다.

If I **had** enough money, I **would buy** a new MP3 player.

내가 돈이 충분히 있다면 새 MP3 플레이어를 살 것이다.

If he **worked** less, he **would be** healthier. 그가 일을 덜 한다면 더 건강할 것이다.

★ 조동사 **may**는 50% 이하의 추측, 확신일 때 사용한다. (**less than 50% certainty**)

It **may** be raining outside. 밖에 아마 비가 올지도 모른다.

This book **may** belong to Jane. 이 책은 아마 Jane의 것일 거야.

★ **to**부정사가 앞에 있는 명사를 꾸밀 때 이를 '부정사의 형용사 용법' 이라 한다.

I have a book **to return** to the library. 나는 도서관에 반납할 책이 있다.

I need something **to eat**. 나는 먹을 것이 필요하다.

∷ Mini Quiz

1 다음 문장 중 틀린 부분을 찾아 바르게 고치시오.

If she had <u>enough</u> money she <u>will</u> buy a jacket <u>for</u> her boyfriend.
  ①   ②   ③   ④

2 다음 중 밑줄 친 <u>may</u>의 쓰임이 <u>다른</u> 하나는?

① <u>May</u> I help you?

② She <u>may</u> be sick.

③ This <u>may</u> be the answer.

④ He <u>may</u> come here.

3 다음 밑줄 친 to부정사의 쓰임 중 <u>다른</u> 하나는?

① I need something <u>to drink</u>.

② Give me something <u>to write</u> with.

③ He gave me the book <u>to read</u>.

④ I went to the store <u>to buy</u> some drinks.

The ancient Egyptian people first used a ring to symbolize an everlasting marriage. [1] Since there are no breaks in a ring, they believed that people who were wearing those rings would live happily ever after. [2] The Egyptians thought that if the ring broke, it would bring bad luck and the marriage would end. [3] They also believed that if a person took the ring off, love would escape from the heart of the person. [4] They thought that blood from one's heart went directly to the fourth finger of the left hand. That is the reason why the fourth finger became the ring finger.

1 **What is the best title for this paragraph?**

① The Importance of a Faithful Marriage Life
② The Real Meaning of Marriage
③ Various Materials for a Ring
④ The Importance of Platonic Love
⑤ The Origin and the Meaning of the Wedding Ring

2 **Why did Egyptians begin to wear a ring?**

① To bring good luck to themselves.
② To live happily forever with their spouse.
③ Because they wanted to show off their wealth.
④ It took a very important role related to the heart.
⑤ It was a new fad.

단어 조사해 오셔~ **Word**

ancient

Egyptian

symbolize

everlasting

marriage

take off

escape

directly

origin

🍴 Drill 1 Grammar

since의 특징

접속사로 사용되는 since는 우리말 '~때문에'로 해석된다. 완료표현 〈have+p.p.〉와 쓰일 때에는 '~이래로, ~이후로'의 뜻이 되므로 조심해야 한다. since는 이미 이유가 잘 알려져 있거나 그 이유가 문장의 나머지 부분보다 덜 중요할 때 주로 쓰인다.

> Since s + v , S + V (since + s + v) 뒤에 올 수도 있다
> ~이기 때문에 …

- **Since** you are honest and diligent, I believe you. 당신이 정직하고 부지런하므로 나는 당신을 믿는다.
- **Since** he has lied to me, I cannot trust him any more.
  그가 나에게 거짓말을 했기 때문에, 나는 그를 더 이상 믿을 수가 없다.

---

1 Since my brother failed the college entrance exam, he has to take it again.

해석 ◯ _____

2 He slept all day, since he read detective stories all night.

해석 ◯ _____

3 버스가 만원이었기 때문에, 나는 집으로 걸어가야 했다. (full, the bus, had to, walk)

영작 ◯ _____

🍴 Drill 2 Translation

1 1번 문장 ◯ _____

2 2번 문장 ◯ _____

3 3번 문장 ◯ _____

4 4번 문장 ◯ _____

Guess what it feels like to forget your whole past. [1] There are actually some diseases which can cause you to lose your memory. [2] One of them is called amnesia. A person with amnesia loses all or part of his memory. [3] Someone with amnesia may not remember anything about 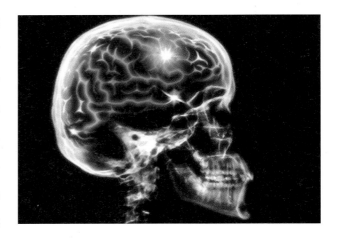 himself including his name, family, or friends. Therefore, amnesia can cause serious problems. Amnesia can last a short time or it can be permanent. If it is caused by an organic brain injury, it may go on for a long time. However, if it is due to a less serious head injury, that form of the disease would not last too long. [4] As well as amnesia, Alzheimer's may cause one to lose one's memory.

1 **Choose the content that best logically follows this paragraph.**

① The Importance of Medical Research
② Memory Loss Problems Related to Alzheimer's
③ Danger of Brain Damage
④ Tips for Improving Memory
⑤ Types of Long-Term Amnesia

2 **According to the paragraph, what can be the worst case?**

① permanent memory loss from amnesia
② an organic brain injury
③ a less serious head injury
④ suffering from Alzheimer's
⑤ none of the above

단어 조사해 오셔~ **Word**

past

disease

cause

amnesia

serious

last

permanent

organic

go on

injury

Alzheimer's

Drill 1 Grammar

2형식 수동태

⟨be + p.p. + 명사 / 형용사 / 동사의 변형 형태(to부정사, 현재분사, 과거분사)⟩의 순서로 오면 2형식 수동태임을 알 수 있게 된다. 억지로 수동태를 껴 맞추어 해석하다 보면 오히려 말이 더 이상하게 될 수 있다. '~로, ~라고'로 해석하거나 'be' 동사 자체의 의미를 살려 해석해도 된다.

• An old man was found dead in his house where few people visited.

　　한 노인이 사람들이 거의 방문하지 않는 그의 집에서 시체로 발견되었다.

• A group of ghosts were said to appear in the deserted house.

　　귀신의 무리가 흉가에서 나타난다고 말해진다.

1　Lee Myung-Bak is thought to be one of the greatest leaders in Korea.

　　해석 ◯ _____

2　Harry Potter was not allowed to use magic outside of Hogwarts School.

　　해석 ◯ _____

3　나의 남자친구는 모든 사람들에게 고릴라라고 불린다. (boyfriend, by everyone, call, gorilla)

　　영작 ◯ _____

 Drill 2 Translation

1　1번 문장 ◯ _____

2　2번 문장 ◯ _____

3　3번 문장 ◯ _____

4　4번 문장 ◯ _____

[1] The use of the Internet is on the rise every year, and this creates many challenges. (a) One of the biggest challenges in the Internet world is security or safety. (b) [2] Businesses, for example, need to make sure that their sites on the Internet are safe for their users. (c) [3] They

need to know who e-mail senders are and whether information coming and going is correct. (d) How the hackers can steal their information is a mystery. (e) [4] While many companies use e-mail because it's a convenient way to communicate, they should take measures to be certain that company secrets remain protected. Described below are some methods that one business is using to meet this challenge.

1 **Choose the best content that follows this paragraph.**

① 기업간 경쟁 방법
② 홈페이지 제작 방법
③ 인터넷 보안 방법
④ 구조 조정의 중요성
⑤ 도전 정신의 중요성

2 (a)~(e) 중, 이 글의 전체 흐름과 관계 없는 문장은?

① (a)
② (b)
③ (c)
④ (d)
⑤ (e)

단어 조사해 오셔~ **Word**

challenge

security

on the rise

safety

make sure

take measures

protect

method

meet

Drill 1 Grammar

명사절로 사용되는 how

중학교부터 고등학교까지 의문사, 관계사, 명사절 다양하게 배워왔지만 정확하게 구별하여 이해하는 학생들이 적은 게 사실이다. "어떠한 경우에 how가 명사절로 사용될까?" how 앞에 명사가 없는 순서일 때 우리말 '어떻게 ~지' 를 붙여 해석하게 된다.

• I wonder how he could enter Harvard University.

나는 그가 어떻게 하버드 대학에 들어갈 수 있었는지 궁금하다.

• I want to know how she learned to play the guitar with her feet.

나는 어떻게 그녀가 발로 기타 치는 것을 배웠는지를 알고 싶다.

1 How she became so busy all of a sudden is a mystery to everyone.

해석 ◯ _____

2 How he could eat two large pizzas and still be hungry is a wonder.

해석 ◯ _____

3 나는 그가 어떻게 그 수학 문제를 풀 수 있었는지 궁금하다. (could solve, the math problem, wonder, how)

영작 ◯ _____

Drill 2 Translation

1 1번 문장 ◯ _____

2 2번 문장 ◯ _____

3 3번 문장 ◯ _____

4 4번 문장 ◯ _____

Among the many theories about the creation of the universe, the big bang theory is the most widely accepted theory which explains the development of the universe. (a) [1] It theorizes that the universe has expanded into its current state from a prior state approximately 20 billion years

ago when there was a huge explosion, which is referred to as the big bang. (b) All matter, energy, space, and even time were produced during the big bang. (c) According to some scientists, the universe will not last for a long time. (d) [2] Although scientists cannot explain yet why or exactly how the big bang happened, they mostly agree that this explosion let the universe expand. (e) [3] As the matter, which was produced during the explosion, was cooled, it formed the particles that made up everything in the universe.

1 Choose the sentence that does **NOT** fit in this paragraph.

① (a) ② (b) ③ (c)

④ (d) ⑤ (e)

2 What is the writer's intention in this paragraph?

① to predict the future from of the universe

② to describe how hard scientists have worked

③ to show the incompetence of scientists because they're not 100% sure

④ to explain the history of the universe

⑤ to explain the most popular theory of the creation of the universe

단어 조사해 오세요~ **Word**

big bang theory

theorize

expand

current

state

prior

approximately

explosion

refer

exactly

particle

Drill 1 Grammar

분사의 형용사적 역할

분사란 '형용사' 와 같다고 설명하는 책들이 대부분이나, 사실 분사는 '명사의 행동, 동작' 을 표현할 때 사용하는 것이다. 영어는 순서에 의해서 결정이 되는데, '-ing / -ed' 형태의 말이 명사 '앞 또는 바로 뒤' 에 위치할 때 -ing는 '~하는, ~하고 있는' 으로, -ed/en 형태는 '~해진, ~된' 으로 해석하면 된다.

~ ed/en + N(명사) '~된, ~진 + 명사' 로 해석 / ~ ing + N(명사) '~하는, ~하고 있는 + 명사' 로 해석

- the **interesting** book   재미있는 책
- a **broken** window   깨진(부서진) 창
- **fallen** leaves   떨어진 낙엽들
- a **running** turtle   달리는 거북이

1   There is a smiling woman in the picture.

해석 ⊙ _____

2   The movie "The War" was the most exciting film in Korea.

해석 ⊙ _____

3   He showed me a broken-down car in the street.

해석 ⊙ _____

4   나는 잠긴 차 안에 있는 이상한 여자를 봤다. (lock, strange, see, in)

영작 ⊙ _____

Drill 2 Translation

1   1번 문장 ⊙ _____

2   2번 문장 ⊙ _____

3   3번 문장 ⊙ _____

Body language is often useful when I travel foreign countries. Usually I can communicate with the people who speak in other languages when I use body language. _____, I have learned that sometimes body language can be misunderstood. Last summer, I was traveling in France. When the hotel manager showed me the room I would stay in and asked me, "Is this room all right?" I made the "Okay" sign with my index finger and thumb to tell him it was okay. The manager looked surprised for a second. Then he said, "I am sorry to hear that. Then, we'll find you another room." At that moment, I didn't understand why he offered me another room. Later I was told that French people use this gesture to indicate "zero" or "useless." From that experience, I learned an important lesson that not all gestures have universal meanings. Most times, gestures are useful when we can't express ourselves verbally. But sometimes they can cause misunderstandings or get you in big trouble!

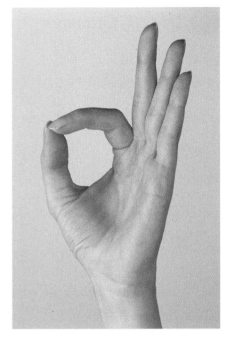

1 Choose the best word to fill in the blank.

① Therefore
② However
③ Moreover
④ For instance
⑤ In other words

2 Which of the followings can you conclude from this passage?

① Body language is an effective way to communicate.
② It is possible to communicate with other people even if you don't speak their language.
③ Using gestures can break the ice between people.
④ Excessive use of gestures may be considered improper and rude.
⑤ You should be careful when you use body language in other countries.

3 Why was the hotel manager surprised?

① Because the writer couldn't speak French.
② Because the writer could only use body language.
③ Because he misunderstood the meaning of the 'Okay' sign.
④ Because he had a lack of experience.
⑤ Because the writer went into the wrong room.

4 What does the underlined 'useless' mean in this passage?

① to save
② none
③ malicious
④ mendicant
⑤ worthless

단어 조사해 오셔~ **Word**

foreign

communicate

misunderstand

index finger

thumb

offer

indicate

useless

universal

gesture

verbally

Review

A **Translate into English.**

1 곧장, 바로 _____

2 고대의 _____

3 달아나다, 사라지다 _____

4 결혼 _____

5 과거 _____

6 질병 _____

7 이어지다, 지속하다 _____

8 영구적인 _____

9 증가되고 있는 _____

10 보호하다 _____

11 방법 _____

12 대처하다 _____

13 이론(학설)을 세우다 _____

14 상태, 형세 _____

15 이전의 _____

16 정확하게 _____

17 오해 _____

18 표현하다 _____

19 언어 _____

20 쓸모없는 _____

B **Translate into Korean.**

1 symbolize _____

2 origin _____

3 everlasting _____

4 take off _____

5 organic _____

6 injury _____

7 cause _____

8 amnesia _____

9 challenge _____

10 security _____

11 make sure _____

12 take measures _____

13 approximately _____

14 explosion _____

15 refer _____

16 current _____

17 lesson _____

18 offer _____

19 index finger _____

20 thumb _____

C **Choose the correct answers to each question.**

1 The ancient Egyptian people first used a ring to _____ an everlasting marriage.
① escape ② symbolize
③ break ④ since

2 A person with _____ loses all or part of his memory.
① amnesia ② past
③ injury ④ brain

3 Usually, gestures are useful when we can't _____ ourselves verbally.
① express ② offer
③ learn ④ cause

D **Translate into English or Korean.**

1 He has to stay at work since he didn't finish his work.

_____

2 My grandfather was thought to be one of the patriots.

_____

3 점수를 더 잘 받는 것이 네 부모님을 기쁘게 하는 방법이다. (how, make somebody happy)

Getting better scores is _____

_____.

4 정원에 떨어진 낙엽을 줍자. (fall, leaf, garden)

Let's pick up _____

_____.

E **Choose the correct words to fill in the blanks.**

1 You have to wear a warm jacket _____ it's cold outside.
① where ② but
③ why ④ since

2 This diet _____ the One Food diet.
① is called ② called
③ is calling ④ to call

3 _____ is very interesting.
① He becomes an astronaut
② How does he become an astronaut
③ How he became an astronaut
④ Become an astronaut

4 It is difficult to take care of _____ babies.
① cry ② cried
③ crying ④ to cry

F **Match the words and the meanings.**

security	last	current	express

1 _____ to continue for a particular length of time

2 _____ to tell or show that what you are feeling or thinking

3 _____ things that are done to keep a person, building, or country safe from danger

4 _____ happening or existing now

CHAPTER 6	DATE	SELF CHECK	TEACHER	PARENTS	CONFIRM
Preview					
Unit 1					
Unit 2					
Unit 3					
Unit 4					
Unit 5					
Review					

Why Does Orange Juice Taste strange After You Brush Your Teeth?
이를 닦은 후에 마시는 오렌지 주스는 왜 이상한 맛이 날까요?

열심히 공부하고 집에 돌아와 이를 닦고, 시원하게 샤워를 했더니 목이 타네요, 냉장고에 있는 시원한 오렌지 주스를 꺼내 한 잔 마시는 순간 허걱! 주스 맛이 왜 이리 시금털털, 떨떠름한 걸까요? 오렌지 주스가 상한 건가요?

이를 닦은 후에 오렌지 주스를 마셔 본 사람이라면 오렌지 주스 맛이 떨떠름한 것을 경험했을 것입니다. 이유가 뭘까요? 그것은 치약 속에 들어있는 라우릴 황산염 나트륨이라 불리는 세정용 화학 약품 때문입니다. 이 SLS는 오렌지 주스 안에 들어있는 천연산에 화학반응을 일으키면서 입안에서 단맛은 온데간데 없어지고 쓴맛이 나게 되는 것입니다. 오렌지 주스 맛을 제대로 즐기려면 이를 닦기 전이나 이를 딱은 후 몇 분 정도는 기다렸다가 드시는 것이 좋아요!

CHAPTER 07

Word 🏠 단어도 모르면서 영어 한다 하지 마!

- punishment *n.* 벌, 응징, 혹사
- proper *a.* 적당한, 예의바른, 고유의
- spare *v.* 용서하다, 할애하다, 아끼다
- order *n.* 순서, 정돈, 질서
- spend *v.* 소비하다, 낭비하다
- stream *n.* 흐름, 경향, 시내, 개울
- import *v.* 수입하다, 의미하다
- defeat *v.* 쳐부수다, 좌절시키다 *n.* 패배
- professional *a.* 직업의, 전문적인
- appropriate *a.* 적당한, 특유한, 고유한

- consider *v.* 생각하다, 고려하다
- play *v.* 놀다, 연주하다, 공연하다
- build *v.* 세우다, 형성하다, 훈련하다
- early *ad.* 일찍이 *a.* 이른, 초기의
- interact *v.* 상호작용하다
- determine *v.* 결심하다, 결정하다
- draw *v.* 당기다, 뽑다, 끌다
- realize *v.* 실감하다, 실현하다, 깨닫다
- admire *v.* 감탄하다, 동경하다
- sink *v.* 가라앉다, 약해지다

⠶ Mini Quiz

1	_____ for the occasion	경우에 꼭 맞는, 형편(자리) 등에 적당한
2	_____ oneself	수고를 아끼다
3	stand in _____ of arrival	도착한 순서대로 서있다
4	three victories and four _____	3승 4패
5	turn _____	프로선수로 전향하다
6	_____ another possibility	또 다른 가능성을 고려하다
7	_____ which way to go	어느 길로 가야 할지 결정하다
8	I didn't _____ it.	나는 그걸 미처 깨닫지 못했다.
9	_____ the view	광경을 보고 감탄하다
10	_____ with customers on-line	온라인상에서 고객들과 대화하다

Grammar 👤 기본 문법도 모르면서 독해한다 하지 마!

★ 이전의 과거(대과거)부터 이후의 과거 시점까지 완료된 일을 나타낼 때 과거완료 〈**had + 과거분사**〉를 사용한다.

My father **had gone** out when I **came** home. 내가 집에 왔을 때 아빠는 외출하신 후였다.

I **had finished** homework when my sister **entered** my room.

내 여동생이 내 방에 들어왔을 때 나는 숙제를 끝마친 후였다.

★ 〈**be + to부정사**〉는 예정, 의무, 운명, 가능, 의도 등을 의미한다.

She **is to arrive** home tomorrow. 그녀는 내일 집에 도착할 예정이다.

You **are to finish** your homework before dinner. 너는 저녁 시간 전까지 숙제를 끝마쳐야 한다.

★ 상관접속사가 들어가는 주어 〈**neither A nor B**〉는 뒤의 주어(**B**)에 동사를 일치시킨다.

Neither she nor you have a red skirt. 그녀도 너도 빨강색 치마는 없다.

Neither you nor I was interested in that movie. 너도 나도 그 영화에는 관심이 없었다.

:: Mini Quiz

1 다음 문장 중 <u>틀린</u> 부분을 찾아 바르게 고치시오.

I <u>have done</u> the dishes <u>when</u> my mother <u>hung</u> up the phone and <u>came</u> to kitchen.
　　①　　　　　　　　②　　　　　　③　　　　　　　　　④

2 다음 밑줄 친 〈be+to부정사〉의 쓰임 중 <u>다른</u> 하나는?

① My dream <u>is to become</u> a doctor.

② We <u>are to leave</u> here next year.

③ Her hobby <u>is to play</u> basketball.

④ His plan <u>is to go</u> to university this year.

3 다음 문장 중 <u>틀린</u> 부분을 찾아 바르게 고치시오.

Neither her sisters <u>nor</u> she <u>go</u> to school because they <u>don't</u> feel well today.
　　①　　　　　　②　　③　　　　　　　　　　④

Is corporal punishment an effective means to discipline students?

Sally: "Spare the rod and spoil the child" is all too true. [1] Not only at home but in the school, physical punishment is sometimes the only way to discipline children. [2] In addition, you can get the proper attention from the one who gets punished as well as from all of his friends or classmates.

John: Some children are so undisciplined that they do not follow any rules. [3] Corporal punishment – unless it is too severe – may be an effective means to teach such children and to maintain order in the classroom.

Cindy: There is a saying that goes: "Those who live by the sword also die by the sword." Love and reason must be the only effective ways to teach children. [4] The only thing children can learn from corporal punishment is that violence can be justified.

1 Who answered the question in positive ways?

① Sally   ② Cindy   ③ Sally, John
④ John, Cindy   ⑤ Sally, John, Cindy

2 What is the aim of this conversation?

① to punish children severely
② to find techniques of corporal punishment
③ to only love children and always stand by their side
④ to discuss pros and cons of physical punishment
⑤ to improve children's exam grades

단어 조사해 오세요~ **Word**

corporal punishment

means

discipline

spare

rod

spoil

attention

undisciplined

severe

violence

justify

 Drill 1 Grammar

명사 + to부정사

부정사에 대해 다양한 문법적인 규칙이 있지만, 한번이라도 우리말 '무엇' 과 같은지 배운 적이 있는가? 영어는 우리말과 달리 순서가 가장 중요한데, 명사 바로 뒤에 나오는 to부정사는 우리말 '~할, ~했던, ~해야 할' 으로 앞말을 꾸며 주며 해석하면 된다.

> N(명사) + to v   '~할, ~했던, ~해야 할 명사'

• The man to sing tonight is Mir. 오늘밤 노래를 부를 사람은 Mir이다.

= The man who will sing tonight is Mir.

위 두 문장의 차이점은? 의미는 똑같다. 그 이유는 두 문장 모두 명사(the man) 뒤에 온 순서이기에 비슷한 역할을 하게 된다.

---

1 There is a gesture to wish good luck.

해석 ◉ _____

2 The only person to cook the food is Yoon-sun.

해석 ◉ _____

3 연습이 외국어를 배우는 유일한 방법이다.

영작 ◉ _____

 Drill 2 Translation

1 1번 문장 ◉ _____

2 2번 문장 ◉ _____

3 3번 문장 ◉ _____

4 4번 문장 ◉ _____

[1] A father took his son to the country (A) to show / showing him how poor people can be. They spent a weekend on the farm of a very poor family. [2] After returning home from their trip, the father (B) was asked / asked his son, "Did you see how poor people can be?" "Yes," the son answered. "We have one dog at home, and they have four. [3] We have a pool in the backyard, and they have a stream (C) that / what has no end. We have imported lamps, and they have the stars." [4] When the little boy was finished, his father sat speechless. The trip had completely defeated the father's purpose.

기출

1 이 글에서 소년에 관한 설명 중, 내용과 일치하는 것은?

① 시골에서 일주일을 보냈다.
③ 아버지의 농장에서 일했다.
③ 시골 사람들의 빈곤함에 놀랐다.
④ 수영장이 있는 농장에서 살았다.
⑤ 시골 환경이 좋다고 생각했다.

2 (A), (B), (C)에서 어법에 맞는 표현을 골라 짝지은 것은?

	(A)		(B)		(C)
①	to show	......	asked	......	what
②	showing	......	was asked	......	what
③	to show	......	asked	......	that
④	to show	......	was asked	......	that
⑤	showing	......	was asked	......	that

단어 조사해 오세요~ **Word**

take

farm

trip

backyard

stream

imported

speechless

defeat

purpose

 **Drill 1** Grammar

2형식 동사의 이해

보통 문법에서는 〈주어＋동사＋보어〉의 형태가 되면 2형식이라고 배우지만, 동사 자체의 이해 없이 문법 주입식은 고급영어로 나아갈 수가 없다. '이동이나, 움직임'을 나타내는 sit, go, come, fall, lie, stand 등의 동사 뒤에 보어가 될 수 있는 말이 오면 우리말 '~인 채로'로 해석한다.

> V[sit, go, come, stand, fall, return 등] **+** 명사, 형용사   '~인 채로'
>   to V, –ing (동작이 필요)

• The man **sat** *listening* to the music over and over all night.

    그 남자는 밤새도록 몇 번이고 반복해서 음악을 듣는 채로 앉아 있었다.

• The handsome man **stood** *smoking* a cigarette.   그 잘생긴 남자는 담배 피는 채로 서 있었다.

---

1   He ran screaming down the street.

    해석 ◯ _____

2   He sat reading comic books all day long.

    해석 ◯ _____

3   그 어린 소년은 아빠가 그의 방으로 들어왔을 때 침대에서 자는 채로 누워있었다. (lie)

    영작 ◯ The young boy _____ on his bed when his father came into his room.

 **Drill 2** Translation

1   1번 문장 ◯ _____

2   2번 문장 ◯ _____

3   3번 문장 ◯ _____

4   4번 문장 ◯ _____

[1] Andres Segovia is the first renowned classical guitarist. He was born in 1893 in Spain. (a) Before the 20th century, people did not consider the guitar as a classical instrument. (b) [2] Most people thought the guitar suitable only for pop music. (c) [3] Even though some classical composers wrote music for the guitar, it was never played in classical concerts. (d) Segovia proved to the world that the guitar can also be a great classical instrument. (e)

1 Choose the best place for the sentence given below.

> Segovia had his first public performance at the age of sixteen and continued having professional classical concerts in many countries.

① (a)   ② (b)   ③ (c)
④ (d)   ⑤ (e)

2 Choose the sentence that explains this paragraph correctly.

① It took almost 10 years for him to make the guitar.
② At that time, many people thought the guitar was appropriate for classical concerts.
③ After the 19th century, people accepted the guitar as a classical instrument.
④ Segovia thought the guitar was suitable for classical music and put on the first classical guitar concert.
⑤ Some composers proved that the guitar was suitable only for pop music.

단어 조사해 오세요~ **Word**

renowned

guitarist

consider

classical

instrument

suitable

even though

composer

play

prove

performance

Drill 1 Grammar

5형식 동사 think의 특징

동사의 뜻만 보고 문장의 형식을 알 수가 있다. 주로 '생각'에 관계된 동사는 5형식 동사가 될 가능성이 크다. 생각의 동사에는 think, believe, guess, expect, find 등이 있는데 목적격보어 자리에 명사, 형용사가 오는 경우는 '개념, 이름, 상태'를 나타내지만, 목적어가 동작, 즉 행동이 필요할 경우 목적격보어 자리에 to부정사를 사용하여 동작을 표현한다. 우리말 '~를 …라고 생각하다' 라고 해석한다.

> V (생각 동사) $+ X + Y$
> 생각하다   X를   Y라고, Y로

- Everybody in Korea thinks Yi Sunsin a great general.

  한국에 있는 모든 사람들은 이순신을 훌륭한 장군이라고 생각한다.

- Many people don't like women to smoke. 많은 사람들은 여자들이 담배 피는 것을 싫어한다.

---

1 I believe the nuclear bomb to be the most evil invention ever created.

해석 ◯ _____

2 The young man thought himself handsome and charming.

해석 ◯ _____

3 모든 학생들은 그를 바보라고 생각한다. (a fool, all the students)

영작 ◯ _____

Drill 2 Translation

1 1번 문장 ◯ _____

2 2번 문장 ◯ _____

3 3번 문장 ◯ _____

[1] Scholars have argued for many years about how a person's personality is formed. [2] This argument has long been known as 'Nature vs. Nurture.' Some scholars argue that one's personality is genetically determined. According to them, one's experience after birth does not change one's personality at all. _____, some other scholars believe that a person's personality is formed after birth. [3] They argue that one's personality is most affected by one's early relationship with one's parents and with culture. [4] These days, however, most scholars agree that neither nature nor nurture solely influences one's personality. Rather, they believe both nature and nurture interactively affect it.

1 **Choose the word or phrase to fill in the blank.**

① And
② Second
③ Instead
④ On the contrary
⑤ In conclusion

2 **Choose the best title for this paragraph.**

① Nature of People
② The Formation of Personality
③ Effect of Culture
④ Research Result of the Scholars
⑤ Relationship of Humans

단어 조사해 오세요~ **Word**

personality

argue

nature

nurture

scholar

genetically

determine

experience

affect

relationship

culture

solely

influence

interactively

 **Drill 1** Grammar

have been + p.p.

완료형의 수동태는 '완료' 라는 문법 지식보다 우리말로 과거에 '~했(었)다' 로 처리하면서 수동의 느낌만 살려 주면 된다. 즉, '~되었다, 되어 왔다' 로 해석하면 된다.

- The Amazon region has been called "the lungs of the world."

  아마존 지역은 '세계의 허파' 라고 불려왔다.

- This history book has been translated into many languages.

  이 역사책은 많은 언어들로 번역되어 왔다.

---

1 The Beatles' songs have been loved by many people all over the world.

해석 ◯ _____

2 Soccer has been called Brazil's national pastime.

해석 ◯ _____

3 모든 입장권이 이미 팔려버렸다. (already, sell, all the tickets)

영작 ◯ _____

Drill 2 Translation

1 1번 문장 ◯ _____

2 2번 문장 ◯ _____

3 3번 문장 ◯ _____

4 4번 문장 ◯ _____

The Titanic was the largest passenger ship ever built in her day. On the 10th of April, 1912, the luxurious ocean liner Titanic sailed on her maiden voyage from Southampton, England to New York. From the very beginning of her construction, the Titanic drew worldwide attention. She was considered as the safest and most luxurious ocean liner. The Titanic was to win the famous Blue Ribbon award after her maiden voyage. (a) It went smoothly at first and the passengers enjoyed the voyage. But, at a quarter to midnight on April 14th, 1912, the ship unfortunately crashed into an iceberg while (b) it was cruising at full speed. (c) It made an enormous rip in the ship's hull, and even the 'safe' construction could not save the vessel.

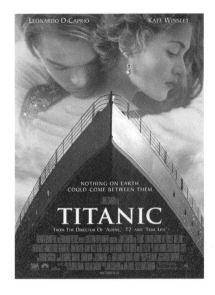

There were approximately 2,224 passengers on board. But the total lifeboat capacity of the vessel was only 1,178. The maiden voyage of the gigantic ocean liner started with others' admiration, _____. Many people who could not board the lifeboats died in the icy cold water of the North Atlantic. The vessels which answered the Titanic's SOS signal were too far from the sinking giant to be of assistance.

Before the Titanic sank, the crew of the Titanic saw the dark outline of a ship passing nearby, and people thought salvation finally came. But this ship did not respond to the distress signals and soon disappeared. And eventually the Titanic sank at 2:20 in the morning. Twenty minutes later, the Cunard Liner Carpathia arrived. But still, a total of 1,513 lives were lost. The Titanic's dream to win the

Blue Ribbon award could not be realized. Instead, the Titanic has been remembered as one of the greatest disasters in maritime history.

---

1 **Which of the following information is NOT true?**

① Titanic was the largest passenger ship in 1912.
② Titanic was supposed to win the Blue Ribbon award.
③ Some people actually survived this terrible disaster.
④ The season was spring when the accident happened.
⑤ Titanic sank because of its unsafe construction.

2 (a)~(c) 중, 밑줄 친 it이 가리키는 대상이 다른 것은?

① (a)   ② (b)   ③ (c)

3 글의 내용을 한 문장으로 요약하고자 한다. 빈칸 (A)와 (B)에 들어갈 말로 가장 적절한 것끼리 짝지은 것은?

> From the very beginning of Titanic's _____(A)_____, the Titanic drew worldwide attention, but it was _____(B)_____ that it crashed into an iceberg during its voyage.

① construction ⋯ prideful   ② construction ⋯ frustrating
③ construction ⋯ exciting   ④ splendor ⋯ frustrating
⑤ splendor ⋯ exciting

4 이 글의 빈칸에 들어갈 말로 가장 적절한 것은?

① which they were proud of
② but the fare was too expensive
③ but it wasn't that great in the indoors
④ but it ended in tragedy
⑤ but it was not warm enough

단어 조사해 오세요~ **Word**

Titanic
ocean liner
luxurious
maiden
voyage
construction
attention
unfortunately
cruise
enormous
rip
hull
vessel
approximately
capacity
admiration
assistance
salvation
respond
distress signal
eventually
disaster
maritime

A   Translate into English.

1   수단, 방법 _____

2   망치다 _____

3   효과적인 _____

4   유지하다 _____

5   농장, 농원 _____

6   뒤뜰 _____

7   말을 못하는 _____

8   목적, 의도 _____

9   구조 _____

10 생각(간주)하다 _____

11 악기 _____

12 공연 _____

13 성격 _____

14 논쟁하다 _____

15 학자 _____

16 결정하다 _____

17 호화로운 _____

18 미경험의, 처녀의 _____

19 수용력, 포용력 _____

20 지원, 도움 _____

B   Translate into Korean.

1   cruise _____

2   undisciplined _____

3   severe _____

4   justify _____

5   stream _____

6   import _____

7   defeat _____

8   take _____

9   guitarist _____

10 suitable _____

11 composer _____

12 prove _____

13 nurture _____

14 genetically _____

15 solely _____

16 influence _____

17 approximately _____

18 admiration _____

19 construction _____

20 enormous _____

C **Choose the correct answers to each question.**

1 _____ the rod and spoil the child.
① Punish
② Maintain
③ Spare
④ Discipline

2 We usually _____ a weekend with parents.
① spend
② defeat
③ import
④ finish

3 Andres Segovia is the first _____ classical guitarist.
① renowned
② prove
③ suitable
④ performance

D **Translate into English or Korean.**

1 This song has been sung by many people.

_____

2 I stood holding a bunch of bananas.

_____

3 나는 앉을 의자를 찾고 있다.
(look for, a chair, sit)

I am _____ on.

4 나는 그가 애국자라고 생각한다.
(a patriot, think)

_____

E **Choose the correct words to fill in the blanks.**

1 Give me something _____ on.
① writing
② to write
③ written
④ write

2 He came _____ a hamburger.
① have
② had
③ eating
④ eat

3 They found him _____.
① is a liar
② a liar
③ was a liar
④ to a liar

4 This book _____ as one of the classics.
① been known
② has been knowing
③ have been known
④ has been known

F **Write the correct words to fill in the blanks.**

1 *a.* violent ➡ *n.* _____

2 *n.* effect ➡ *a.* _____

3 *v.* perform ➡ *n.* _____

4 *v.* argue ➡ *n.* _____

5 *v.* construct ➡ *n.* _____

6 *v.* admire ➡ *n.* _____

CHAPTER 7	DATE	SELF CHECK	TEACHER	PARENTS	CONFIRM
Preview					
Unit 1					
Unit 2					
Unit 3					
Unit 4					
Unit 5					
Review					

Why Do Snakes Dart Out Their Tongues?
뱀은 왜 혀를 낼름거리는 거예요? 메롱으로 우리를 놀리는 건가요?

'동물의 왕국' 이나 '디스커버리 채널' 등을 볼 때면, 여러 가지 종류의 뱀들이 등장하는데 작은 놈이든, 사람보다 더 큰 놈이든 간에 똑같이 혀를 낼름거리는 것을 볼 수 있습니다. 사람들한테 '약 오르지롱' 하며 놀리는 걸까요? 땅에서도 나무에서도 심지어 먹이에 접근할 때도 혀를 낼름거리는데 도대체 왜 그런 걸까요?

뱀이 혀를 낼름거리며 기어다니는 것을 보면 정말로 소름이 쫙 돋아날 정도로 무섭습니다. 사실 누군가를 해치려거나 놀리려는 의도로 그런 행동을 하는 것은 아닙니다. 뱀은 무척 날쌔고 예민해 보이지만 감각 기관이 그리 발달하지 못한 신경이 무딘 동물입니다. 뱀은 혀를 이용해 먹이를 찾고, 유기물의 냄새를 맡고 맛을 느끼게 해주는 아주 중요한 감각 기관 역할을 합니다. 짝을 찾을 때도 가장 많이 사용하는 것이 바로 혀입니다. 말하자면 뱀의 혀는 곤충의 더듬이와 비슷한 역할을 하고 있는 것이지요.

그래서 항상 혀를 낼름거리면서 사물의 위치를 파악하고 공기 중에 흩어져 있는 냄새를 혀를 이용하여 코와 입천장에 있는 냄새를 인지하는 두 개의 액낭에 보냅니다. 이 액낭들은 혀의 끝과 각각 연결되어 있어 공중에 떠다니는 극소량의 냄새를 감지하여 먹이나 짝을 찾아내는 것입니다. 그리고 먹이를 잡을 때는 유연성이 뛰어난 턱뼈를 늘려 먹이를 물거나, 몸으로 먹이를 칭칭 감아서 사냥을 한답니다. 최근 조사에 따르면 뱀은 혀로 음파를 탐지할 수도 있어서 먹이감에 가까이 다가갈 수 있다고 합니다.

CHAPTER 08

Word 🏠 단어도 모르면서 영어 한다 하지 마!

☐ **already** *ad.* 이미, 벌써

☐ **latest** *a.* 최신의, 최근의

☐ **discourage** *v.* 낙담시키다

☐ **knowledge** *n.* 지식, 견문, 학문

☐ **rush** *v.* 돌진하다, 서두르다

☐ **forecast** *v.* 예상하다, 예보하다

☐ **progressive** *a.* 전진하는, 진보적인

☐ **motivate** *v.* 동기를 주다, 자극하다

☐ **movement** *n.* 동작, 운동, 동향

☐ **occur** *v.* 발생하다, 머리에 떠오르다

☐ **solar** *a.* 태양의

☐ **phenomenon** *n.* 현상, 사건

☐ **appreciation** *v.* 진가, 감상, 감사, 존중

☐ **factor** *n.* 요인, 요소, 원인

☐ **appear** *v.* 나타나다, ~인 듯하다

☐ **disappoint** *v.* 실망시키다, 좌절시키다

☐ **scene** *n.* 장면, 경치, 현장

☐ **contaminate** *v.* 오염시키다, 더럽히다

☐ **offend** *v.* 성나게 하다, 위배되다

☐ **investigate** *v.* 조사하다, 수사하다, 연구하다

❖ Mini Quiz

1 get deeply _____   크게 낙담하다

2 Fires often _____ in winter.   화재는 겨울에 자주 발생한다.

3 _____ is power.   아는 것이 힘이다.

4 _____ out of school   학교에서 (아이들이) 우르르 쏟아져 나오다

5 _____ changes   점진적인 변화

6 _____ energy   태양에너지

7 _____ his ability   그의 능력의 진가를 알다

8 _____ the crime   범죄를 수사하다

9 the _____ of an accident   사고 현장

10 _____ against the custom   관습에 어긋나다

Grammar 기본 문법도 모르면서 독해한다 하지마!

★ 시간의 부사절에서는 현재시제를 사용하여 미래를 표현한다.

After I graduate, I will work with my father. 나는 졸업한 후 아버지와 함께 일할 것이다.
When he comes home, she will tell him. 그가 집에 오면, 그녀가 그에게 말할 것이다.

★ 방법을 나타내는 관계부사 **how**는 선행사 **the way**와 함께 쓰이지 않으며 명사절을 이끈다.

This is **how we solve the problem**. 이것이 우리가 그 문제 해결하는 방법이다.
    (how = the way in which)
How I look in this party is important. 이 파티에서 내가 어떻게 보이느냐가 중요하다.
(how = the way in which)

★ 현재 진행형이 가까운 미래의 확정된 일을 나타내는 경우를 살펴보자.

They **are leaving** from Seoul tomorrow. 그들은 내일 서울을 떠날 것이다.
He **is coming** home soon. 그는 곧 집에 올 것이다.

:: Mini Quiz

1 다음 문장 중 틀린 부분을 찾아 바르게 고치시오.

   I will do my best after I will finish this project.
   ①   ②   ③   ④

2 다음 문장 중 틀린 부분을 찾아 바르게 고치시오.

   I told him the way how she accomplished the project.
   ①   ②   ③   ④

3 다음 괄호 안에서 적절한 표현을 고르시오.

   The plane to L.A. [is taking off / have took off] tomorrow morning.

In a meeting of Animal Space Scientists, the chimpanzee proudly announced. "We sent a rocket to the moon. [1] It stayed there for a whole month before making the long trip back to Earth." [2] "That's nothing," said the fox. "We already sent our spaceship to start the first colony on Mars." "We can beat you both," said the pig. "We're going to send a rocket straight to the sun." The chimpanzee and the fox laughed loudly and said. "Don't be silly. [3] The rocket will melt before it gets there." "No, it won't," said the pig. [4] "We're sending it up at night."

기출

1 이 글에서 필자의 어조로 가장 적절한 것은?

① 분석적
② 부정적
③ 감상적
④ 사실적
⑤ 해학적

2 돼지가 여우와 침팬지를 이길 수 있다고 확신한 이유로 가장 적절한 것은?

① The pig's rocket was the latest model.
② Because the other animals were discouraged.
③ Because the pig thought that space has day and night.
④ Because the pig had a great knowledge about space.
⑤ The pig's rocket was already on its way to the sun.

단어 조사해 오세요~ **Word**

proudly

announce

trip

spaceship

colony

beat

straight

laugh

silly

melt

🍴 Drill 1 Grammar

시간의 부사절 **before**, 시간의 부사절에 대해 조금 더 알아보자!

before ~하기 전에	when ~할 때	while ~하는 동안에, ~인 반면에
after ~하고 나서	as ~할 때, ~함에 따라서	since ~이래로, ~이기 때문에
once 일단 ~하면	until[till] ~할 때까지	

- It will not be long **before** your dream *comes* true. 네 꿈이 실현되기까지 오래 걸리지 않을 것이다.
- It has been 10 years **since** I *saw* you last. 네가 너를 마지막으로 본 이래로 10년이 흘렀다.

1 What are you going to do after school is over?

해석 ◉ _____

2 그녀는 학교를 졸업한 후에, 좋은 직업을 가질 것이다.

영작 ◉ _____

3 After watching the movie, all the people in the movie theater got very angry.

해석 ◉ _____

🍴 Drill 2 Translation

1 1번 문장 ◉ _____

2 2번 문장 ◉ _____

3 3번 문장 ◉ _____

4 4번 문장 ◉ _____

Unexpectedly, a storm formed over the ocean. [1] Nobody could really expect it because the forecast had said the weather would be clear for the afternoon. [2] On the sea, there was a ferry boat which delivered tourists twice a day to a small island from the mainland. [3] The larger the

waves became, the more frightened the people on the boat were. Suddenly, a wave the size of a great mountain almost turned the ship over. People became panicked, and they all rushed to the lifeboats. Crews and male passengers helped women and children climb into the lifeboats. [4] Among them, there was a 12 year-old boy, Tom, who was about to climb into the boat with his mother. Then he saw the horrified women and children behind him. He did not think there would be enough space in the lifeboat for all of them. So Tom decided to swim to shore.

1 Choose the matched word that best describes Tom's personality in this paragraph.

① patriotic
② progressive
③ hard-working
④ sacrificial
⑤ selfish

2 Which describes the overall mood of this paragraph?

① exciting
② disappointing
③ sporting
④ motivating
⑤ alarming

단어 조사해 오셔~ **Word**

unexpectedly

among

expect

forecast

deliver

mainland

frighten

turn over

crew

be about to

horrify

space

🍴 Drill 1 Grammar

비교급의 주요 구문 〈the + 비교급 ~, the + 비교급 ~〉

'~하면 할수록, 더욱 더 ~하다' 로 해석한다.

> The + 비교급 + S + V , the + 비교급 + S + V
> (원인) ~하면 할수록   (결과) 더욱 더 ~하다

- **The more** you eat, **the fatter** you become. 네가 더 많이 먹으면 먹을수록 살은 더욱 더 찐다.

- **The fresher** the fruit is, **the better** it tastes. 과일이 더 신선할수록, 그것은 맛이 더 좋다.

---

1 The harder you study, the better grades you will get.

해석 ⊙ _____

2 네가 더 열심히 공부할수록, 너는 너의 꿈에 점점 더 가까워져 간다. (the harder, the closer, your dream, get)

영작 ⊙ _____

3 The longer he waits to take a shower, the smellier he becomes.

해석 ⊙ _____

🍴 Drill 2 Translation

1 1번 문장 ⊙ _____

2 2번 문장 ⊙ _____

3 3번 문장 ⊙ _____

4 4번 문장 ⊙ _____

Have you ever seen an eclipse of the Sun? (a) It is called a solar eclipse. 'Solar' means 'of the Sun.' (b) ¹ A solar eclipse happens when the Sun's light is blocked from the Earth. ² Do you know why it is blocked? It is because of the movements of both the Earth and the Moon. The Moon circles around the Earth. At the same time, both the Earth and the Moon travel around the Sun. (c) We cannot live without the Sun. (d) During its movement, the Moon sometimes passes between the Earth and the Sun. When it does, the Sun's light is blocked by the Moon. (e) ³ This means that the Sun, the Earth and the Moon make a single line with the Moon in the middle. ⁴ When the Sun's light is completely blocked, the Earth becomes dark. This darkness may persist for two to several minutes. Then, as the Moon moves, the sunlight appears again. A solar eclipse is a spectacular phenomenon.

1 **Choose the sentence that does not belong in this paragraph.**

① (a)   ② (b)   ③ (c)

④ (d)   ⑤ (e)

2 **Choose the best main idea for the paragraph.**

① A solar eclipse is a spectacular phenomenon.

② Have you ever seen an eclipse of the Sun?

③ A solar eclipse occurs when the Sun's light is blocked by the Moon.

④ We cannot live without the Sun.

⑤ The Moon sometimes passes between the Earth and the Sun.

단어 조사해 오세요~ **Word**

eclipse

solar eclipse

block

movement

completely

persist

several

appear

spectacular

phenomenon

 **Drill 1** Grammar

접속사 why

접속사 why는 명사절을 이끌어 주어 또는 목적어 역할을 할 수 있다. 이러한 경우에 주어와 목적어가 길어지므로, 문장의 실제 동사를 찾아 끊어 읽을 수 있어야 한다.

- [Why ancient Egyptians built pyramids] *remains* a mystery.
  고대 이집트인들이 피라미드를 왜 지었는지가 미스터리로 남아있다.

- Do you *know* why Christina left early? Christina가 왜 일찍 떠났는지를 아니?

---

1 I don't know why she had to leave me at that time.

해석 ◉ _____

2 This is why Lee Myung-bak became the president of Korea.

해석 ◉ _____

3 나는 왜 그가 그 이상한 여자를 사랑했는지 정말로 궁금하다. (really wonder, the strange woman, why)

영작 ◉ _____

Drill 2 Translation

1 1번 문장 ◉ _____

2 2번 문장 ◉ _____

3 3번 문장 ◉ _____

4 4번 문장 ◉ _____

[1] Korean people call it a blind date, in which more than two girls and an equal number of boys have a date together, called a "meeting." Usually during the "meeting," they have a cup of tea all together first in order to get to know each other better. Then, they pick their date partners according to an agreed rule. When they make their decisions, it seems that appearance is the most important factor. [2] One day, I overheard one college student talking about his date partner, and I noticed all he was interested in was how she looked and what she was wearing. [3] But I'd like to advise the young people; they must understand that beauty is in the eyes of the beholder and that appearance does not reflect the good quality of a person at all. Therefore, they should make an effort to learn about their partners even if they are disappointed with their partners' looks. [4] If they do so, they will be able to have appreciation beyond "God's failed work."

1 **What does the underlined phrase "God's failed work" mean?**

① being cursed by God

② a plain appearance

③ the fact that the partner is not a church-goer

④ meeting a wrong partner

⑤ being late for a blind date

2 **What do young people care most about in a blind date?**

① economical ability

② appearance

③ smartness

④ beauty

⑤ richness

단어 조사해 오셔~ **Word**

pick

decision

it seems that

factor

overhear

beholder

appearance

reflect

quality

make an effort

disappoint

looks

appreciation

beyond

 **Drill 1** Grammar

관용적 표현 It seems that ~

It은 가주어가 되고, that은 명사절인 진주어인 구문이다. 대단한 문법적인 역할보다 만날 때마다 정확하게 해석할 수 있으면 된다. 우리말 '~처럼 보이다' 로 해석한다.

It seems that ... ~처럼 보이다	It appears that ... ~처럼 보이다
It happens that ... 우연히 ~하다	It follows that ... ~라는 결론이 된다

- **It seems that** she *knows* about the secret. 그녀가 그 비밀을 아는 것처럼 보인다.
- **It happened that** I *sat* beside a beautiful woman on the train.
  나는 우연히 기차에서 아름다운 여자 옆에 앉았다.

1 It seems that she likes to talk with a ghost.

해석 ◎ _____

2 It seems that people in Korea really like hamburgers or pizza.

해석 ◎ _____

3 그는 우표 수집을 좋아하는 것 같다. (seems, stamps, collecting)

영작 ◎ _____

Drill 2 Translation

1 1번 문장 ◎ _____

2 2번 문장 ◎ _____

3 3번 문장 ◎ _____

4 4번 문장 ◎ _____

In many mystery books and movies, fingerprints at the crime scene play a very important role to catch the offender. (a) In a movie, you may see that investigators dust everywhere to search for fingerprints. And when <u>they</u> do, they never miss a single print. _____, the weapon used for the crime is often found near the scene. (b) Usually, the police use latex gloves when they pick up the weapon in order not to contaminate the valuable evidence. (c) Then, a few hours later, they have all the information of the offender. Those movies make us think that crime investigation is a piece of cake. (d) First, smart criminals don't leave their fingerprints or any other evidence behind. Second, if they left fingerprints, it is very unlikely that those prints are in the police database unless <u>they</u> are ex-convicts. (e) Therefore, don't trust what you see in the movies too much.

1 The below sentence has been omitted from the paragraph. The answer choices within the paragraph indicate possible places where the omitted sentence can be inserted. Choose the best possible answer.

> But in real life, it usually takes longer than a week to find good evidence, and there are more unresolved cases than resolved cases.

① (a)   ② (b)   ③ (c)
④ (d)   ⑤ (e)

2 What is the writer trying to explain?

① Comparing the crime investigation of books or movies with real situations
② Explaining the wisdom and cautiousness of the offenders
③ Only ex-convicts are easy to arrest.
④ Investigations aren't so difficult because police officers use latex gloves.
⑤ Finding evidence is the most important process.

3 Choose a phrase to fill in the blank.

① On the contrary   ② For example
③ In addition   ④ The consequence of
⑤ Because of

4 이 글에서 밑줄 친 첫 번째 they와 두 번째 they가 가리키는 것을 가장 잘 짝지은 것은?

첫 번째 they		두 번째 they
① investigators	……	movies
② criminals	……	fingerprints
③ investigators	……	criminals
④ criminals	……	criminals
⑤ investigators	……	fingerprints

단어 조사해 오세요~ **Word**

fingerprint

play an important role

offender

investigator

dust

latex gloves

scene

contaminate

valuable evidence

a piece of cake

database

ex-convict

unresolved

case

Review

A **Translate into English.**

1 발표하다 _____

2 여행 _____

3 식민지 _____

4 녹다 _____

5 예상하다 _____

6 일기예보 _____

7 나르다, 배달하다 _____

8 선원 _____

9 일식 _____

10 막다, 차단하다 _____

11 지속하다 _____

12 나타나다 _____

13 요소, 요인 _____

14 결정 _____

15 우연히 듣다 _____

16 특성, 특질 _____

17 범죄자 _____

18 수사관, 조사자 _____

19 현장, 장소 _____

20 전과자 _____

B **Translate into Korean.**

1 proudly _____

2 beat _____

3 straight _____

4 silly _____

5 unexpectedly _____

6 mainland _____

7 frighten _____

8 turn over _____

9 spectacular _____

10 phenomenon _____

11 several _____

12 movement _____

13 looks _____

14 beholder _____

15 make an effort _____

16 reflect _____

17 valuable evidence _____

18 dust _____

19 fingerprint _____

20 unresolved _____

C **Choose the correct answers to each question.**

1 We are going to send a rocket
_____ to the sun.
① colony ② silly
③ melt ④ straight

2 On the sea, there was a ferry boat which
_____ tourists twice a day to a
small island from the mainland.
① delivered ② rushed
③ turned ④ frightened

3 People should make an effort to learn
about their partners _____ they
are disappointed with their partners'
looks.
① unless ② even if
③ so ④ but

D **Translate into English or Korean.**

1 The colder it gets, the warmer you have
to keep yourself.

2 Do you know why they didn't come to the
party?

_____

3 눈이 오면 나는 나가서 놀 것이다. (it, snow)
I will go out and play _____.

4 그 아이는 빵을 좋아하는 것처럼 보인다.
(seem, the child, bread)
It _____.

E **Choose the correct words to fill in the blanks.**

1 What are you going to do after you
_____ your homework?
① finish ② will finish
③ would finish ④ finished

2 _____ you eat, the fatter you will be.
① Much ② More
③ Most ④ The more

3 That is _____.
① do not drink tap water
② why don't people drink tap water
③ why people don't drink tap water
④ not drink tap water

4 I think you know the answer to this
question.
= It _____ you know the answer to
this question.
① seems that
② happens that
③ doesn't seem that
④ doesn't happen that

F **Write the correct words to fill in the blanks.**

| appearances | beat | valuable |

1 We will win against that team.
= We will _____ that team.

2 Don't judge by looks.
= Don't judge by _____.

3 Try not to contaminate useful evidence.
= Try not to contaminate _____
evidence.

CHAPTER 8	DATE	SELF CHECK	TEACHER	PARENTS	CONFIRM
Preview					
Unit 1					
Unit 2					
Unit 3					
Unit 4					
Unit 5					
Review					

You Don't Have to Overeat to Enjoy Dinner!
오바하지 마란 말이야!

Q. 얼마 전 TV에서 어떤 오락 프로그램을 보고 있었는데요. 근데 게스트로 나온 가수가 별로 웃기지도 않는 얘기를 혼자 신나서 떠들어대자 다른 게스트들이 그 사람에게 '오바하지 말라' 고 호통을 치더라구요. 생각해 보니까 언제부터인지 우리 주변에는 '오바하다' 라는 말이 참 많이 쓰이고 있는 것 같아요. 제 생각에는 over라는 단어에서 나온 콩글리쉬 같은데... 영어에서는 '오버하다' 라는 말을 실생활에서 정말로 사용하나요?

A. 친구들끼리 또는 TV프로그램에서 보면 언제부턴가 우리의 말이나 행동이 지나칠 때, 어떤 일에 너무 신경 쓰거나 과민반응을 보이거나 무리를 할 때 '오바한다' 는 말을 많이 쓰곤 하는데요. over에 '초과' 의 의미가 있는 것을 보고 이런 말을 쓰기 시작한 것 같습니다. 영어에서는 접두사 over를 이용해서 '오바하다' 라는 말을 만들기도 하는데, 어떤 행동이 지나쳤을 때는 overdo, 지나치게 물건을 많이 사거나 소비하는 행위를 overbuy, 무리하게 많이 먹었을 때 overeat을 쓸 수 있습니다. 우리가 흔히 술을 많이 먹고 구토하는 것을 '오바이트' 라고 하는데 이는 overeat의 일본식 발음에서 비롯된 것입니다. overeat은 '과식하다' 의 의미이고, '구토하는 것' 은 vomit이죠. 일반적으로 실생활에서 접두사 over-를 이용한 동사가 그리 많은 편은 아니구요. overcome(극복하다)처럼 over-를 붙인다고 해서 무조건 '지나다' , 즉 '오바하다' 라는 뜻이 되는 건 아닙니다. 일상생활에서 '오바하다' , 즉 말이나 행동이 '지나치다' 라는 뜻으로 가장 많이 쓰이는 표현은 go too far를 씁니다. '터무니없다'(be extravagant)는 뜻의 go overboard를 쓰기도 합니다. 그래서 "어제 술 먹고 너무 오바했어." 라는 말은 When you drank yesterday, you went too far. 혹은 ~ you went overboard.라고 할 수 있습니다. 그 외에도 too far로 타동사 take나 carry를 수식해 take(carry) something too far라고 해도 '~이 너무 지나치다' 라는 뜻이 된답니다.

CHAPTER 09

Word 🏠 단어도 모르면서 영어 한다 하지 마!

- **respond** *v.* 대답하다, 응하다
- **film** *v.* 촬영하다 *n.* 필름, 얇은 막
- **literally** *ad.* 글자 뜻대로, 정말로
- **overlay** *v.* 씌우다, 감추다, 놓다
- **democracy** *n.* 민주주의, 민주정치
- **sight** *v.* 발견하다 *n.* 시력, 풍경
- **enormous** *a.* 거대한, 엄청난
- **possess** *v.* 소유하다, 지니다
- **method** *n.* 방법, 방식, 순서
- **migrate** *v.* 이주하다, 이동하다

- **detail** *n.* 세부, 사소한 일
- **direct** *v.* 지도하다, (주의를) 돌리다
- **promising** *a.* 장래성 있는, 좋아질 것 같은
- **urgent** *a.* 긴급한, 절박한
- **unique** *a.* 유일한, 독특한
- **vivid** *a.* 생생한, 선명한, 발랄한
- **on a regular basis** 정기적으로
- **host** *v.* ~을 주최하다 *n.* 주인
- **match** *v.* 경쟁하다 *n.* 경쟁상대, 경기
- **title** *n.* 제목, 직함, 선수권

∷ Mini Quiz

1 The weather is ＿＿＿＿＿＿.　　　　　　　　　날씨가 좋아질 것 같다.

2 on either a(n) ＿＿＿＿＿ or an occasional ＿＿＿＿＿　　정기적 혹은 비정기적으로

3 The views are ＿＿＿＿＿ breathtaking.　　그 광경은 정말로 아슬아슬했다.

4 a(n) ＿＿＿＿＿ amount of work　　엄청난 양의 일

5 a scientific ＿＿＿＿＿　　과학적인 방법

6 have bad ＿＿＿＿＿　　눈(시력)이 나쁘다

7 describe in ＿＿＿＿＿　　상세하게 설명하다

8 ＿＿＿＿＿ message　　긴급한 전갈

9 ＿＿＿＿＿ color　　선명한 색

10 a(n) ＿＿＿＿＿ personality　　개성

Grammar  기본 문법도 모르면서 독해한다 하지 마!

★ **2형식 문장 중 감각동사는 〈감각동사 + 형용사〉 또는 〈감각동사 + like + 명사〉로 표현한다.**

I **feel good** today. 오늘은 몸 상태가 좋다.

It **sounds like a good idea**. 그것은 좋은 아이디어처럼 들린다.

★ **시간 전치사 for는 '~동안'이라는 의미로 숫자가 포함된 기간과 함께 사용하고, during은 '~하는 중, ~내내' 라는 의미이며 특정한 기간과 함께 사용한다.**

I will finish this book **during the winter vacation**. 나는 겨울방학 동안 이 책을 끝낼 것이다.

We are going to stay at grandmother's **for two weeks**. 우리는 할머니 댁에 2주 동안 머무를 것이다.

★ **강한 추측을 나타내는 조동사 must be(~임에 틀림없다)와 cannot be(~일 리가 없다)에 대해 살펴보자.**

It **must** be true. 그것은 사실임에 틀림없다.

She **cannot** be at home. 그녀가 집에 있을 리 없다.

:: Mini Quiz

1 다음 문장 중 틀린 부분을 찾아 바르게 고치시오.

He <u>looks</u> <u>like</u> <u>very</u> <u>ill</u> today.
　　① 　② 　③ 　④

2 다음 밑줄 친 전치사의 쓰임 중 틀린 것은?

① I have used this dictionary <u>for</u> thirteen years.

② You and I have been together <u>during</u> ten years.

③ She slept <u>for</u> four hours yesterday.

④ I will be here <u>during</u> the holidays.

3 다음 괄호 안에서 적당한 표현을 고르시오.

Jane is honest and clever so she [must / cannot] be the thief.

How would you respond if someone says humans can fly? Some people really can – at least in movies. [1] For example, you've probably seen Superman flying through the sky in a movie. Surely, people in that movie do not literally fly. [2] But moviemakers know some tricks to make them look like they are flying. [3] A few decades ago, when technology was not as developed as now, people used a trick in films.  [4] First, they filmed the sky in which clouds or stars moved quite fast. Then the actors who pretended to fly were filmed. After that, the film with the actors was overlaid on the film with the sky. [5] So the image of the actors was put over the image of the sky. But nowadays, the tricks the moviemakers use have become more complicated, thanks to the technological development.

1 What does the paragraph above describe about movies?

① Violence
② Recreational Feature
③ Location
④ Recording
⑤ Special Effects

2 Write True or False.

(1) _____ Moviemakers still use tricks today.
(2) _____ Flying scenes were filmed in the sky.
(3) _____ Actors were usually filmed before clouds or stars were.

단어 조사해 오셔~ **Word**

at least

probably

literally

trick

decade

technology

film

pretend

overlay

complicated

🍴 Drill 1 Grammar

명사 + -ing (현재분사의 후위 수식)

현재분사는 명사 앞 또는 명사 뒤에서 명사를 수식하여 형용사와 비슷한 역할을 한다. 현재분사는 능동과 진행의 뜻이 있고, 동사처럼 수식어를 취할 수 있다. 또한 주격보어와 목적격보어로도 쓰일 수 있다.

- The man [standing *over there*] is the famous Superman. 저기에 서있는 남자가 그 유명한 슈퍼맨이다.

- There are girls [singing *in the rain*]. 빗속에서 노래를 하고 있는 소녀들이 있다.

---

1   I respect people doing volunteer work.

해석 ◎ _____

2   The man sitting in front of me at the movie theater was snoring.

해석 ◎ _____

snore 코를 골다

3   아기를 팔로 안고 있는 여자가 버스를 기다리고 있다. (holding, her arms, waiting, the bus)

영작 ◎ _____

🍴 Drill 2 Translation

1   1번 문장 ◎ _____

2   2번 문장 ◎ _____

3   3번 문장 ◎ _____

4   4번 문장 ◎ _____

5   5번 문장 ◎ _____

There are so many places you can visit in London. [1] To begin with, the Houses of Parliament are located on the north side of the Thames River, which runs through London. After touring the Parliament, you may want to see the Big Ben, a huge clock at one end of the Parliament. [2] It is famous for its huge bell, which weighs about 13.5 tons. The Buckingham Palace in London, the home of the royal family, is very beautiful. [3] You can also visit the Tower of London, which used to be a prison for many notorious criminals. Other than these monuments, visitors in London may also be interested in the Tower Bridge and the British Museum. [4] London also has many beautiful parks, such as the Hyde Park, which is the largest park in London.

1 **Choose the best title for this paragraph.**

① The Home of British Democracy
② Visitors in London
③ Kings and Queens
④ The Houses of Parliament
⑤ Many Sights in London

2 런던에 관한 이 글의 내용과 일치하지 <u>않는</u> 것은?

① The Big Ben is famous for its enormous bell.
② There are lots of tourists visiting London.
③ London has many places to visit.
④ Hyde Park is the largest park in London.
⑤ Buckingham Palace is the house of the royal family.

단어 조사해 오세요~ **Word**

to begin with

House of Parliament

be located on

Thames River

Big Ben

weigh

Buckingham Palace

royal family

notorious

criminal

monument

Hyde Park

🍴 Drill 1 Grammar

보충 설명하는 관계사절 : ~~, which ...

관계대명사나 관계부사 앞에 콤마(,)가 있으면 계속적 용법으로 쓰인 것이다. 제한적 용법에서는 관계사절을 먼저 해석한 후 선행사를 꾸며 주는 방식으로 해석하지만, 계속적 용법은 부연설명을 하는 것이므로 앞에서부터 차례대로 해석한다. 또한 계속적 용법 which는 앞에 있는 단어, 구, 절 또는 형용사를 받을 수 있으므로 주의를 요한다.

- She used five names, which were not all her real ones.

  그녀는 5개의 이름을 사용했다. 그런데 그것들은 모두 그녀의 실제 이름은 아니었다.

- I bought a new bed, which was very comfortable. 나는 새로운 침대를 샀다. 그런데 그것은 매우 편안했다.

1   He wrote her a love letter, which she sent back unopened.

해석 ◎ _____

2   I drank a bottle of water, which turned out to be pee.

해석 ◎ _____

pee 오줌

3   그녀는 내게 조언을 했다, 그런데 그것은 내가 정말로 필요한 것이었다. (which, needed, I, much, so)

영작 ◎ She gave me some advice, _____

🍴 Drill 2 Translation

1   1번 문장 ◎ _____

2   2번 문장 ◎ _____

3   3번 문장 ◎ _____

4   4번 문장 ◎ _____

[1] Some kinds of birds fly great distances every year. When autumn is almost over, they start migrating.

(A) During the fall, they leave the Northern Hemisphere and fly thousands of miles to the Southern Hemisphere.

(B) [2] It is amazing because they never fail to fly in the right direction, and they always return to the same place every year.

(C) After spending winter in the warm south, they return to their homes in the Northern Hemisphere every spring.

[3] Scientists do not really understand how those birds can do this, but they believe that migratory birds must have a very detailed map in their brains.

1 **Choose the right order of the sentences (A), (B) and (C).**

① (C) – (B) – (A)
② (A) – (B) – (C)
③ (C) – (A) – (B)
④ (B) – (A) – (C)
⑤ (A) – (C) – (B)

2 이 글을 통해서 알 수 있는 것은?

① Details of Northern Hemisphere
② Movements of migratory birds
③ Schedule of the scientists
④ Birds' methods of flying
⑤ Changes of weather in the Northern Hemisphere

단어 조사해 오셔~ **Word**

distance

autumn

migrate

Northern Hemisphere

Southern Hemisphere

fail to

direction

migratory

Drill 1 Grammar

동명사 구문

〈동사 + -ing〉형태가 문장에서 주어, 목적어, 보어, 전치사의 목적어로 사용될 경우 이를 문법적으로 '동명사' 라고 한다.

- **Reading** in a dark room *is* not bad for the eyes. 어두운 방에서 책을 읽는 것은 눈에 나쁘지 않다.
- The only way to successful weight control *is* exercising regularly.
  성공적인 체중 조절의 유일한 방법은 규칙적으로 운동하는 것이다.

---

1 Making good grades requires studying hard.

   해석 ○ _____

2 You should give up watching TV if you want to go to a college.

   해석 ○ _____

3 그녀는 CNN의 여성 뉴스 진행자가 된 것을 자랑스러워 한다. (a news anchorwoman, becoming, for CNN)

   영작 ○ _____

 Drill 2 Translation

1 1번 문장 ○ _____

2 2번 문장 ○ _____

3 3번 문장 ○ _____

¹One winter night I found myself lost in the fog and in a part of the city I didn't know. Then, I met a man and asked him to direct me. ²He said okay and we walked together, with his hand on my elbow. ³When we arrived at the address I had given, I said goodbye, thanking him. ⁴As I turned to shake his hand, I realized he could not see my hand, and indeed the way we had come. The stranger who had led me so surely through the fog was blind. 기출

1 필자가 느낀 점을 한 문장으로 요약하고자 한다. 빈칸 (A)와 (B)에 가장 적절한 것끼리 짝지은 것은?

> ⇒ To one who must live in a world of ___(A)___ , the way ahead is as ___(B)___ in the thickest fog as in the brightest sunshine.

(A)		(B)
① darkness	......	dangerous
② darkness	......	clear
③ business	......	clear
④ business	......	promising
⑤ information	......	dangerous

2 What is the mood of this author?

① curious and scared
② excited and urgent
③ surprising and grateful
④ unique and vivid
⑤ relaxed and bored

단어 조사해 오세요~ **Word**

fog
be lost
direct
elbow
address
stranger
blind
thick
promising

🍴 Drill 1 Grammar

분사구문의 부대상황 〈with + 명사 + 전명구 / 분사(-ing / -ed)〉

전치사 with가 목적어를 갖는 형태로 '가지다'의 뜻이 아닌 경우가 있다. 또한 목적어 뒤에는 '현재분사, 과거분사, 전명구, 형용사' 등이 올 수 있다. 의미 전달을 간결하게 하기 위해 전치사 with가 생략되는 경우도 있다.

- She looked at me **with** *anger* **in her eyes.**   그녀는 분노가 눈에 가득한 채로 나를 쳐다보았다.
- The man standing there **with** *a ball* **in his hands** is a famous soccer player.
  공이 손에 있는 채로 저기에 서있는 남자는 유명한 축구선수이다.

1   The old man listened to the sound of rain, with his eyes closed.

해석 ◎ _____

2   그 여배우는 다리를 꼰 채로 의자에 앉아 있었다. (crossed, her legs, the actress, sat on)

영작 ◎ _____

3   We saw a ghost sitting on the bench, with chin in hand and elbow on knee.

해석 ◎ _____

🍴 Drill 2 Translation

1   1번 문장 ◎ _____

2   2번 문장 ◎ _____

3   3번 문장 ◎ _____

4   4번 문장 ◎ _____

The Federation Internationale de Football Associations (FIFA) is the organization which makes the rules of football. In 1929, the FIFA decided to open international football competitions on a regular basis. They named the series of the competitions the World Cup. So it

was given the name World Cup. In 1930, Jules Rimet, the president of FIFA, decided the first World Cup tournament would be held in Uruguay, celebrating the century of its independence. Thirteen nations sent their teams, and the host country Uruguay became the first champion of the Jules Rimet Trophy that year. After the 1938 tournament in France, the World Cup was not played again until 1950. The 2002 World Cup championship was special. It was the first time the games were played in Asia. _____(A)_____ It was a sporting championship to remember!

The Wimbledon tournament must be one of the most famous international sporting competitions. Among many players, there was a young French tennis player in 1919. Suzanne Lenglen lost just a few matches and won the championship that year. She went on to win 31 Grand Slam titles for twelve years. She was also famous for wearing shorter skirts than any other player. _____(B)_____ Another woman, Gertrude Ederle was the first female who swam the English Channel. It took 14 hours to swim the channel. A Norwegian figure skater Sonia Henie won three consecutive gold medals in the Olympics.

1 How many countries participated in the first World Cup? Write in English.

2 Choose the most suitable sentences to fill in the blanks (A) and (B).

① (A) However, it cost a fortune to organize the World Cup.
(B) So other female players imitated her.

② (A) On the contrary, people in France congratulated the first World Cup played in Asia.
(B) Also her tennis racket brand became very famous.

③ (A) There were many excellent soccer players in Asia because they had a long history in soccer.
(B) She donated all her prize money to the indigent people.

④ (A) It was also the first time that two countries, Korea and Japan, hosted the World Cup together.
(B) She became the first female tennis celebrity.

⑤ (A) The 2002 FIFA World Cup was watched by almost 30 billion people worldwide.
(B) She became the first female soccer player.

3 The Jules Rimet Trophy is related to _____.

① Wimbledon tournament
② English Channel
③ Olympic
④ Football World Cup
⑤ International matches

4 How many athletes are mentioned in the 2nd paragraph?

① one person
② two persons
③ three persons
④ four persons
⑤ five persons

단어 조사해 오셔~ **Word**

federation

association

organization

competition

tournament

hold

celebrate

independence

host country

Jules Rimet Trophy

celebrity

the English Channel

consecutive

A Translate into English.

1 속임수 _____

2 ~인 체하다 _____

3 복잡한 _____

4 과학기술 _____

5 왕실, 황족 _____

6 악명 높은 _____

7 범죄자 _____

8 무게가 나가다 _____

9 거리, 간격 _____

10 가을 _____

11 방향 _____

12 ~하는 데 실패하다 _____

13 안개 _____

14 길을 잃다 _____

15 짙은, 두꺼운 _____

16 팔꿈치 _____

17 개최하다 _____

18 유명인사, 유명인 _____

19 연속적인 _____

20 경축하다, 축하하다 _____

B Translate into Korean.

1 at least _____

2 overlay _____

3 literally _____

4 decade _____

5 to begin with _____

6 be located _____

7 enormous _____

8 possess _____

9 migrate _____

10 migratory _____

11 Northern Hemisphere _____

12 detail _____

13 direct _____

14 address _____

15 promising _____

16 blind _____

17 tournament _____

18 host country _____

19 independence _____

20 competition _____

C **Choose the correct answers to each question.**

1 The moviemakers use some
_____ to make actors look like
they are flying.
① violence   ② tricks
③ details   ④ cameras

2 The Houses of Parliament are
_____ on the north side of the
Thames River.
① weighed   ② begun
③ located   ④ huge

3 The 2002 World Cup championships
were _____ in two countries,
Korea and Japan.
① held   ② hold
③ host   ④ compete

D **Translate into English or Korean.**

1 There is a baby sleeping in a car.

_____

2 She has two cars, which are a Mercedes-
Benz and a BMW.

_____

3 식후에 초콜릿을 먹는 것은 그의 습관 중 하나이다.
(eat, chocolate, meal)

_____ is one of his habits.

4 그 여자는 아이를 팔에 안고 앉아 있었다.
(in, with, a baby)

The woman was sitting _____ .

E **Choose the correct words to fill in the blanks.**

1 Do you know that girl _____ in the
hall?
① dancing   ② be dancing
③ danced   ④ be danced

2 I enjoy _____ snow-boarding in
winter.
① going   ② to go
③ gone   ④ go

3 They like to eat steak with a potato
_____ .
① mash, baking, or french fried
② mash, bake, or french fry
③ mashing, baking, or french frying
④ mashed, baked or french fried

4 I want to give you this book. It was
written by my father.
= I want to give you _____ was
written by my father.
① which, this book
② this book, which
③ this book what
④ which book

F **Translate into Korean.**

1 keep one's distance

_____

2 hold on   _____

3 go in the wrong direction

_____

CHAPTER 9	DATE	SELF CHECK	TEACHER	PARENTS	CONFIRM
Preview					
Unit 1					
Unit 2					
Unit 3					
Unit 4					
Unit 5					
Review					

Why Do Some Chickens Lay Brown Eggs and Others Lay White Eggs?
어떤 닭은 왜 갈색 달걀을, 또 어떤 닭은 흰색 달걀을 낳는 거예요?

시골에서 자랐다면, 아침마다 닭울음소리와 함께 닭장에 가보면 어김없이 따끈따끈한 온기가 느껴지는 알을 발견하곤 했을 것입니다. 그런데 왜? 달걀이 흰색과 갈색이 있는지 궁금하지 않나요? 달걀 안의 내용도, 맛도 똑같은데 왜 색깔이 다른 걸까요?

흰색 달걀과, 갈색 달걀의 색깔에 대한 원인은 항상 의문이었습니다. 색깔의 결정적인 원인을 제공하는 것은 암탉입니다. 굳이 달걀을 확인하지 않아도 암탉을 보면 색깔을 미리 예상할 수가 있다고 합니다. 암탉의 귓불을 가만히 살펴보면 귓불의 색깔이 흰색인 닭과 갈색인 닭이 있을 것입니다. 갈색 또는 흰색의 알이 나오는 것은 바로 암탉 귓불의 색과의 일치입니다. 미국인들은 대부분 흰색 달걀을 선호해서 닭 벼슬이 하나인 흰 레그혼이 가장 인기 있는 알 낳는 닭이 되었는데, 이 레그혼은 상당히 작으며 다른 암탉보다 빨리 성숙하게 자란다고 합니다. 흰색 달걀이 갈색 달걀보다 더 건강에 좋거나, 더 좋은 영양 성분이 들어있는 것은 아니지만, 사람들은 대부분 갈색 달걀을 꺼려하는 편견이 있다고 하네요.

CHAPTER

10

Word 🏠 단어도 모르면서 영어 한다 하지 마!

- **belief** *n.* 믿음, 신뢰, 신앙
- **annoy** *v.* 화나게 하다
- **cloth** *n.* 천, 헝겊
- **tell** *v.* 말하다, 구별하다
- **advance** *n.* 진보 *v.* 나아가다 *a.* 미리 하는
- **notice** *v.* 알아채다 *n.* 통지, 주의
- **hand out** 나누어 주다, 분배하다
- **shock** *v.* 깜짝 놀라게 하다 *n.* 충격
- **dismay** *n.* 당황, 근심, 두려움
- **puzzle** *v.* 곤혹하게 하다 *n.* 수수께끼

- **restore** *v.* 복구하다, 되돌려 주다
- **label** *v.* 라벨을 붙이다 *n.* 라벨
- **reach** *v.* 도착하다, 내밀다
- **consider** *v.* 잘 생각하다, 고려하다
- **essential** *a.* 필수의 *n.* 본질적 요소
- **risk** *n.* 위험, 모험
- **pleased** *a.* 좋아하는, 만족스러운
- **satisfy** *v.* 만족시키다, 채우다
- **gift** *n.* 선물, 타고난 재능
- **opinion** *n.* 의견, 견해, 판단

∷ Mini Quiz

1   a person of many _____   다재다능한 사람

2   public _____   여론

3   get _____ by bad manners   버릇없는 태도에 화가 나다

4   in _____   미리, 선금으로

5   come as a(n) _____   충격적이다 (충격으로 다가오다)

6   a high _____ of an accident   사고가 날 높은 위험성

7   the _____ to speak English   영어를 말하는 데 있어 꼭 필요한 요소들

8   without _____   통지 없이

9   I cannot _____ her from her sister.   나는 그녀와 그녀의 여동생을 구별할 수 없다.

10   in〔with〕_____   걱정하여

Grammar

기본 문법도 모르면서 독해한다 하지 마!

★ 물질명사의 수량은 〈수사 + 단위 + of + 물질명사〉로 표시하고 수사와 단위로 단/복수를 나타낸다.

May I have **a loaf of bread**? 빵 한 덩어리 주시겠어요?

Put **three spoons of sugar** in my coffee please. 제 커피에 설탕 세 스푼을 넣어 주세요.

★ 과거진행은 〈**was/were + -ing**〉 과거의 다른 행동이 시작될 시점에 이미 진행 중이었던 동작을 의미한다.

I **was walking** down the street when you **called**. 나는 네가 전화했을 때 길을 걷고 있었다.

I **was cleaning** my room when my mother **came** home.
엄마가 집에 오셨을 때 나는 내 방을 청소하고 있었다.

★ 형용사, 부사의 원급을 이용한 동등비교 〈**as + 원급 + as** (~만큼 …한)〉는 비교 대상이 비슷할 때 쓴다.

This city is **as large as** Seoul. 이 도시는 서울만큼 크다.

She can cook **as well as** you. 그녀는 너만큼 요리를 잘한다.

:: Mini Quiz

1 다음 문장 중 틀린 부분을 찾아 바르게 고치시오.

He drank two glass of water because he was thirsty.
　　①　　②　　③　　　　　④

2 다음 문장 중 틀린 부분을 찾아 바르게 고치시오.

She was eating a hamburger when they will see a bug in her hamburger.
　①　②　　　　　③　　④

3 다음 괄호 안에서 어법에 맞는 것을 고르시오.

My boyfriend eats as [more / most / much] steak as Ho-dong.

You can learn many interesting things about animal behavior. [1] Sometimes you may not easily understand the reason why they behave in certain ways. [2] However, that makes it very exciting to learn something new about animal behavior. Sometimes what we think about animals may not be true. The following is a

typical example of a false belief about animal behavior. In a bullfight, a matador shakes a piece of red cloth to upset a bull. When the angry bull rushes at the matador, the matador quickly steps to one side and kills it with his sword. [3] Many people believe that the red color makes a bull angry. However, a bull is actually _____. It cannot tell one color from another. Instead, the bull is annoyed by the movement of the cloth. No matter what color it is, any moving cloth would make the bull angry.

1 **Choose the best word to fill in the blank.**

① wild   ② sweet   ③ gentle

④ color-blind   ⑤ warm-hearted

2 **Choose the sentence which does NOT make sense in the paragraph.**

① Sometimes, it is not easy for people to understand animal behavior.

② A matador uses a red cloth in a bullfight.

③ The bull is annoyed by the shaking cloth, not the color.

④ Many people think the red color makes the bull comfortable.

⑤ The matador kills the bull with a sword.

단어 조사해 오세요~ **Word**

behavior

behave

false

belief

matador

sword

annoy

tell

instead

movement

no matter what

 **Drill 1** Grammar

make 동사의 특징

make는 동사 뒤에 오는 '단어의 순서에 따라 문장이 결정된다'. 3형식, 4형식, 5형식 문장의 동사로 사용되는데 이를 문법적으로 암기하지 말고 이해가 우선되어야 한다. make는 일단 기본 뜻인 '만들다' 의 의미로만 해석하는 게 좋다.

> make + X (목적어) - X를 만들다   make + X (목적어) + Y (형용사) - X를 Y하게 만들다

목적어인 명사(X)를 Y(형용사)한 상태로 만들다' 의 뜻으로 5형식 문장이 된다.

- I made a box.   나는 박스를 만들었다.

- She makes me *happy*.   그녀는 나를 행복한 상태로(행복하게) 만든다.

- Does she make you *crazy*?   그녀가 당신을 미치게 만드나요?

---

1   We can make the world better.

해석 ◯ _____

2   The smell of food made us hungry.

해석 ◯ _____

3   그녀의 미소는 항상 나를 행복하게 만든다. (makes, happy, her smile)

영작 ◯ _____

Drill 2 Translation

1   1번 문장 ◯ _____

2   2번 문장 ◯ _____

3   3번 문장 ◯ _____

[1] Everybody thought that Mr. Wilson would be the last teacher who would give a test without advance notice. Today, we all realized how wrong we had thought about him because <u>he did it today</u>. [2] When all the students sat down, Mr. Wilson announced that there would be a quiz before the lecture. I was in such a state of shock

that I could not even speak a word. Math is my weakest subject. While Mr. Wilson was handing out the quiz, I kept saying to myself, "Don't panic. You will be alright." But as soon as I read the questions on the quiz, I almost got a panic attack. I could not even answer a single question. Although I totally screwed up on Mr. Wilson's pop quiz, I think I have become a better person as I learned something from it. [3] Two valuable lessons I learned today are not to make assumptions about others and _____.

1 **What does the underlined 'he did it today' mean?**

① He announced a test tomorrow.
② He did not give a test.
③ He gave a test without notice in advance.
④ He did not feel OK today.
⑤ He didn't do well on the test.

2 이 글의 빈칸에 들어갈 말로 가장 적절한 것은?

① to go to school always no matter what happens
② to always be prepared
③ to be close to all the teachers
④ study extra for math
⑤ not to panic during test

단어 조사해 오세요~ **Word**

advance

notice

realize

announce

lecture

panic

screw

valuable

assumption

Drill 1 Grammar

2형식 동사의 이해

2형식 동사로 대부분의 학생들이 'be동사' 만을 생각하는 경향이 있다. 동사는 크게 2가지로 나뉘는데 '동작동사(일반동사)' 와 연결동사(linking verb = be동사)' 이다. 연결동사는 be동사 이외에 많은 형태가 있는데, 정확한 이해가 되지 않을 경우 영작과 회화에 적잖은 어려움이 있을 수 있다. stay, remain, keep, continue, rest 등의 동사를 잘 보면 거의 모두 '정지 or 계속' 의 뜻을 나타내고 있다. 따라서 이러한 동사는 우리말 '계속 ~이다' 의 뜻으로 해석하는 것이 좋다.

stay, keep + [형용사 / -ing / to V] (보어로 올수 있는 3가지 형태) - 계속 ~이다

- The milk kept *fresh* for several hours. 우유는 몇 시간 동안 계속해서 신선했다.
- The dead body of the Stone Age man **remained** *perfect* in the ice.
  석기시대 사람의 시체가 얼음 속에 계속 완벽한 상태로 남아 있었다.

---

1 Dead bodies keep fresh much longer inside pyramids.

   해석 ◉ _____

2 The students wish that the weather will stay fine when they go camping.

   해석 ◉ _____

3 콧물이 계속 흐른다. (keep, running, my nose)

   영작 ◉ _____

Drill 2 Translation

1 1번 문장 ◉ _____

2 2번 문장 ◉ _____

3 3번 문장 ◉ _____

[1] One man and his little son were driving along a country road. Suddenly, a hare jumped into the road. Even though the man tried his best not to hit the hare, his car hit it. As soon as he heard the thumping sound, he stopped the engine and got out of the car. To his dismay, he found that the hare was dead. The man cried out, "The hare is dead! It's my fault!" [2] His little son, who was sitting in the passenger seat, came out of the car and saw the dead hare. The boy went back to the car, and returned with a spray can. The boy sprayed the contents of the can onto the dead hare. [3] The man got puzzled and asked his son, "What are you doing, son?" The boy proudly showed the can to his father. [4] The label of the can said, "Hair Spray. Restores Life to Dead Hair."

1 Choose the pair of meanings of 'Restores Life to Dead Hair.' that correspond to the actual meaning of the label on the can and the son's interpretation of the label.

What the label meant	What the son understood
① Revives a dead hare.	Restores the hare's fur.
② Restores human hair.	Revives a dead hare.
③ Revives a dead hare.	Restores human hair.
④ Restores the hare's fur.	Revives a dead hare.
⑤ Restores human hair.	Restores the hare's fur.

2 What is the mood of this paragraph?

① blessed and satisfying ② urgent but relaxing
③ loving and sacrificing ④ sorrowful but humorous
⑤ happy and exciting

단어 조사해 오세요~ **Word**

country road

hare

as soon as

thumping sound

dismay

content

get puzzled

proudly

label

restore

 **Drill 1** Grammar

~, who ...

문장 중간에 콤마로 분리되면서 who가 나오면 계속적 용법으로 쓰인 것이다. 보통은 앞에 있는 명사를 꾸며주면서 해석 하지만 계속적 용법은 콤마 앞에 있는 명사와 who를 한 단어의 주어로 취급하여 '그런데 주어 + 동사는 ~' 으로 쭉 해석해 내려간다.

• She has a daughter, who became a wrestler.

　　그녀는 딸이 있다, 그런데 그 딸이 레슬링 선수가 되었다.

• I met an old friend of mine, who didn't recognize me at first.

　　나는 나의 옛 친구를 만났다, 그런데 그 (옛)친구는 처음에 나를 알아보지 못했다.

1　He had a son, who became a good lawyer.

　　해석 ◗ _____

2　I love my girlfriend, who always gives me some money.

　　해석 ◗ _____

3　나는 Dennis에게 공을 패스했지만, 그런데 Dennis는 그걸 놓쳐버렸다. (passed, missed, who)

　　영작 ◗ _____

Drill 2 Translation

1　1번 문장 ◗ _____

2　2번 문장 ◗ _____

3　3번 문장 ◗ _____

4　4번 문장 ◗ _____

[1] American people think that a boy becomes an adult when he reaches 18, but Eskimos think differently. (a) Eskimos used to live in igloos, which are the houses made of blocks of snow, but it has become hard to find igloos in Alaska nowadays. (b) The polar bear is a

very dangerous animal. [2] Some of them are over 9 feet long and weigh over 1,300 pounds. (c) [3] Therefore, it is very challenging and risky to kill a polar bear by oneself. (d) An Eskimo boy is not considered as an adult man until he kills a polar bear by himself. (e) Killing a polar bear is considered as the proof that the boy has developed the _____ which are necessary to be a hunter – and a man.

1 Choose the numbered sentence that does not belong in this paragraph.

① (a)   ② (b)   ③ (c)
④ (d)   ⑤ (e)

2 이 글의 빈칸에 들어갈 말로 가장 적절한 것은?

① ice blocks and gifts
② opportunities and human relationships
③ skills and bravery
④ talents and tools
⑤ victory and essential skills

단어 조사해 오세요~ **Word**

adult

Eskimo

igloo

polar bear

challenging

consider

proof

necessary

🍴 Drill 1 Grammar

조동사 used to / would

used to는 현재에는 지속되지 않는 과거의 습관이나 상태를 나타낸다. 우리말 '~하곤 했(었)다' 로 해석하면 된다. 그러나 '지금은 안 한다' 를 내포하고 있음에 주의한다. would는 미래를 나타내는 will의 과거 용법 외에 '과거에는 ~했지만 지금은 안 한다' 를 표현하는 뜻으로도 쓰인다. 전통적인 영문법에서는 흔히 used to는 '과거의 습관' 을 나타내고, would 는 '과거의 불규칙적인 습관' 을 나타낸다고 설명하는 경우가 많은데, 실제 원어민들에겐 정말로 웃긴 얘기로 많은 비웃음을 사곤 한다. 규칙이냐, 불규칙적이냐에 관계없이 과거의 습관을 표현할 때 used to나 would 둘 다 사용한다. 단, 과거의 상태를 나타내는 동사일 경우 would는 쓸 수 없다는 것에만 주의하자.

- I used to eat meat, but now I'm a vegetarian. 나는 예전에 고기를 먹곤 했다, 하지만 지금은 채식주의자다.

- There used to be a tall tree here. (The tall tree is not here anymore.)
  이곳에 큰 나무가 있었다. (지금은 없다.)

---

1   Tropical rain forests used to cover as much as 14% of the Earth's land. But they cover less than 6% now.

　　해석 ⬦ _____

2   My father used to carve a pumpkin and dress up like Spider-man every Halloween.

　　해석 ⬦ _____

3   나는 미국 팝 가수들에 열광하곤 했었다. (American pop singers, crazy about)

　　영작 ⬦ _____

🍴 Drill 2 Translation

1   1번 문장 ⬦ _____

2   2번 문장 ⬦ _____

3   3번 문장 ⬦ _____

(A)

Mr. Clark is very (a) pleased / pleasing that his ten-year-old daughter is good at learning foreign languages. He sends his daughter for private foreign language lessons every evening. However, she has a lot of homework and now finds it very hard to do everything. She wanted to stop

(b) to go / going for Japanese and Arabic lessons, but her father would not listen. "You must learn as much as you can while you are young," he said. She has become stressed and anxious.

(B)

Rick Bell was six, but he was very good at mathematics. Rick liked to play with his friends and enjoyed reading and writing more than mathematics. He dreamed of being a football player. Mr. Bell refused to listen to him. He insisted that his son (c) goes / go to a special school for the gifted where he could develop his talent for mathematics. After a year at the school, even his son's teachers agreed that he was unhappy.

기출

1 글 (A)와 (B)가 자녀 교육에 대해 공통으로 시사하는 바로 가장 적절한 것은?

① 봉사 정신을 함양해야 한다.

② 조기 교육을 해야 한다.

③ 본인의 의사를 존중해야 한다.

④ 지식 교육을 우선해야 한다.

⑤ 외국어 교육을 강화해야 한다.

2 글 (A)의 밑줄 친 Japanese and Arabic lessons에 상응하는 것을 (B)에서 고를 때, 가장 적절한 것은?

① football

② friends

③ reading

④ writing

⑤ mathematics

3 (a), (b), (c) 각 네모 안에서 어법상 적절한 것끼리 짝지은 것은?

	(a)	(b)	(c)
①	pleased	to go	goes
②	pleasing	going	go
③	pleased	going	goes
④	pleased	going	go
⑤	pleasing	to go	goes

4 (B)에 관한 내용 중 글의 내용과 일치하지 <u>않는</u> 것은?

① Rick was unsatisfied at the special school.

② Rick's dream was to become a football player.

③ Rick liked reading books and writing.

④ Mr. Bell was good at learning foreign languages.

⑤ Mr. Bell objected to Rick's opinion.

단어 조사해 오셔~ **Word**

be good at

private

Arabic

anxious

refuse

insist

the gifted

talent

agree

Review ☺

A **Translate into English.**

1 행동 _____

2 잘못된, 틀린 _____

3 믿음, 확신 _____

4 검, 칼 _____

5 강의 _____

6 값진, 귀중한 _____

7 생각, 판단 _____

8 공포, 공황 (상태) _____

9 (야생) 산토끼 _____

10 당황, 불안감 _____

11 자랑스럽게 _____

12 라벨, 꼬리표 _____

13 성인, 어른 _____

14 용기, 대담함 _____

15 북극곰 _____

16 증거 _____

17 ~을 잘하다 _____

18 거부하다, 거절하다 _____

19 동의하다 _____

20 불안한 _____

B **Translate into Korean.**

1 matador _____

2 tell _____

3 instead _____

4 behave _____

5 announce _____

6 screw _____

7 realize _____

8 assumption _____

9 satisfied _____

10 get puzzled _____

11 thumping sound _____

12 restore _____

13 challenging _____

14 igloo _____

15 opportunity _____

16 weigh _____

17 insist _____

18 gift _____

19 talent _____

20 Arabic _____

C Choose the correct answers to each question.

1 In a bullfight, a matador shakes a piece of red cloth to _____ a bull.
① upset   ② trick
③ refuse   ④ behave

2 I was in such _____ that I could not even speak a word.
① bed   ② comfortable
③ happy   ④ shock

3 To his _____, he found that the hare was dead.
① hare   ② dismay
③ label   ④ content

D Translate into English or Korean.

1 This music makes me sleepy.

_____

2 She has two sons, who are twins.

_____

3 샐러드는 그가 집에 올 때까지는 신선하게 유지될 것이다. (stay, salad, fresh)

_____ until he comes home.

4 나는 저녁에 공원으로 산책을 나가곤 했다.
(go, used, for, to, a walk)

I _____ to the park in the evening.

E Choose the correct words to fill in the blanks.

1 You always _____ me happy.
① make   ② to make
③ making   ④ will be made

2 My dog kept _____ so I took it to the vet.
① snores   ② snoring
③ snore   ④ snored

3 I gave my best wishes to _____ is my best friend.

= I gave my best wishes to Carol, and she is my best friend.
① who, Carol   ② Carol, who
③ which, Carol   ④ Carol, which

4 I _____ drink wine on my birthday.

= Before, I drank wine on my birthday, but I don't these days.
① have to   ② can
③ used to   ④ will

F Write the synonyms for each word.

| essential | incorrect |
| irritate | announcement |

1 _____ false

2 _____ annoy

3 _____ notice

4 _____ necessary

CHECK
BOX

CHAPTER 10	DATE	SELF CHECK	TEACHER	PARENTS	CONFIRM
Preview					
Unit 1					
Unit 2					
Unit 3					
Unit 4					
Unit 5					
Review					

Why Does the Skin on Our Fingers and Toes Wrinkle After Bathing?
목욕을 하고 나면 왜 손가락과 발가락이 쭈글쭈글해지는 거죠?

어렸을 때 아버지를 따라가 대중목욕탕에 가서 목욕을 할 때, 큰 욕조에 몸을 담그고 아버지는 콧노래를 부르곤 하셨습니다. 한증막에도 가고, 냉탕에도 몸을 담그면서 즐거운 목욕을 마친 후 옷을 입으면서 손을 보니 헉! 손과 발이 모두 온통 쭈그렁 할머니처럼 됐지 뭡니까! 도대체 왜 그런걸까요?

사실 피부는 모두 쭈글쭈글해지지만, 손가락과 발가락은 신체 어느 부위보다도 주름이 많이 보이는 곳이죠. 손이랑 발에는 각질층(죽은 세포층)이 두껍게 발달되어 있는데, 상당 시간 물에 불리면 이 죽은 피부가 팽창하게 됩니다. 수분을 흡수해서 팽창하게 되는 거죠! 팽창하지 않는 피부는 없지만, 손발의 거친 피부에 주름이 가장 많이 보이게 되는 것입니다.

CHAPTER 11

Word 🏠 단어도 모르면서 영어 한다 하지 마!

- **involve** *v.* 포함하다, 관련시키다
- **individual** *n.* 개인 *a.* 개인의, 독특한
- **consequence** *n.* 결과, 결론, 중요성
- **alternative** *n.* 양자택일, 다른 방안
- **pleasure** *n.* 즐거움, 유쾌함, 만족
- **cottage** *n.* 시골집, 작은 별장
- **carpet** *n.* 카펫 *v.* 양탄자를 깔다
- **mode** *n.* 방법, 양식, 모드
- **rub** *v.* 비비다, 마찰하다, 문지르다
- **inflate** *v.* 부풀리다, 팽창시키다

- **creature** *n.* 창조물, 생물
- **review** *v.* 복습하다 *n.* 평론, 비평
- **suitable** *a.* 적당한, 어울리는
- **problematic** *a.* 문제가 있는, 의심스러운
- **predict** *v.* 예언하다, 예보하다
- **analyze** *v.* 분석하다, 분해하다
- **award** *v.* 수여하다 *n.* 상
- **consist** *v.* 이루어져 있다, 존재하다
- **purpose** *n.* 목적, 용도, 취지
- **fortune** *n.* 운, 재산

∷ Mini Quiz

1	_____ needs	개개인의 요구들
2	propose a(n) _____	대안을 제시하다
3	strange _____ of life	색다른 생활 방식
4	night _____	야행성 동물
5	_____ the last lesson	지난 수업을 복습하다
6	a(n) _____ site	적당한 장소
7	_____ earthquakes	지진을 예측하다
8	_____ industry trends	업계 동향을 분석하다
9	win a(n) _____	수상하다
10	for business _____	업무상 (사업 목적으로)

Grammar 👤 기본 문법도 모르면서 독해한다 하지 마!

★ 조동사 **might**는 **may**의 과거형이 아니라, 현재나 미래의 불확실한 사실을 언급할 때 쓸 수 있다.

He **might have** the key. 그가 열쇠를 가지고 있을지도 몰라.

Jane **might want** to go with us. Jane이 우리랑 같이 가고 싶어할지도 모르겠어.

★ 관계부사 **where**는 접속사와 부사역할을 하며 선행사가 장소(**the place**)일 때 쓴다. 〈**where = in〔at, on〕 + which**〉이다.

This is the city. I was born there. ○ This is the city **where** I was born.

이곳이 내가 태어난 도시이다.   = in which

This is the place **where** we used to play. 여기는 우리가 예전에 놀던 곳이다.

　　　　　　　　　　　= at which

★ 수동태 문장에서 행위자가 일반인일 때 혹은 불특정인이거나 확실하지 않을 경우 〈**by + 목적어**〉를 생략한다.

Both French and English are spoken in Canada **(by Canadians)**.

캐나다에서는 불어와 영어가 둘 다 사용된다.

Many people were killed in the incident **(by a criminal)**. 많은 사람들이 그 사고로 죽었다.

∷ Mini Quiz

1 다음 해석에 맞게 빈칸을 채울 때 가장 적절한 것을 고르시오.

Minjung ＿＿＿＿＿＿＿＿ be late for school if she doesn't leave now.

지금 떠나지 않으면 민정이는 학교에 지각할지도 모른다.

① must 　　② might 　　③ should 　　④ shall

2 다음 문장 중 틀린 부분을 찾아 바르게 고치시오.

He works two miles away from the city which he lives.
　①　　②　　③　　④

3 다음 괄호 안에서 어법상 옳은 것을 고르시오.

Not long ago, some pieces of rock from outer space [discovered / were discovered] in Australia.

[1] If scarcity exists, choices must be made by individuals and societies. (a) Therefore, people prefer to be employed by a trading company. (b) [2] These choices involve "tradeoffs" and necessitate an awareness of consequences of those tradeoffs. (c) [3] For example, suppose that you have $25 to spend and have narrowed your alternatives to a textbook or a date. (d) Scarcity prohibits the purchase of both and imposes a tradeoff − a book or a date. Each choice has a consequence. (e) The textbook might enable you to increase your knowledge, and the date might mean an evening of merriment.

기출

1 What is the best main idea of this paragraph?

① rational choices
② good textbooks
③ good exports
④ an ideal society
⑤ bargain sales

2 이 글에서 전체 흐름과 관계 없는 것은?

① (a)　　　　② (b)　　　　③ (c)
④ (d)　　　　⑤ (e)

단어 조사해 오셔~ **Word**

scarcity

involve

individual

tradeoff

necessitate

awareness

consequence

alternative

prohibit

purchase

impose

merriment

🍴 Drill 1 Grammar

목적격보어로 쓰이는 부정사

출제 빈도가 높은 5형식 동사는 확실한 이해가 필요하다. 동사가 force, tell, ask, advise, allow, expect, order, cause, enable 등의 공통점은 대부분 '명령군' 에 속한다. 우리말 '~가 …하도록〔하게〕 하다' 로 해석되며 목적격보어 자리에 '동작, 행위' 가 필요해서 'to부정사' 형태를 써야 한다는 점을 반드시 암기해 두어야 한다.

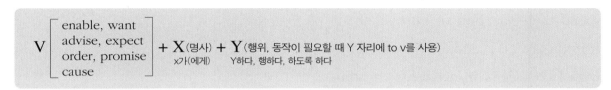

V $\begin{bmatrix} \text{enable, want} \\ \text{advise, expect} \\ \text{order, promise} \\ \text{cause} \end{bmatrix}$ + X (명사) + Y (행위, 동작이 필요할 때 Y 자리에 to v를 사용)

                             x가(에게)   Y하다, 행하다, 하도록 하다

- Money **enables** *us* **to do** a lot of things.   돈은 우리가 많은 것을 할 수 있게 해 준다.

- Mom **ordered** *me* not **to hang** out with bad friends.   엄마는 나에게 나쁜 친구들과 어울리지 말라고 명령했다.

---

1   I warned her not to smoke in public places.

       해석 ⊙ _____

2   The government forced the people to pay taxes every year.

       해석 ⊙ _____

3   의사는 경고했다 아버지에게 끊으라고 담배를. (의사는 아버지에게 담배를 끊으라고 경고했다.)
    (warned, smoking, to quit)

       영작 ⊙ _____

🍴 Drill 2 Translation

1   1번 문장 ⊙ _____

2   2번 문장 ⊙ _____

3   3번 문장 ⊙ _____

We have all grown up, (A) known / knowing that people are different. [1] They spend their money in different ways, while seeking different pleasures. A couple may spend their vacation in Europe; their friends are (B) content / contenting with two weeks in a cottage by the sea. [2] A woman may save her household money to carpet her bedrooms; her neighbor may save hers to buy a second car. [3] Different modes of consumer behavior – different ways of spending money – do not surprise us. [4] We have been brought up to believe that such differences are (C) that / what makes life interesting. 기출

1 **Choose the best main idea of this paragraph.**

① 다양한 소비 유형
② 원만한 대인 관계
③ 치밀한 휴가 계획
④ 넉넉한 가계 수입
⑤ 효과적인 실내 장식

단어 조사해 오세요~ **Word**

household

consumer behavior

way

seek

content

mode

2 (A), (B), (C)에서 어법에 맞는 표현을 골라 짝지은 것은?

	(A)	(B)	(C)
①	knowing	content	that
②	knowing	contenting	that
③	knowing	content	what
④	known	content	that
⑤	known	contenting	what

Drill 1 Grammar

···, ~ing

문장 중간에 쉼표로 분리하여 나오는 -ing는 우리말 '~하면서'를 붙여 해석한다. 분사구문의 형태이다.

- We have all grown up, **knowing** that people are different.

  우리 모두는 사람들이 서로 다르다는 것을 알면서 성장했다.

- My father was sitting on the sofa, **reading** a newspaper.

  나의 아버지께서는 신문을 읽으면서 소파에 앉아 계셨다.

---

1 He sat for a long time, listening to the sound of the rain.

해석 ◎ _____

2 Kelly read the newspaper, eating her breakfast.

해석 ◎ _____

3 나의 형은 MP3를 들으면서 공부했다. (the MP3 player, listening to)

영작 ◎ _____

Drill 2 Translation

1 1번 문장 ◎ _____

2 2번 문장 ◎ _____

3 3번 문장 ◎ _____

4 4번 문장 ◎ _____

Bees, wasps, and mosquitoes make buzzing sounds with their wings. [1] But crickets and grasshoppers make noises by rubbing their legs or snapping their wings. [2] The reason why these insects make those sounds is to communicate. Many insects have

ears, which look very different from our ears. [3] Often, those ears seem to be in places where they don't belong. A cricket's ears are on its front pair of legs, and a grasshopper's ears are on its belly. Frogs must be the first creatures which developed voice during the process of evolution. A frog has a vocal sac. The frog inflates the sac by closing its mouth and nostrils. In this way, the frog can blow the sac up like a balloon and make sounds by deflating it quickly.

1 **What kind of writing is this paragraph?**

① a newspaper article
② a discussion
③ a book review
④ a description
⑤ a novel

2 **Write True or False.**

(1) _____ Ears of insects are located in different places.
(2) _____ A frog makes noise with its head.
(3) _____ A cricket has a vocal sac on its front legs.

단어 조사해 오셔~ **Word**

wasp

buzz

cricket

grasshopper

snap

belong

belly

creature

evolution

vocal sac

inflate

nostril

deflate

 **Drill 1** Grammar

관계대명사 which

관계사 which가 선행사에 따라 어떻게 변하며, 격은 무엇에 따라 결정되는지 등의 설명으로 머리가 아주 아팠던 적이 있을 것이다. 영어는 문법적인 기능 이전에 영어와 한국어의 기계적인 유사성, 즉 구조론적인 측면이 더 중요하다. which는 여러 가지로 쓰일 수 있지만 관계사로 사용되려면 which 앞에 반드시 '명사'가 있어야 한다. which 앞에 명사가 있는 위치를 확인하고 우리말 '~하는, 했던'을 붙여 앞에 있는 명사를 꾸며 주면서 해석하면 된다.

• We *saw* **the temple** [**which** *was built* 1000 years ago].   우리는 1000년 전에 지어진 사원을 보았다.
  V₁(진짜 동사)   V₂ (절 안에서만 역할을 하는 동사)

• Kindness *is* **the language** **which** the deaf can hear and the blind can see. [*Mark Twain*]
  친절은 귀머거리가 들을 수 있고 장님이 볼 수 있는 언어이다.

---

1   The books which I bought yesterday were very interesting.

해석 ◌ _____

2   Jason bought me this ring which I'm wearing.

해석 ◌ _____

3   이것이 그 책이니, 네가 일전에 그 책을 찾고 있었던? (이것이 네가 일전에 찾고 있었던 책이니?)
(the other day, look for)

영작 ◌ _____

 **Drill 2** Translation

1   1번 문장 ◌ _____

2   2번 문장 ◌ _____

3   3번 문장 ◌ _____

(a) Weather is very important to live our lives. (b) ¹Meteorologists, scientists who study the weather, analyze the air, wind, and rain, etc and predict the weather in the near future. Pilots must know how airplanes might

Tomorrow	Sat	Sun
Clear	Clear	Rain
37°/25°	43°/32°	45°/39°
Precip 0%	Precip 10%	Precip 30%

be affected by the bad weather. (c) Bad weather can be problematic. ²In order to grow healthy crops, farmers need the sunlight and enough amount of rain. ³An early frost can ruin the whole crop if the harvest season hasn't come yet. (d) ⁴Thick fog can cause accidents for cars and boats. But for children, the bad weather can be fun. (e) On dry and hot days, they can go swimming. On snowy and cold days, they can go skiing.

1 **Choose the sentence that best summarizes this paragraph.**

① (a) ② (b) ③ (c)
④ (d) ⑤ (e)

2 **According to the paragraph, why is weather so important?**

① Because people rely on the weather each day.
② People can die from bad weather conditions.
③ Weather can influence humans in many ways.
④ Children need to have a suitable environment in which to play.
⑤ Meteorologists need to keep their honorable jobs.

단어 조사해 오세요~ **Word**

meteorologist

analyze

predict

be affected by

crop

ruin

harvest season

go skiing

 **Drill 1** Grammar

조동사 must

조동사 must는 'necessity, prohibition, 95% certainty' 와 같이 필요, 금지, 확신 등을 표현할 때 사용한다. must be는 '~임에 틀림없다' 는 뜻으로 객관적인 확신(95% certainty)을 가지고 표현할 때 사용되므로 〈must + 동사원형〉과 구별할 줄 알아야 한다. must not은 '강한 금지' 를 나타낸다.

• You **must be** tired after your long trip. 너는 장거리 여행을 한 후여서 피곤함에 틀림없다.

• Everybody **must** wear a seatbelt on this KTX train. 모든 사람은 KTX 열차에서 좌석 벨트를 착용해야 한다.

---

1   You must study hard if you are to get good grades.

    해석 ◯ _____

2   They must be happy to be working for their company.

    해석 ◯ _____

3   너는 학교에 올 때에는 교복을 입어야 한다. (come, when, the uniform, wear, to school)

    영작 ◯ _____

Drill 2 Translation

1   1번 문장 ◯ _____

2   2번 문장 ◯ _____

3   3번 문장 ◯ _____

4   4번 문장 ◯ _____

The Nobel Prizes, except the peace prize, are presented in Stockholm by the king or queen of Sweden. The Nobel Prizes must be the greatest award given to scholars. Each year, the Nobel Prizes are awarded in the fields of chemistry, physics, physiology or medicine, economics, and literature. Occasionally, prizes are not given or are awarded later. The winners are selected by groups of distinguished scholars from several European countries, including Sweden and Norway.

The peace prize is presented in Oslo by the king or queen of Norway. The prizes consist of a medal, a certificate, and a cash award.

The prizes were established by Alfred Nobel, a Swedish chemist who invented dynamite, an explosive. Nobel had invented dynamite for peaceful purposes, _____ people soon discovered that dynamite could be a powerful weapon in war, this misuse of his invention saddened Nobel. The invention had brought him great wealth, and he decided to use the money to award anyone who worked for peace and the good of mankind. Before he died in 1896, he wished that the yearly income from the fortune should be divided into various annual awards.

1 이 글의 빈칸에 들어갈 말로 가장 적절한 것은?

① therefore
② in consequence of
③ but
④ to begin with
⑤ in addition

2 Why was Nobel sad after inventing dynamite? Write in English.

3 Choose the best title of this passage.

① Explanation of Nobel Prize Nominees
② Life of Alfred Nobel
③ Kinds of Fields of Nobel Prize
④ Effects to the World by Nobel Prize
⑤ Establishment and History of Nobel Prize

4 What does the underlined word 'misuse' refer to?

① use of Nobel's money
② use of dynamite for peaceful purposes
③ use of the Nobel Prize
④ use of the dynamite in wars
⑤ use of the medal and certificate

단어 조사해 오서~ **Word**

Nobel Prize

Stockholm

award

field

chemistry

physics

physiology

economics

literature

occasionally

distinguished

consist of

certificate

establish

explosive

purpose

misuse

sadden

income

fortune

be divided into

Review ☺

A   **Translate into English.**

1   지각, 인지, 인식   _____

2   강요하다   _____

3   금지하다   _____

4   즐거움   _____

5   가구, 가계   _____

6   ~에 만족하다   _____

7   방법, 방식   _____

8   찾다, 구하다   _____

9   귀뚜라미   _____

10   마땅한 장소에 있다   _____

11   진화   _____

12   배, 복부   _____

13   망쳐놓다, 파괴하다   _____

14   예상하다   _____

15   분석하다   _____

16   농작물   _____

17   물리학   _____

18   증명서   _____

19   목적, 의도   _____

20   설립하다, 만들다   _____

B   **Translate into Korean.**

1   necessitate   _____

2   tradeoff   _____

3   consequence   _____

4   scarcity   _____

5   consumer behavior   _____

6   mode   _____

7   carpet   _____

8   cottage   _____

9   creature   _____

10   vocal sac   _____

11   nostril   _____

12   grasshopper   _____

13   be affected by   _____

14   harvest season   _____

15   meteorologist   _____

16   airplane   _____

17   economics   _____

18   distinguished   _____

19   misuse   _____

20   fortune   _____

C Choose the correct answers to each question.

1 The _____ of his fall was a broken leg.
① consequence
② alternative
③ merriment
④ tradeoff

2 The reason why the insects make sounds is to _____.
① inflate   ② buzz
③ snap   ④ communicate

3 An early frost can _____ the whole crop if the harvest season hasn't come yet.
① analyze   ② predict
③ ruin   ④ harvest

D Translate into English or Korean.

1 An electronic dictionary enables me to study English easier.

_____

2 What are you doing sitting out here?

_____

3 Alex가 말했던 그 빌딩 앞에서 만나자. (which, building, in front of)

Let's meet _____
Alex talked about.

4 너는 엄마 말씀을 들어야 한다.
(listen to, mom, your, must)

_____

E Choose the correct words to fill in the blanks.

1 My parents _____ a perfect score on the final exam.
① expect to get me   ② expect me to get
③ expect get me   ④ expect me get

2 I study English, _____ to music.
① listen   ② listens
③ listening   ④ to listen

3 My mom bought that skirt. Hyoree wore the same skirt on TV.

= My mom bought _____ Hyoree wore on TV.
① the same skirt who
② which the same skirt
③ which
④ the same skirt which

4 • You _____ not drink alcohol because you are not an adult.

• He _____ be a criminal because he looks guilty.
① have to   ② must
③ used to   ④ will

F Write the synonyms and antonyms for each word.

misuse	ruin	occasionally

1 frequently   ⇔   _____

2 wrong use   =   _____

3 destroy   =   _____

CHAPTER 11	DATE	SELF CHECK	TEACHER	PARENTS	CONFIRM
Preview					
Unit 1					
Unit 2					
Unit 3					
Unit 4					
Unit 5					
Review					

You Have to Go!
네가 가라!

Q. 중고등학교 시절에 보면 언제나 영문법에서는 '～해야 한다' 라는 뜻의 조동사로는 must, have to, have got to, should, ought to가 있잖아요. 분명히 현대영어에서는 활용이 다를 것 같은데, 어떤 동사가 어느 정도의 강도로 표현하는지, 그래서 어느 상황에 어떻게 골라 써야 하는지 잘 모르겠어요. 이 동사들의 차이점에 대한 설명이 있는 영어책이나 사전은 없나요?

A. 좋은 질문이네요. 보통의 영문법에서는 '～해야 한다' 의 뜻으로 설명이 되어 모두 다 같은 뜻으로 착각할 수 있습니다. 물론 해석상의 뜻은 같습니다. 그러나 활용에서는 차이가 있다는 것이지요. 문법(Grammar)과 활용법(Usage) 사이에는 차이가 있습니다. 여러분이 배우는 것은 영문법 수준인데, 그 영문법이라는 게 일본식 영문법을 아무런 여과없이 받아들인 것들이 대부분이죠. 한국 영어에 여러 가지 일본식의 잘못된 영문법의 잔재가 아직도 남아 있는 것입니다.

must, have to, should, ought to 등은 한결같이 '～해야 한다' 라고만 되어 있어, 특히나 회화에서 잘못 사용하기 쉬운 표현들입니다. 사실 이 조동사들의 용법에는 '추측' 이나 '예상' 등 다양한 것들이 있지만, '의무, 필요' 의 용법에 대해서만 설명드리기로 하겠습니다. 그나마 다행히도 현대 영어에서는 should와 ought to를 큰 구별 없이 사용하고 있으며, must와 have to의 경우에도 마찬가지입니다. 따라서 크게 〈should와 ought to〉, 〈must와 have to〉 두 그룹으로 나눠서 생각해 볼 수 있습니다. 다만 have to가 더 일반적으로 사용되며 must는 좀더 formal한 인상을 주게 됩니다. 보통은 어떤 일을 하는 게 좋겠다(advisability) 정도의 가벼운 뉘앙스일 때는 should나 ought to를 사용하고, 강한 확인(95% certainty)을 가지고 '반드시 ～해야 한다' 고 단정적으로 말할 때는 must나 have to를 사용합니다. 이처럼 must와 have to는 단정적이고 강한 어투이기 때문에 일상생활에서 너무 많이 사용하면 상대방의 기분을 상하게 할 수 있으니 주의해야 합니다.

CHAPTER 12

Word 🏠 단어도 모르면서 영어 한다 하지 마!

- **invention** *n.* 발명품, 발명
- **behave** *v.* 행동하다, 처신하다
- **transfer** *v.* 옮기다, 갈아타다
- **grant** *v.* 주다, 인정하다, 승인하다
- **convince** *v.* 확신시키다, 납득시키다
- **imagine** *v.* 상상하다, 가정하다
- **confident** *a.* 자신만만한, 확신하고 있는
- **realize** *v.* 이해하다, 실현하다
- **stage** *n.* 단계, 시기, 무대
- **anxious** *a.* 걱정하는, 열망하는

- **sensitive** *a.* 민감한, 예민한
- **research** *v.* 연구하다 *n.* 연구, 조사
- **expense** *n.* 지출, 비용, 경비
- **outstanding** *a.* 눈에 띄는, 저명한
- **setting** *n.* 주위의 상태, 환경
- **provide** *v.* 공급하다, 준비하다
- **temperature** *n.* 온도, 체온
- **function** *n.* 기능, 역할, 행사
- **radiate** *v.* (빛, 열을) 발하다, 분출시키다
- **solar** *a.* 태양의, 태양광선의

∷ Mini Quiz

1 ＿＿＿＿＿＿＿＿ yourself. 　　　　　행동 조심해라.

2 ＿＿＿＿＿＿＿＿ to line number 3 　　3호선으로 갈아타다

3 If this is ＿＿＿＿＿＿＿, what next? 　이것은 그렇다 치고(인정하는데), 다음은?

4 I'm ＿＿＿＿＿＿＿. 　　　　　　　나는 확신해.

5 a(n) ＿＿＿＿＿＿＿ manner 　　　자신 있는 태도

6 a(n) ＿＿＿＿＿＿＿ look 　　　　걱정스러운 표정

7 traveling ＿＿＿＿＿＿＿ 　　　　여행 경비

8 a(n) ＿＿＿＿＿＿＿ figure 　　　두드러진 인물

9 the social ＿＿＿＿＿＿＿ of education 교육의 사회적 기능

10 ＿＿＿＿＿＿＿ energy 　　　　　태양 에너지

Grammar 기본 문법도 모르면서 독해한다 하지마!

★ 관계대명사 **whose**는 선행사가 사람이고 소유격 역할을 할 때 사용한다.

I have **a friend whose father** is a doctor. 나는 아버지가 의사인 친구가 있다.

A child whose parents are dead is called an orphan. 부모님이 돌아가신 아이는 고아라고 불린다.

★ 관계대명사 **what**은 선행사를 포함하고 있으며 'all that / anything that / the thing(s) which' 등과 같은 의미이다.

What I say is always true. 내가 말하는 것은 항상 사실이다.
= The thing which

He will buy **what** she wants. 그는 그녀가 원하는 것을 사 줄 것이다.
= anything that

★ 전치사 **in**은 넓은 장소 / 월, 계절, 년, 세기 / 시간(시간경과) / 언어(표현방법) / 스타일(착용) 등의 앞에 쓸 수 있다.

in the United States / **in summer** / **in recent years** / **in English**
미국에서   여름에   최근에   영어로

Look at the lady **in red.** 저 빨간 옷을 입은 여자를 봐.

:: Mini Quiz

1 다음 문장 중 틀린 부분을 찾아 바르게 고치시오.

Look at the girl who shoes do not match each other.
　①　　　②　　　③　　　④

2 다음 두 문장의 의미가 같도록 빈칸에 알맞은 것은?

They have to be responsible for the things which they have done.

= They have to be responsible for ＿＿＿＿＿ they have done.

① what　　　　② which　　　③ that　　　　④ who

3 다음 밑줄 친 단어 중 어법에 어긋난 것은?

① I usually go skiing in winter.　　② You will have a test in five minutes.

③ He followed the man in black.　　④ I go to church in Sunday.

The Broadway show "The Farnsworth Invention" is about one boy, whose last name was Farnsworth, and (a) <u>what he invented</u> in 1930. It was one of the products which (b) <u>have greatly influenced</u> our life in modern society. It affects the way people think, behave and (c) <u>communicate with each other</u>. ² Nowadays, it is impossible to imagine a day without it even though it has been only about seventy years (d) <u>since it had become a part</u> of people's lives. ³ Until 1922, scientists had tried to find a way to transfer pictures with sound, but they could not think of any possible means. However, a 14 year-old American boy, Farnsworth, came up with an idea about how pictures could be (e) <u>electronically transmitted</u>. Eventually, he invented <u>this product</u> and was granted the patent for this electronic product in 1930.

1 **What does the underlined part 'this product' mean?**

① radio

② television

③ movie

④ book

⑤ computer

2 (a)~(e) 중, 어법상 <u>어색한</u> 것을 찾아 바르게 고치시오.

invention

product

influence

modern society

behave

transfer

means

come up with

electronically

transmit

eventually

grant

patent

 **Drill 1** Grammar

과거완료(had +p.p.)

과거완료(had p.p.)는 과거 이전부터 과거의 어느 시점까지의 동작이나 상태의 완료, 경험, 계속을 나타내거나, 과거에 발생한 두 일 중에서 먼저 일어난(더 과거) 일을 표현한다. 접속사를 활용해 두 가지 일을 표현할 때 나중에 발생한 일은 '과거'로 표현하고 더 이전(훨씬 더 과거)에 일어난 일은 〈had +p.p.〉로 표현한다. '~했다, 했었다'의 과거로 해석하면 된다.

- The game **had** already **started** when I **arrived** at the stadium.
  had + p.p. (먼저 일어난 일)　　　　　　　V과거 (나중에 일어난 일)
  그 시합은 내가 경기장에 도착했을 때 이미 시작되었다.

- The wedding reception **had ended** by the time Dennis **got** there.
  Dennis가 그곳에 도착했을 무렵, 결혼식은 끝나 있었다.

1　Mr. Smith had lived in Chicago for 6 years before he moved to Seattle.

　　해석 ◑ _____

2　A strange woman walked into the room. I had never seen her before.

　　해석 ◑ _____

3　After I had finished my homework, I went out for dinner.

　　해석 ◑ _____

4　I arrived at the party at 8 o'clock last night. Christine wasn't there. She went home at 7 o'clock.

　　영작 ◑ When I _____ at the party last night, Christine _____ already _____ home.

 **Drill 2** Translation

1　1번 문장 ◑ _____

2　2번 문장 ◑ _____

3　3번 문장 ◑ _____

Teens surround themselves with _____ audiences. They imagine others are as interested in them as they are in themselves. **Believing** that everyone is watching them, teenagers are extremely self-conscious. A young boy, for example, may believe that he is unattractive because of his nose.

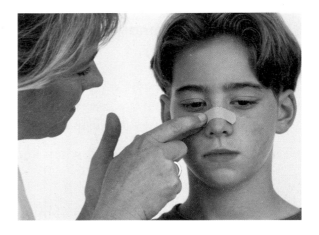

[1] Nothing can convince him that other people are paying no attention to his nose at all. [2] Also, when **chatting** with friends, some teenage girls are too expressive, talking and laughing loudly, playing to their unreal audiences. They gradually realize, however, that others are not really interested in them. [3] Teenagers' behavior changes when they realize others are too busy with their own lives to be watching them. (기출)

1 **Choose the best word to fill in the blank.**

① loud
② busy
③ friendly
④ imaginary
⑤ attractive

2 **How does the teenagers' behavior change?**

① Gradually, when they realize that other people hate them.
② Gradually, as they grow up and recognize that others are too busy.
③ When they are focused on by others during a conversation.
④ When they are confident about themselves in society.
⑤ By being influenced in positive ways by their friends.

단어 조사해 오셔~ **Word**

audience

imagine

extremely

self-conscious

unattractive

convince

pay attention to

behavior

🍴 Drill 1 Grammar

분사구문

분사가 이끄는 어구가 문장에서 부사의 역할을 할 때 이를 문법적으로 분사구문이라 한다. 이 경우 분사는 의미상 동사와 접속사 역할을 겸하게 된다. 분사구문은 주로 문장 앞에 온다. 영어는 순서(위치, 자리)가 가장 중요한 언어라고 설명했다. -ing 형태가 문장 맨 앞에 나와서 쉼표로 분리될 때, 쉼표 옆에 있는 명사(주어)를 꾸미면서 우리말 '~하는, ~한, ~ㄴ'을 붙여 해석해 주면 된다.

> ~ ing ......, S(명사) + V ......
> '~하는, ㄴ + 명사' 로 해석

- **Picking** up a stone, *he* threw it at the ghost. 돌을 주운 그는 그것을 귀신에게 던졌다.
- **Living** next door, *I* seldom see him. 옆집에 살고 있는, 나는 좀처럼 그를 보지 못한다.

---

1 Being poor, I cannot afford to buy a car.

해석 ◎ _____

2 Surfing the Internet on your computer, you could get a lot of information.

해석 ◎ _____

3 공원에서 걷고 있던, 나는 우연히 그녀를 만났다. (happened to, in the park, walking)

영작 ◎ _____

🍴 Drill 2 Translation

1 1번 문장 ◎ _____

2 2번 문장 ◎ _____

3 3번 문장 ◎ _____

[1] Some research results indicate that stress associated with college entrance exams is negatively related to the psychological development and self-identity of adolescents, and in extreme cases it may increase the risk of mental disorders. [2] There are many reasons why Korean students feel anxious and stressed about the exam. [3] Many Korean people think

that higher education assures a person's success in his or her life. Therefore, most Korean parents are concerned too much about their children's academic achievement. Young people generally become very sensitive during adolescence, and the pressure to do well on the college entrance exams and their parents' excessive expectations become extremely burdensome to them.

1 **What is the best title of this paragraph?**

① Developmental Stages of Adolescents
② Teenagers' Sensitivity to Adults
③ The Importance of a College Education
④ Relations Between Teenagers and Their Parents
⑤ The Burden of Entering a College on Adolescents

2 **Why is higher education considered important in Korea?**

① It makes students responsible with their study.
② Koreans believe that it guarantees a successful life.
③ It forces the students to try harder.
④ Koreans are worried about peer pressure from other countries.
⑤ It can make students sensitive.

단어 조사해 오세요~ **Word**

indicate

associate

college entrance exam

be related to

psychological

self-identity

adolescent

mental disorder

anxious

assure

sensitive

pressure

excessive

burdensome

Drill 1 Grammar

명사 + -ed/-en (과거분사의 후치수식)

과거분사는 수동, 완료의 의미를 나타내며, 특히 동사의 과거형과 같은 형태의 과거분사가 주어를 수식하는 경우에 이를 동사로 잘못 착각하지 않도록 주의해야 한다. 명사 다음에 -ed가 연이어 나온다면 명사를 꾸며 주면서 우리말 '~된, ~진, ~하게 된'으로 앞의 명사를 꾸며 주며 해석해야 한다. 명사가 행동이나 동작이 필요로 할 때 사용되는데, 명사가 사람이나 생물체가 아닌 사물 또는 행위를 할 수 없는 명사가 오면 '-ed/-en'을 사용하게 된다.

- Knowledge [learned by hard study] *is* long remembered.

  진짜 동사 아니야!   진짜 동사야!

  열심히 공부해서 배운(배워진) 지식은 오래 기억된다.

- These books [made in Korea by the publishing firm, We're books], *are* very useful. 위아북스 출판사에 의해 한국에서 만들어진 이 책들은 굉장히 유익하다.

---

1 The man injured in the traffic accident was taken to the hospital.

해석 ◎ _____

2 I met a handsome Italian man named Bob.

해석 ◎ _____

비교 ◎ I met a handsome Italian man who was named Bob.

(명사(뒤)에 who 순서가 같아 역할이 똑같다는 것을 알 수 있다. 영어는 기능보다는 순서가 더 중요한 조건이다.)

3 그 테러범, 체포된, 경찰관에 의해, 지난주, 죽었다, 감옥에서. (지난주 경찰관에 의해 체포된 그 테러범이 감옥에서 죽었다.) (the police officer, died, in jail, arrested, the terrorist)

영작 ◎ _____

 Drill 2 Translation

1 1번 문장 ◎ _____

2 2번 문장 ◎ _____

3 3번 문장 ◎ _____

[1] If you want to go abroad to study a foreign language, there are a number of things you should consider before making a decision. [2] First, you should decide which country you want to go to. For instance, in recent years, many Asian students have been going to the United States to learn

English. If you study in the United States, you will be able to practice English both in and out of the classroom. [3] In addition, you can meet people from all around the world so you are in an English-speaking setting 24 hours a day. [4] You may also have an opportunity to learn about different cultures. On the other hand, you should know there is also a disadvantage of going to the United States – the high cost.

1 **What will be the next topic of this paragraph?**

① various advantages to learning English in America
② outstanding learning ability of Asian students
③ inexpensive tuition for American universities
④ expenses for learning English in America
⑤ reasons why the U.S.A. is good for learning English

2 **Choose the main idea of this paragraph.**

① Learning foreign languages is a difficult job.
② At the moment, there are many Asian students studying English.
③ Studying abroad provides many opportunities for students.
④ There are advantages and disadvantages of studying abroad.
⑤ Learning other cultures is important.

단어 조사해 오셔~ **Word**

go abroad

foreign language

a number of

consider

make a decision

setting

opportunity

disadvantage

cost

outstanding

tuition

 **Drill 1** Grammar

조건의 부사절 if

조건의 부사절 if와 가정법의 if를 구별해서 사용할 줄 알아야 한다. if는 명사절에도 사용되므로 많은 독해를 통해 정확한 이해가 필요한 부분이다. 조건의 부사절의 if는 우리말 '만약 ~라면' 으로 해석하고, 부사절 안에 있는 동사는 미래시제 대신 현재시제를, 미래완료 대신 현재완료를 써서 표현해야 한다.

- **If** it *is* sunny tomorrow, we will go swimming.   내일 날씨가 맑으면 우리는 수영하러 갈 것이다.

- **If** I *have read* your book, I will return it on Sunday.
  내가 너의 책을 다 읽으면, 나는 그것을 일요일에 돌려줄 것이다.

---

1   If it rains tomorrow, we won't go on a picnic.

　　해석 ◎ _____

2   I'm sorry, but you can't see the doctor if you don't have an appointment.

　　해석 ◎ _____

3   Jason이 회사에 또 늦게 도착하면 사장님은 화를 낼 것이다. (the boss, arrive, at work, angry)

　　영작 ◎ _____

Drill 2 Translation

1   1번 문장 ◎ _____

2   2번 문장 ◎ _____

3   3번 문장 ◎ _____

4   4번 문장 ◎ _____

Greenhouses are useful to grow plants and vegetables especially in the winter season. Greenhouses are usually built with glass or plastic roofs and walls so that sunlight can get in and the heat is retained inside.

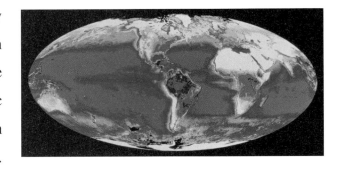

The air inside the greenhouse is continuously heated up by the incoming sunlight like the air inside a car parked outside in summer. This keeps the plants and vegetables warm enough to live in winter.

The huge difference of temperature between the Earth and outer space is because of certain gases in the Earth's atmosphere which trap the solar radiation. The process of trapping the warm temperatures next to the Earth is called the greenhouse effect. Without those gases, heat would escape back into space and the Earth's average temperature would be about 60 degrees colder. Because of the function of those gases, they are referred to as greenhouse gases.

The Earth's atmosphere is the layer of the air around the Earth. (a) Greenhouse gases in the atmosphere do what the glass or plastic roofs and walls of a greenhouse do. (b) Solar radiation enters the Earth's atmosphere, passing through the blanket of greenhouse gases. When it reaches the Earth's surface, it warms air, land and water. (c) Therefore, the water evaporates faster as the greenhouse temperature rises. (d) Some of the solar radiation radiates back into space, but much of it remains trapped in the atmosphere by the greenhouse gases, causing our world to heat up. The greenhouse effect is important. (e) Without the greenhouse effect, the Earth would not be warm enough for humans to live on.

1 **Choose the best main idea for this article.**

① Usefulness of the greenhouse
② Recognizing the formation of the Earth
③ Elucidation of the greenhouse effect
④ How to control temperature in a greenhouse
⑤ Temperature differences of the Earth and outer space

2 세 번째 단락에서 (a)~(e) 중, 전체 흐름과 관계 없는 문장은?

① (a)　　　　② (b)　　　　③ (c)
④ (d)　　　　⑤ (e)

3 **Which of the following information is <u>NOT</u> true?**

① 지구와 우주의 온도 차이는 복사열 방출을 막는 어떤 특정한 기체 때문이다.
② 온실효과란 지구의 온도를 유지하는 과정을 말한다.
③ 대기중의 온실가스는 비닐하우스와 같은 원리가 적용된다.
④ 복사열은 거의 대부분 우주로 방출되고 일부는 대기에 머물러 지구를 따뜻하게 만들어 준다.
⑤ 온실은 밖으로 나가는 열을 차단하여 겨울에도 식물들이 잘 자랄 수 있게 해 준다.

단어 조사해 오셔~ **Word**

greenhouse effect

retain

continuously

outer space

atmosphere

escape

average temperature

function

refer to

solar radiation

temperature

radiate

trap

elucidation

Review 😊

A **Translate into English.**

1 발명(품) _____

2 방법, 수단 _____

3 특허(권) _____

4 제품, 상품 _____

5 관중, 관객 _____

6 설득하다 _____

7 행동, 행위 _____

8 ~에 신경 쓰다 _____

9 연구, 조사 _____

10 보장(보증)하다 _____

11 압박(감) _____

12 부담이 되는 _____

13 기회 _____

14 수업료 _____

15 단점 _____

16 눈에 띄는 _____

17 계속 유지하다 _____

18 막다, 붙잡다 _____

19 대기 _____

20 온도 _____

B **Translate into Korean.**

1 transfer _____

2 transmit _____

3 grant _____

4 influence _____

5 unattractive _____

6 extremely _____

7 self-conscious _____

8 imagine _____

9 be associated with _____

10 mental disorder _____

11 indicate _____

12 be related to _____

13 make a decision _____

14 setting _____

15 a number of _____

16 foreign language _____

17 function _____

18 solar radiation _____

19 outer space _____

20 escape _____

C **Choose the correct answers to each question.**

1 The _____ of parents on their children is important.
① means
② invention
③ influence
④ patent

2 You have to _____ your teacher in class.
① convince
② imagine
③ make a decision
④ pay attention to

3 The criminal _____ from prison.
① escaped
② referred
③ radiated
④ assured

D **Translate into English or Korean.**

1 Turning to the right, you will find the house.

_____

2 He is an artist just returned from France.

_____

3 어제까지만 해도 나는 그 소문에 대해 들어 보지 못했어. (never, hear about, rumor)

Until yesterday, I _____ .

4 만약 네가 규칙적으로 조깅을 한다면 살이 빠질 것이다. (regularly, jog)

_____, you will lose some weight.

E **Choose the correct words to fill in the blanks.**

1 I went to the box office, but they _____ all the tickets. I couldn't buy any tickets.
① will sell
② have sold
③ had sold
④ sell

2 _____ the news, she turned pale with fright.
① Hears ② To hear
③ Heard ④ Hearing

3 He has a large house _____ of stone and brick.
① building ② built
③ build ④ will build

4 If we _____, we'll catch the bus.
① have hurried ② hurry
③ will hurry ④ had hurried

F **Write the proper words in the blanks.**

1 a wide range of _____ 다양한 상품

2 effective _____ 효과적인 수단

3 _____ skin 민감성 피부

4 blood _____ 혈압

5 high _____ 비싼(높은) 가격

6 dual _____ 이중 기능

CHAPTER 12	DATE	SELF CHECK	TEACHER	PARENTS	CONFIRM
Preview					
Unit 1					
Unit 2					
Unit 3					
Unit 4					
Unit 5					
Review					

Please Don't Call Me Honkey!
욕은 싫어요!

Q. 얼마 전 미국에 있는 친척집에 영어공부도 할 겸 놀러 갔는데요. 미국인 녀석들이 저만 보면 혼자말로 가끔 Chink라고 하는 거예요. 이놈들이 무슨 말을 하는 건지 몰라, 사전을 찾아보니 '중국인'을 가리키는 속어라고 되어 있던데요, 어느 정도로 나쁜 말인가요? 저한테 욕한 게 맞죠? 복수해야 되니까 알려주세요!

A. 예전에 한번 미국이 UN 인권위원회(Human Rights Commission)에서 비난을 받은 적이 있었습니다. 툭하면 다른 나라의 인권문제를 걸고넘어지던 미국으로서는 참으로 황당한 상황이 아니었을까 합니다. '인종의 도가니'(Melting Pot)라고 비유될 만큼 세계 거의 모든 인종이 모여 사는 다문화, 다민족 국가인 미국에서는 인종차별(Racial Discrimination)을 법으로 금하고 있으나, 순수 백인 혈통들의 마음 속 깊이 자리 잡은 우월의식과 유색인종을 무시하는 마음은 변하지 않는 것 같습니다. 얼마 전 TV에서 봤는데요, 미국인들이 동양여성 특히 한국여성에 관심이 많은데 그 이유는 한번 같이 놀고 싶고, 자기보다 낮은 인종이 신기해서라고 말하는 것을 보고, 받은 충격은 이루 말할 수 없었습니다. Chink는 '중국인'을 비하해서 부르는 말입니다. 우리말의 '짱깨, 띠놈' 정도로 보시면 됩니다. 우리 눈에 외국인들을 보면 모두 비슷비슷하게 생긴 것처럼 보이듯이, 그네들에게도 동양인들은 모두 비슷해 보인다고 합니다. 따라서 일본인이나 한국인에게도 Chink라고 하는 경우가 많습니다. 가장 대표적인 인종차별적 표현으로는 '흑인'을 지칭하는 nigger가 있고, '일본인'을 가리켜 Jap 또는 Nip, '멕시코인'을 포함해서 '라틴 아메리카계 사람들'을 뜻하는 Spic, '폴란드 사람'을 가리키는 말로 Polack 등이 자주 쓰이는 편입니다. 한국을 비롯한 동양인들에게는 Gook이라고 부르며 멸시하기도 합니다. 이에 질세라 흑인을 비롯한 소수민족들은 '백인'을 Honkey라고 부르죠. 하지만 이런 표현은 교양 없는 아주 버릇 없는 사람들이 쓰는 표현이니, 그런 놈을 만나면 따귀 100대 정도는 때려 줘야 속이 후련하겠죠.

CHAPTER 13

Word 🏠 단어도 모르면서 영어 한다 하지 마!

- **sneeze** *v.* 재채기하다 *n.* 재채기
- **force** *v.* 강요하다 *n.* 힘, 영향력
- **skip** *v.* 뛰어다니다, 건너뛰다
- **irritate** *v.* 짜증나게 하다, 자극하다
- **react** *v.* 반응하다, 반동하다
- **conduct** *v.* 행동하다 *n.* 행위, 지도
- **potential** *a.* 가능한 *n.* 잠재능력
- **indicate** *v.* 가리키다, 나타내다
- **concern** *n.* 걱정, 관심 *v.* 관계가 있다
- **ban** *n.* 금지, 반대 *v.* 금지하다

- **outlaw** *n.* 무법자 *v.* 불법화하다
- **masculine** *a.* 남자의, 남성다운
- **factor** *n.* 요인, 요소, 원인
- **perceive** *v.* 지각하다, 이해하다
- **particular** *a.* 특별한, 상세한
- **area** *n.* 범위, 지역, 영역
- **tradition** *n.* 전통, 관례, 전설
- **trick** *n.* 속임수, 장난, 재주 *v.* 속이다
- **fool** *n.* 바보 *v.* 장난치다, 놀리다
- **exist** *v.* 존재하다, 나타나다, 생존하다

❖ Mini Quiz

1	in _____	힘을 다하여, (법적으로) 유효하여, 시행중인
2	be slow to _____	반응하는 데 느리다
3	a code of _____	행동 수칙
4	full _____	최대 잠재능력, 무한한 가능성
5	full of _____	매우 걱정되는
6	key _____	중요한 요인
7	_____ code	지역번호
8	hand down a(n) _____	전통을 물려주다
9	still _____	아직 (멸종하지 않고) 존재하다
10	fall for a(n) _____	속다

Grammar 기본 문법도 모르면서 독해한다 하지 마!

★ 동사 -ing형 중 동명사는 〈목적, 용도 (~하기 위한)〉의 의미로 쓰이고 현재분사는 〈상태, 동작 (~하고 있는)〉의 의미로 쓰인다.

This train has a **sleeping** car. 〔동명사〕 이 기차에는 침대차가 있다.

Be quiet. There is a **sleeping** baby. 〔현재분사〕 조용히 해. 잠자는 아기가 있어.

★ 비교급을 사용하는 비교문장에서 '~보다'를 나타내는 **than** 대신 **to**를 사용하는 경우가 있다.

prefer	senior	junior	major	minor	
interior	exterior	posterior	superior	inferior	] + to

He is **senior to** me by five years. 그는 나보다 다섯 살 많다.

I **prefer** red wine **to** white. 나는 백포도주보다 적포도주를 더 좋아한다.

★ 시간 강조 구문 : 〈It is〔was〕 + 시간 + when ~ (~한 때는(시기는) 바로 ~이(었)다)〉

It was 4 a.m. **when** I felt somebody lying beside me.
내 옆에 누군가가 누워있다는 것을 느낀 것은 바로 새벽 4시였다.

It was last year **when** we went to China. 우리가 중국을 갔던 때는 바로 작년이었다.

∷ Mini Quiz

1 다음 문장 중 틀린 부분을 찾아 바르게 고치시오.

It was last night when we see a strange woman in the library.
　①　　　②　　③　　④

2 다음 해석과 같아지도록 빈칸에 들어갈 단어를 고르시오.

She went on a trip in the weeks ＿＿＿＿＿＿＿ her death. 그녀는 죽기 몇 주 전에 여행을 떠났다.

① prior　　　　　　　　② prior to

③ prior than　　　　　　④ than

3 다음 밑줄 친 표현 중 쓰임이 다른 하나는?

① waiting room　　　　② knitting needle

③ sleeping car　　　　④ dancing girl

If you sneeze in public, someone will say 'God bless you.' The reason is simple. [1] A sneeze is an explosion of air from the lungs. [2] When something irritates the nasal nerve, your brain sends a signal to force the air out of your lungs through your nose and mouth. The speed of air is quite fast; you sneeze at over 160 kmph (100 mph). [3] And while you sneeze, the lungs cannot take air in and the heart skips a beat. So if you can't stop sneezing, you may die! In addition, the air which comes out through your nose and mouth may carry germs. Therefore, within a second the germs can be passed on to others. [4] So it is courteous as well as hygienic to cover your mouth with a handkerchief while sneezing.

1   **What may be spread when you sneeze?**

① spittle
② nose drippings
③ nasal nerve
④ germs
⑤ all of the above

2   **Fill in the blank from the above passage.**

We sneeze because _____ .

단어 조사해 오셔~ **Word**

sneeze

explosion of air

lung

irritate

nasal nerve

force

in addition

germ

courteous

hygienic

spittle

Drill 1 Grammar

상관 접속사

> not only [just, merely] X but (also) Y X뿐만 아니라 Y도 = Y as well as X

- The professor **as well as** the students was glad that there was no class that day.
  학생들뿐만 아니라 교수님도 그 날 수업이 없어서 기뻤다.

- Flour is used to make paste **as well as** to bake bread.
  밀가루는 빵을 굽기 위해서뿐만 아니라 풀을 만들기 위해서도 사용된다.

---

1 Remember that people judge you by your words as well as by your actions.

해석 ◎ _____

2 She as well as you has to attend the conference.

해석 ◎ _____

3 그녀의 남편뿐만 아니라 그녀도 스페인어를 말할 수 있다. (her husband, Spanish)

영작 ◎ _____ 〈as well as 이용〉

_____ 〈not only, but (also) 이용〉

Drill 2 Translation

1 1번 문장 ◎ _____

2 2번 문장 ◎ _____

3 3번 문장 ◎ _____

4 4번 문장 ◎ _____

[1] Plants (a) <u>are known to</u> react to environmental pressures such as wind, rain, and even human touch. [2] Coastal trees, for example, become shorter and (b) <u>stronger in</u> response to strong winds and heavy rainfall. [3] In a laboratory study conducted at Stanford

University, the same changes <mark>in plant growth patterns</mark> (c) <u>were brought</u> about by (d) <u>touched plants</u> twice a day. [4] The researchers also found that these growth changes (e) <u>resulted from</u> gene activation. Their findings indicate that this gene actuation did not occur unless there was _____.

---

1 **Choose the best answer to fill in the blank.**

① fresh air
② enough sunlight
③ direct stimulation
④ some water
⑤ growth potential

2 (a)~(e) 중, 어법상 <u>어색한</u> 것을 찾아 바르게 고치시오.

단어 조사해 오셔~ **Word**

react

environmental pressure

in response to

rainfall

conduct

be brought about

gene

actuation

finding

indicate

stimulation

potential

🍴 Drill 1 Grammar

주어의 앞뒤에 수식어구가 오는 경우

주어의 앞뒤에서 형용사뿐 아니라 다양한 구와 절이 주어를 수식함으로써 주어가 길어지는 경우가 있다. 이때 해석을 위해서는 먼저 동사의 위치를 파악한 후, 주어부를 찾고, 주어를 수식하는 수식어구를 확인한다. 명사 뒤에 오는 〈전치사 + 명사〉 수식어구는 우리말 '~하는, ~ㄴ'을 붙여 앞에 명사를 수식해 주면서 해석한다.

- **The tools** *for analyzing information* weren't even available until the early 1990s.

  정보 분석을 위한 도구들은 1990년대 초가 지나서야 비로소 이용가능하게 되었다.

- **A teacher** *without students* is like **a fish** *out of water*.

  학생이 없는 선생님은 물 밖에 있는 물고기와 같다.

---

1 Place your watch on the table in front of you or keep your eye on the clock in the back of the room.

   해석 ◎ _____

2 The rescue team found the lost hikers in the forest at eleven o'clock.

   해석 ◎ _____

3 옆집에 사는 가족은 이사 가기를 원한다. (move out, in the next house)

   영작 ◎ _____

🍴 Drill 2 Translation

1 1번 문장 ◎ _____

2 2번 문장 ◎ _____

3 3번 문장 ◎ _____

4 4번 문장 ◎ _____

People have always been concerned a lot about their hair. [1] In ancient times, people preferred curly hair to straight hair. Men even curled their beards. Irons were used to curl hair and beards. In England, in King Henry VIII's time, men had a variety of concerns

about long hair. But the King outlawed long hair. [2] Instead, he issued an order for men to have short hair, grow and trim beards and to curl their mustaches. [3] But it was not long before men were allowed to have long hairstyles again when James I became the King in 1603. [4] In the 19th century, men started to think that short hair was more masculine than long hair. _____, women have never been banned from growing long hair. Long and beautiful hair was considered as the crowning glory of their appearance. Nevertheless, short hair sometimes became the craze.

1 **Choose the best phrase to fill in the blank.**

① In addition
② On the contrary
③ Moreover
④ Unfortunately
⑤ Therefore

2 **Why did men prefer shorter hair later on?**

① Because long hair was inconvenient.
② People wanted to disobey King James I.
③ They wanted to honor the deceased King Henry VIII.
④ People wanted to show the difference between men and women.
⑤ They thought short hair symbolized masculinity.

단어 조사해 오세요~ **Word**

prefer A to B

curly

iron

a variety of

concern

outlaw

issue an order

trim

masculine

ban

crowning glory

appearance

nevertheless

craze

🍴 Drill 1 Grammar

> It will not be long before ~ 얼마 안가 ~
> It will be a long time before ~ 얼마 지나서야 ~
> It will be some time before ~ 얼마가 지나서야 ~

- **It was not long before** he was appointed professor. 얼마 안가 그는 교수로 임명되었다.
- **It was not long before** we met again by chance. 얼마 안가 우리는 다시 우연히 만나게 되었다.
- **It will be a long time before** we meet again. 얼마가 지나서야 우리는 다시 만날 것이다.
- **It will be some time before** the terrible smell goes away. 얼마 지나서 그 끔찍한 냄새는 사라질 것이다.

---

1 It was not long before the ship sank to the bottom of the ocean.

    해석 ◯ _____

2 It was not long before the big boxer knocked the little boxer down. The referee counted to ten and the match was over.

    해석 ◯ _____

3 얼마 안가 비가 그쳤다. (It was not long before)

    영작 ◯ _____

🍴 Drill 2 Translation

1 1번 문장 ◯ _____

2 2번 문장 ◯ _____

3 3번 문장 ◯ _____

4 4번 문장 ◯ _____

Our sense of smell is nowadays being used for various purposes. (a) [1] One area **in which** smells achieve particular results is marketing. (b) [2] For some time manufacturers have taken advantage of our sense of smell to sell more household goods. (c) [3] They spend millions of dollars hunting for the right aroma as they believe perfume influences the way consumers perceive a brand. (d) In addition,

painting walls with a white color may be effective to help patients relax in the waiting room of a dental office. (e) In one survey, people were asked what they had considered most when they bought a detergent. The scent of the detergent was found to be the most important factor.

---

1 **Choose the sentence that does <u>NOT</u> belong in this paragraph.**

① (a)   ② (b)   ③ (c)

④ (d)   ⑤ (e)

2 **According to the paragraph, why is the smell of a product so important?**

① The smell of the products affects our health.

② Our clothes should always smell good.

③ Most consumers are persuaded by scent of the product.

④ All newly made products should smell fresh.

⑤ The smell of the product is more important than the color.

단어 조사해 오세요~ **Word**

sense of smell

various

area

particular

manufacturer

household goods

aroma

take advantage of

right

consumer

perceive

survey

detergent

scent

factor

Drill 1 Grammar

전치사 + 관계대명사

관계사 앞에 전치사가 오는 경우에, 문장에 정확한 이해가 없으면 독해에 답답함을 느낄 때가 있다. 영어에서 전치사는 항상 〈전치사 + 명사〉가 덩어리로 짝을 이루어야 하는데 전치사와 함께 쓰인 '명사'가 선행사가 되어 절 속에 있을 때, 전치사는 관계대명사 바로 앞이나 관계사절의 끝에 올 수 있다.

끝에 전치사가 올 경우 관계대명사는 생략될 수 있다. 영어는 '순서'에 의해 결정된다고 설명했던 것처럼 〈명사 + 전치사 + 관계사〉의 순서가 되면 앞의 명사를 꾸며 주면서 우리말 '~하는, ~했던, ~ㄴ'을 붙여 해석한다. 왜냐하면 명사 뒤에 어떤 말이 나오든지 문법적인 기능보다는 그러한 순서에 의해 우리말 '무엇'과 같은지를 아는 게 우선이기 때문이다.

> N(명사) + 〔전치사 + 관계사 … V₁(절 안의 동사) ....〕 V₂(진짜 동사) : '~하는, ㄴ, ~했던'으로 해석

- This is **the woman** [**about whom** I told you.] 이 사람이 내가 네게 말했던 그 여자이다.
- Soccer is **a sport** [**of which** I am very fond.] 축구는 내가 매우 좋아하는 스포츠이다.

---

1 Language is the means by which people communicate with other people.

해석 ◯ _____

2 The newspaper is the source from which the public gets its knowledge about the world.

해석 ◯ _____

3 The professor lectured on a topic in which I was interested.

해석 ◯ _____

4 여기가 내가 졸업한 학교이다. (graduated, from)

영작 ◯ _____

Drill 2 Translation

1 1번 문장 ◯ _____

2 2번 문장 ◯ _____

3 3번 문장 ◯ _____

Have you ever wondered why April 1st is called April Fools' Day? No one knows exactly. But we know that we are allowed to fool our friends and neighbors on April Fools' Day, like sending them on absurd errands, or trying to make them believe that something false is true.

There are many theories about the origin of April Fools' Day. Some people say that April Fools' Day started in France. France was one of the first countries that used the new calendar. In 1564, Charles IX changed the date of the new year from April 1st to January 1st, according to the new calendar. Some people didn't receive the news for several years or didn't believe the change in the date, for news traveled on foot at that time. So some people continued to celebrate New Year's Day on April 1st. In France, some people made fun of those poor, _____ people by sending mock gifts, and inviting them to celebration parties which did not exist. Those who were fooled were called "April fools." This "April Fools" tradition was passed on to England and Scotland in the 18th century and eventually made its way to the American colonies.

Now April Fools' Day is celebrated all over the world. April Fools' Day has become common and a great day for fun!

1 **In France, who did people call "April Fools"?**

① the people who were very foolish
② the people who continued to celebrate New Year's Day on April 1st
③ the people who couldn't read the new calendar
④ the people who changed New Year's Day to January 1st
⑤ the people who celebrated New Year's Day in the 16th century

2 이 글의 주제로 가장 적절한 것은?

① What people do on April Fools' Day
② Change of April Fools' Day by Charles IX
③ History and explanation of April Fools' Day
④ People adapting to the new April Fools' Day
⑤ Reasons for the creation of the April Fools' Day

3 이 글의 빈칸에 들어갈 말로 가장 적절한 것은?

① insulted
② acknowledged
③ abused
④ perceived
⑤ misinformed

4 **Which information is NOT mentioned in the paragraph?**

① Charles IX changed the date of the new year from April 1st to January 1st.
② Charles IX was the first to use the new calendar.
③ In general, most people weren't offended by the trick on April Fools' Day.
④ The 'April Fools' tradition was passed on to England and Scotland.
⑤ Nowadays, April Fools' Day is celebrated all over the world.

Review 😊

A **Translate into English.**

1 재채기하다 _____

2 자극하다 _____

3 세균 _____

4 예의바른 _____

5 반응하다 _____

6 강우량 _____

7 유전자 _____

8 자극 _____

9 고대의 _____

10 관심 _____

11 사내다운 _____

12 외모, 출현 _____

13 제조업자 _____

14 다양한 _____

15 조사 _____

16 향기, 냄새 _____

17 터무니없는, 어리석은 _____

18 기원, 유래 _____

19 존재하다 _____

20 명령, 순서 _____

B **Translate into Korean.**

1 hygienic _____

2 nasal nerve _____

3 force _____

4 lung _____

5 conduct _____

6 finding _____

7 potential _____

8 indicate _____

9 outlaw _____

10 trim _____

11 issue an order _____

12 nevertheless _____

13 particular _____

14 household goods _____

15 factor _____

16 take advantage of _____

17 mock _____

18 be passed _____

19 common _____

20 errand _____

C **Choose the correct answers to each question.**

1 If you sneeze in _____, someone will say 'God bless you.'
① private   ② public
③ addition   ④ a hurry

2 Plants are known to _____ to environmental pressures.
① react   ② conduct
③ indicate   ④ find

3 The color white may be _____ to help patients relax.
① various   ② masculine
③ ancient   ④ effective

4 We are allowed to _____ our friends on April Fools' Day.
① order   ② exist
③ fool   ④ force

D **Translate into English or Korean.**

1 The man in this room is your boss.

_____

2 It will be some time before he realizes the truth.

_____

3 그뿐만 아니라 그녀도 많이 먹었다. (as well as)

_____ a lot.

4 이것이 내가 관심 있어 하는 음악 장르 중 하나이다. (be interested in)

This is one of the music genres _____

_____ .

E **Choose the correct words to fill in the blanks.**

1 You as well as I _____ happy with the news.
① am   ② was
③ are   ④ be

2 The doughnuts on the table _____ delicious.
① were   ② is
③ was   ④ am

3 He came home soon.
= It was not _____ before he came home.
① long time   ② long
③ time   ④ short

4 I need a paper _____ I can write something down.
① which on   ② on which
③ which   ④ on

F **Which word doesn't correspond with the other words?**

1 ① lung   ② nose
③ germ   ④ mouth

2 ① react   ② conduct
③ indicate   ④ actuation

3 ① beard   ② masculine
③ mustache   ④ whisker

4 ① aroma   ② scent
③ perfume   ④ factor

CHECK
BOX

CHAPTER 13	DATE	SELF CHECK	TEACHER	PARENTS	CONFIRM
Preview					
Unit 1					
Unit 2					
Unit 3					
Unit 4					
Unit 5					
Review					

Why Do Military Personnel Salute One Another?
왜 군인들은 서로 경례를 하는 건가요?

저자도 최전방에서 군무를 했었습니다. 부산에서요!(일본과 최전방이죠^.^) 그런데 모든 군인들은 서로 만나게 되면 "충성", "돌격", 그리고 "단결" 등의 구호를 붙이면서 인사를 나누는데, 그냥 고개 숙여 인사하지 않고 소리를 지르며 서로 경례를 하는 걸까요?

이 질문에 대한 정확한 답은 없습니다. 경례의 방법은 시대와 문화에 따라 다양했습니다. 오늘날과 같은 경례 방법 즉 오른손을 이마 혹은 모자챙에 올리는 경례는 아주 최근의 형태입니다. 18세기 말엽까지는 상급자에게 경례를 할 때는 반드시 모자를 벗고 했습니다. 이는 중세 기사들이 왕 앞에서 투구를 벗던 관습에서 유래된 것이죠. 지금의 오른손을 들어 올리는 경례는 고대 유럽에서 유래되었을 것이라 생각하는 전문가들이 있습니다. 이 시대 사람들은 무기를 지니고 다니는 일이 많았기 때문에, 그 당시에 특히 남성들은 오른 팔을 들어 올려서 자신이 지니고 있는 칼이나 무기를 사용할 의도가 없다는 것을 상대방에게 보여 주는 관습이 있었습니다. 사실 모자를 살짝 들어 올리거나 손을 흔드는 것 그리고 악수를 하는 것과 같은 여러 가지 몸짓들은 아마도 무기를 갖고 있지 않다는 것을 보여 주는 방법들이었을 것이라고 추정하고 있습니다.

가장 재미있는 유래로는 옛날 영국에서 여왕에게 훈장을 수여받는 수병들에게 여왕의 아름다운 얼굴을 보고 반하지 않기 위해 훈장을 받을 때 오른손으로 눈을 가리라는 명령에서 비롯되었다는 얘기도 있습니다.

빠르고 정확한 독해를 위한

Just
READING

정답

1

신석영 지음

CHAPTER 01

Preview

Word • Mini Quiz

1. discontinue	2. argument
3. split	4. range
5. effort	6. harsh
7. revolve	8. publish
9. separate	10. agreement

Grammar • Mini Quiz

1. ③   2. ④   3. playing

Unit 1

Answers

1. ⑤   2. ③

Word

root 뿌리, 근원
stay 머무르다, ~인 채로 있다
run down 흘러내리다
form 형성하다, 만들다
various 다양한, 여러 가지의
harsh 황량한, 가혹한, 거친
environment 환경, 주위, 상황

Drill 1 • Grammar

1. 김치는 만들기에 어렵지 않다.
2. This car is not safe to drive.
3. 문법이 어렵기 때문에 영어는 배우기에 쉽지 않다.

Drill 2 • Translation

1. 나무는 여러 가지 면에서 우리의 생활에 매우 중요하다.
2. 만일 나무가 없다면, 빗물은 산에서 빨리 흘러내려와 때때로 집들을 쓸어버릴 것이다.
3. 셋째로, 나무는 보기에 아름답다.
4. 그것들이 없다면, 지구는 훨씬 더 황량한 환경이 될 것이다.

Unit 2

Answers

1. ①   2. (1) F (2) T

Word

prism 프리즘
split 쪼개다, 분할하다
spectrum 스펙트럼, 분광
mixture 혼합, 혼합물
form 만들다, 이루다, 형성하다
raindrop 빗방울
argument 논쟁, 주장
agreement 일치, 조화

Drill 1 • Grammar

1. 읽을 몇 권의 책들이 있다.
2. 일주일에는 7일이 있다.
3. There were lots of people waiting for a bus.

Drill 2 • Translation

1. 1666년에, 뉴턴은 햇빛을 여러 가지 색으로 나누기 위해 유리 프리즘을 사용했다.
2. 이렇게 함으로써, 그는 하얀빛이 무지개의 모든 색깔의 혼합이라는 것을 보여 줄 수 있었다.
3. 사실상, 무지개에는 수백만 개의 색이 있다.
4. 하지만 우리는 그것들 중 몇 개의 이름만을 가지고 있다.

Unit 3

Answers

1. ③   2. ①

Word

honor 명예
universal 전 세계의 (전 인류의)
common 공통의
valuable 가치가 있는
regardless of ~에 상관(관계)없이
justice 정의

courtesy 예의
broaden 넓히다
expand 확장하다, 발전하다
experience 경험(하다)

Drill 1 • Grammar

1. 나는 네가 다음번에 더 잘할 것이라는 걸 믿는다.
2. 문제는 그가 아프다는 것이다.
3. That she will enter a good college in the future is possible.

Drill 2 • Translation

1. 해외에서 여행하는 동안에 당신은 문화적인 차이에 상관없이 전 세계적으로 공통된 가치가 있다는 것을 알게 될 것이다.
2. 그러나 어떤 나라의 몇몇 사람들은 다른 나라의 사람들이 같은 가치체계를 가지고 있다는 것을 이해하지 못한다, 왜냐하면 그 가치들이 만들어지고 다루어지는 방식이 다르기 때문이다.
3. 새로운 경험은 우리가 사물을 다르게 보도록 해 주기 때문에 여행은 항상 우리의 마음을 넓히고 발전시킨다.

Unit 4

Answers

1. ②
2. to educate people and bring necessary changes to the country

Word

aware 알아차리고 있는, 알고 있는
press 신문, 출판물
publish 출판하다
in an effort to do ~하려는 노력으로
educate 교육하다
necessary 필요한
for a while 잠시 동안
due to ~때문에
lack 부족, 결핍
in spite of ~에도 불구하고

Drill 1 • Grammar

1. 영화배우들은 10대들에 의해 사랑받는다.
2. 숙제는 (나에 의해) 곧 끝마쳐질 것이다.
3. This dress was designed by Andre Kim.
4. The book is read by many teenagers.

Drill 2 • Translation

1. 1883년이 한국 언론의 역사에서 가장 중요한 연도라는 사실을 알고 있는 사람은 드물다.
2. 국민을 교육하고 국가에 필요한 변화를 가져오기 위한 노력의 일환으로 그 해에 한국에서 신문이 최초로 발행되었다.
3. 그 짧은 역사에도 불구하고 그 신문은 한국인들의 뉴스를 접하는 방법을 영원히 바꿔놓았다.

Unit 5

Answers

1. ④
2. The sun is the center of the solar system.
3. ①
4. ⑤

Word

planet 행성
gravity 중력
revolve 회전하다
asteroid 소행성
comet 혜성
meteor 유성
form 형성하다
gaseous 가스 상태의
approach ~에 다가가다
separate 분리하다
condense 응축하다
accumulate 축적하다
radioactive 방사성의
release 방출하다
unique 특이한, 독특한
feature 특징
typical 전형적인, 대표적인
crust 〔지질〕 지각

Review

A.

1. various
2. root
3. stay
4. environment
5. form
6. raindrop
7. mixture
8. offer
9. honor
10. universal

11. broaden
13. for a while
15. effort
17. separate
19. inner

12. valuable
14. lack
16. gravity
18. hold
20. planet

B.

1. 거친, 가혹한
3. 흘러나오다
5. 햇빛
7. 프리즘
9. 예의
11. ~와 상관(관계)없이
13. 교육하다
15. ~때문에
17. 응축하다, 압축하다
19. 방출하다, 놓아주다

2. ~없이
4. 환경
6. 무지개
8. 쪼개다, 분할하다
10. 경험
12. 공통의
14. 알아차리고 있는, 알고 있는
16. 가스의, 기체상태의
18. 축적하다, 누적하다
20. ~로 구성되다

C.

1. ②   2. ④   3. ②

D.

1. 이 책은 공부하기에 어렵다.
2. 당신을 찾는 한 남자가 있다.
3. Everybody knows that this game is fun.
4. This building was built in the 1700s.

E.

1. ③   2. ④   3. ①   4. ④

F.

1. ④   2. ③

CHAPTER 02

Preview

Word • Mini Quiz

1. complex
3. increase
5. between / and
7. necessity
9. culture

2. supply
4. development
6. helpful
8. exchange
10. certain

Grammar • Mini Quiz

1. makes
2. ① interesting → interested
3. ④

Unit 1

Answers

1. ①   2. ①

Word

in short 간단히 말해
occupy 점령하다, 차지하다
play a role 역할을 하다
interaction 상호관계
conflict 대립, 분쟁
frustrate 좌절시키다
occur 일어나다
essential 본질적인
fulfill 수행하다
multiple 다수의

Drill 1 • Grammar

1. 따뜻한 물에서 목욕하는 것은 여러분을 진정시키는 것을 돕는다.
2. She helped me (to) finish the project.
3. 목표는 여러분이 지속적으로 동기부여 되도록 도울 것이다.

Drill 2 • Translation

1. 당신은 한 가족의 구성원이고 지역 야구팀의 선수이며 그리고 당신 학교의 학생이다.
2. 일반적으로, 당신은 자신에게 기대되는 것이 무엇인지 알기 때문에 당신의 각각의 역할을 수행하는 데 어려움을 거의 갖지 않는다.

3. 당신이 상충하는 여러 역할들을 요구받을 때, 당신은 아주 불편하게 느끼고 때때로 좌절감을 느낄 수 있다.

Unit 2

Answers

1. ⑤   2. ①

Word

medicine 약
advance 진보, 발전
agricultural 농업의
chemistry 화학
food supply 식량 공급
pollute 오염시키다
air transportation 항공 교통
impress 감동시키다
frighten 겁먹게 하다
air crash 비행기 추락
undoubtedly 의심할 바 없이, 틀림없이

Drill 1 • Grammar

1. 그 돌은 너무 무거워서 나는 그것을 움직일 수 없었다.
2. Minsu is such a good student that all the teachers think he is special.
3. 그는 천재여서 그의 친구들은 그가 그 문제를 풀 수 있다고 믿는다.

Drill 2 • Translation

1. 과학자들은 농화학 분야에서 큰 발전을 이루어 식량 공급을 크게 증가시켰다.
2. 그런데 우리의 강은 너무 오염되어서 심지어 수영조차 할 수 없다.
3. 우리는 이제 우주에 갈 수 있다는 사실에 흥분해 있다.
4. 하지만 우리는 또한 틀림없이 또 다른 면을 보게 될 것이다.

Unit 3

Answers

1. ⑤   2. ③

Word

Egyptian 이집트 사람, 이집트의
pay 지불하다
tax 세금

ancient 고대의
Roman 로마의
government 정부
include 포함하다
gender 성별
escape 벗어나다, 탈출하다
in addition 게다가

Drill 1 • Grammar

1. 그 도둑은 알아채이지 않기 위하여 그의 머리를 검은 모자로 덮었다.
2. 나는 학교에 늦지 않기 위하여 급히 전철역으로 갔다.
3. He ate his breakfast and hurried to the bus stop in order to catch the bus.

Drill 2 • Translation

1. 기원전 300년에 이집트 사람들은 고대 로마 정부에게 많은 세금을 내야만 했다.
2. 로마 사람들은 미래의 납세자가 도망가지 못하게 하기 위해서 생일이나 성별과 같은 모든 납세자들의 정보를 기록해 두었다.
3. 납세자들은 토지, 농작물, 가축과 물건을 포함하여 그들이 가진 모든 것에 대해 세금을 내야 했다.
4. 오늘날 사람들이 세금에 대해 불평한다면, 그들에게 고대 이집트에서 태어나지 않은 것이 다행이라고 말해 줄 수 있다.

Unit 4

Answers

1. ④   2. ⑤

Word

be interested in ~에 관심이 있다
make friends 친구를 사귀다
custom 풍습
communicate 의사소통하다
local 지역의
professional 프로의, 전문가의
for instance 예를 들어
international 국제의
culture 문화
reason 이유

Drill 1 • Grammar

1. 숙제를 하지 않는 것은 성적에 좋지 않다.
2. To watch television is to waste time.
3. 입을 벌리고 음식을 먹는 것은 몇몇 문화에서는 무례한 행동으로 간주된다.

Drill 2 • Translation

1. 첫째로, 다른 나라의 문화나 역사에 관심이 있는 사람들이 외국어 배우기를 원한다.
2. 둘째로, 다른 나라로 여행하기를 원하는 사람들이 그 나라에 살고 있는 사람들과 의사소통하기 위해서 외국어 배우기를 원할지도 모른다.
3. 여행자가 그 지방의 언어를 말할 수 있다면 그 지역 사람들과 친구가 되는 것이 틀림없이 훨씬 더 쉬울 것이다.
4. 예를 들어, 몇몇 국제적인 회사들은 직원들이 서로 더 잘 의사소통하기 위해서 적어도 두 개의 언어를 말할 수 있길 원한다.
5. 하지만, 사람들이 외국어를 배우는 가장 중요한 이유는 그것이 다른 사람들과 그들의 문화를 더 잘 이해하도록 도와줄 것이기 때문이다.

Unit 5

Answers

1. ②
2. ①
3. (1) T (2) F (3) F
4. ⑤

Word

article 물건, 물품
item 품목, 종목
naval 해군
chief (조직, 집단의) 장
be fond of ~을 좋아하다
session (활동의) 지속기간
regularly 규칙적으로, 자주
weaver 직조공
loom 직기, 베틀
knit 짜다, 뜨다
waistcoat 조끼

Review

A.

1. structure
2. conflict
3. guide
4. essential
5. advance
6. chemistry
7. pollute
8. impress
9. Egyptian
10. ancient
11. government
12. escape
13. professional
14. custom
15. international
16. local
17. knit
18. charge
19. regularly
20. disturb

B.

1. 상호관계
2. 좌절시키다
3. 일어나다
4. 수행하다
5. 비행기 추락
6. 틀림없이
7. 농업의
8. 겁먹게 하다
9. 지불하다
10. 포함하다
11. 성별
12. 게다가
13. 예를 들어
14. 문화
15. 친구를 사귀다
16. ~에 관심이 있다
17. (신문) 기사, 물건, 물품
18. 해군의
19. (활동의) 지속기간
20. (조직, 집단의) 장

C.

1. ③
2. ②
3. ②

D.

1. 그녀는 그녀의 엄마가 세탁하는 것을 도와드렸다.
2. 그는 그녀를 놀라게 하기 위해 여자 친구에게 목걸이를 사 주었다.
3. She practiced the piano hard in order to be a pianist.

E.

1. ③
2. ③
3. ④
4. ①

F.

1. local
2. regularly
3. essential
4. advance

CHAPTER 03

Preview

Word • Mini Quiz

1. survive	2. notice
3. value	4. commercial
5. own	6. experience
7. tempted	8. appearance
9. deal	10. concentrate

Grammar • Mini Quiz

1. what to eat
2. ③ which → who
3. ②

Unit 1

Answers

1. ④   2. ②

Word

approximately 대략
look for ~을 찾다, 구하다
dense 밀집한
protect 보호하다
notice 알아차리다
tribe 부족
comprise of ~으로 구성되다
Tasaday 타사다이족
completely 완벽하게
crop 농작물
protect 보호하다
discover 발견하다
traditional 전통의

Drill 1 • Grammar

1. 당신이 기부하는 어떤 것도 가난한 사람들에게는 크게 도움이 될 것이다.
2. 그녀는 내가 만나기를 원했던 여자가 아니다.
3. The story (that) I read last night was very horrible.

Drill 2 • Translation

1. 남자들이 입고 있었던 것은 작은 나뭇잎뿐이었다.
2. 그들이 살고 있던 동굴은 정글로 완전히 막혀 있어서 이 동굴은 심지어 몇 야드 밖에서조차 눈에 띄지 않았다.
3. 그들은 심지어 사냥하는 것이나 농작물을 심는 방법도 알지 못했다.
4. 그들은 발견되지 않고 그렇게 오랫동안 어떻게 살 수 있었을까?

Unit 2

Answers

1. ③   2. ④, ⑤

Word

greenhouse 온실
temperature 온도
moisture 수분, 습기
control 조절하다, 관리하다
throughout ~동안 내내
outdoor 야외의
nowadays 오늘 날에는
commercial 상업상의, 판매를 목적으로 하는

Drill 1 • Grammar

1. 영어로 연설하는 것은 쉽지 않다.
2. 네가 다른 사람의 충고를 듣는 것이 필요하다.
3. It is important to travel to other countries.

Drill 2 • Translation

1. 지붕과 벽이 유리나 플라스틱으로 만들어진 온실은 종종 hothouse(핫 하우스) 또는 유럽에서는 glasshouse(글라스 하우스)라고 불린다.
2. 온실에서는 온도와 빛, 습도가 조절될 수 있기 때문에 그 안에서 많은 종류의 식물과 야채가 일 년 내내 자랄 수 있다.
3. 사람들이 온실을 짓는 이유는 연중 어느 때나 야채와 식물을 기를 수 있기 때문이다.
4. 그러나 또한 사람들이 자신의 야채를 기르기 위해 만든 작은 온실도 있다.

Unit 3

Answers

1. ④   2. ①

Word

invent 발명하다
photophone 광선전화
beam 광선, 빛
operate 작동하다, 작용하다
reflect 반사하다
vibration 진동
receiver 수화기
signal 신호

Drill 1 • Grammar

1. 언어를 잘 배우기 위하여, 너는 인터넷을 최대한 활용해야 한다.
2. 철학을 이해하기 위해서, 당신은 열린 마음과 추상적인 사고를 가져야만 한다.
3. To buy a gift for his girlfriend, Dennis went to the department store.

Drill 2 • Translation

1. 하지만 전화기가 그의 유일한 발명품이 아니라는 것을 아는 사람은 그리 많지 않다.
2. 전화기는 전기를 사용하여 전선을 통해 소리를 전달하는 반면에 광선전화는 음파를 전달하기 위해서 공중에서 이동하는 광선을 사용했다.
3. 광선전화를 작동시키기 위해서 벨은 햇빛을 반사하도록 만들어진 거울 가까이에서 말했다.
4. 그리고 수화기는 빛의 진동을 전자신호로 바꾸도록 되어 있었고 이어폰은 전자신호를 다시 소리로 바꾸어 주었다.

Unit 4

Answers

1. ⑤   2. ③

Word

consumer 소비자
commercial 광고방송
medicine 약
employ 사용하다, 쓰다
in addition 게다가
product 상품, 제품
advertise 광고하다

regret 후회하다
immediately 즉시, 즉각
deal 거래

Drill 1 • Grammar

1. (그 버스에 있는) 죄수들은 매우 위험한 죄수들이다.
2. (하늘에) 별이 하나도 없었다.
3. When I was young, I lived (in the country).

Drill 2 • Translation

1. 광고사업에 종사하는 사람들은 언제나 소비자들이 상품을 구입하도록 유혹하기 위해 모든 수단을 활용한다.
2. 어떤 다른 광고방송은 그들의 상품이 다른 것보다 더 좋다는 것을 확신시키기 위해 도표와 그래프를 사용한다.
3. 예를 들어, 매트리스를 광고하는 광고방송은 우리가 어떤 특정한 종류의 매트리스에서 잔다면 그 다음날 기분이 더 좋아질 것이라고 말한다.

Unit 5

Answers

1. ③   2. ①
3. (1) F   (2) T   (3) F
4. You can save on expenses and study in a better environment than at universities.

Word

graduate from ~을 졸업하다
sudden 갑작스러운
expense 지출, 비용
community college 지역 전문대학
concentrate 집중하다
meanwhile 한편(으로는)
extracurricular 일과 이외의, 과외의
adequate 적합한, 알맞은
specialize 특수화하다, 전공하다
require 필요로 하다
society 사회
university 대학교

Review

A.

1. notice   2. completely

3. discover   4. comprise
5. greenhouse   6. temperature
7. control   8. outdoor
9. broaden   10. justice
11. expand   12. common
13. employ   14. advertise
15. immediately   16. convince
17. sudden   18. adequate
19. specialize   20. concentrate

B.

1. 밀집한   2. 전통의
3. ~을 찾다, 구하다   4. 대략
5. 상업상의   6. 수분, 습기
7. ~동안, ~내내   8. 요즘에
9. 예의   10. 가치 있는
11. 주의하지 않는, 영향을 끼치지 않는
12. 전 세계의
13. 소비자   14. 상품, 제품
15. 게다가   16. 광고방송

17. 일과 이외의   18. 필요로 하다
19. 지출, 비용   20. 한편

C.

1. ②   2. ④   3. ③

D.

1. 이 교실에 있는 학생들은 매우 똑똑하다.
2. 이것이 그 여자가 얘기했던 책이다.
3. The book that you read was written by my grandfather.

E.

1. ①   2. ①   3. ④   4. ②

F.

1. advertise   2. approximately
3. operate   4. moisture

CHAPTER 04

Preview

Word • Mini Quiz

1. put on   2. role
3. various   4. come up with
5. recover   6. emerged
7. resources   8. demand
9. defend   10. threaten

Grammar • Mini Quiz

1. clean
2. ② fluency → fluently
3. ②

Unit 1

Answers

1. ③   2. ④

Word

various 다양한
purpose 목적
deceive 속이다
religious 종교의
represent 나타내다, 상징하다
demon 악마
ancient 고대의
audience 관중
occasion 행사
Halloween 할로윈

Drill 1 • Grammar

1. 그는 몇 권의 책을 사기 위하여 서점에 갔다.

2. 윤선이는 숙제를 끝내기 위해 늦게까지 잠을 자지 않았다.

3. 그는 고등학교 때 그의 첫사랑을 만나기 위하여 그 식당으로 갔다.

4. Many students attend university to get a good job.

Drill 2 • Translation

1. 이것들을 쓰면 당신은 다른 사람이 된 것 같은 느낌이 들 것이다.

2. 옛날에 사냥꾼들은 동물을 속이기 위해 이것들을 썼다.

3. 또한, 고대 그리스와 로마의 배우들은 그들이 연기하고 있는 역할이 무엇인지를 관중들에게 보여 주기 위해 이것들을 쓰곤 했다.

Unit 2

Answers

1. ⑤   2. ④

Word

argue 주장하다

hemisphere 반구 (뇌의 반쪽)

according to ~에 따라

tend to ~하는 경향이 있다

linguistic 언어의

ability 능력

injury 손상, 부상

compare to ~와 비교하다

recover 회복하다

permanently 영구히

utilize 이용하다, 활용하다

cell 세포

Drill 1 • Grammar

1. 내가 시골길을 운전해 가고 있을 때, 나는 이상한 여자를 봤다.

2. 비가 올 때, 그들은 주로 고무 부츠를 신는다.

3. When I was a child, I studied Spanish.

Drill 2 • Translation

1. 몇몇 과학자들은 언어를 사용할 때 남자들은 단지 뇌의 왼쪽만 사용하는 반면 여자들은 뇌의 양쪽을 사용하는 경향이 있다고 주장한다.

2. 결과적으로, 과학자들에 의하면, 여자들이 더 나은 언어능력을 나타내는 경향이 있다.

3. 그들의 연구결과를 보면 여자들은 남자들에 비해 말할 때 더 많은 수의 단어를 사용하고 더 빨리 적절한 단어를 생각해내는 경향이 있다.

4. 게다가, 여자들은 남자들에 비해 뇌에 있는 더 많은 세포조직을 이용하기 때문에 영구적인 손상이 더 적을 것 같다.

Unit 3

Answers

1. ③   2. ⑤

Word

activity 활동

increase 증가하다

Antarctica 남극대륙

emerge 나타나다, 일어나다

impact 영향

tourist 관광객

threaten 위협하다

wild creature 야생동물(생물)

natural 자연의

resource 자원

continent 대륙

Drill 1 • Grammar

1. Karen은 MP3 플레이어를 잃어버렸다.

2. Jason과 Emma는 1999년에 결혼했다. 그들은 9년 동안 행복한 결혼생활을 했다.

3. I have studied English for five years.

Drill 2 • Translation

1. 남극대륙에서 인간의 활동이 증가함에 따라 새로운 문제들이 생겨났다.

2. 비록 남극대륙을 방문하는 사람들의 수가 그리 많지는 않지만, 그렇게 한 몇몇 사람들이 큰 영향을 끼쳤다.

3. 관광객들은 종종 쓰레기를 남겨두고, 때때로 너무 크게 소음을 내는 것으로 야생생물들을 위협한다.

4. 하지만 가장 심각한 문제는 천연자원에 대한 끊임없는 인간의 욕구가 대륙 전체를 위협하고 있다는 것이다.

Unit 4

Answers

1. ①, ②   2. ④

Word

concern 걱정하다

defense 방어, 방위

communist 공산주의자

Soviet Union 소비에트 연방 (구소련)

nuclear weapon 핵무기

launch 발사하다
satellite 인공위성
threaten 위협하다
as a consequence 그 결과
budget 예산(안)
exploration (우주의) 개발, 연구
decade 10년(간)

Drill 1 • Grammar

1. 너는 말을 물까지 이끌고 갈 수 있으나 말이 물을 마시도록 강요할 수는 없다.
2. 그 장군은 병사들에게 조국을 위해 용감하게 싸울 것을 명령했다.
3. The teacher asked his students to read a lot of books.

Drill 2 • Translation

1. 엎친 데 덮친 격으로 1957년에 소비에트 연방은 세계최초의 인공위성인 스푸트니크 1호를 우주에 발사시켰다.
2. 미국 사람들은 위협을 느꼈고 그래서 정부에게 국방과 우주공학에 더 많은 돈을 쓰도록 요구하였다.
3. 10년 후 미국은 마침내 역전하여 1969년에 달에 최초로 인간을 보냈다.

Unit 5

Answers

1. ③   2. ②   3. ①   4. ③

Word

Copernicus 코페르니쿠스(폴란드의 천문학자로서, 지동설의 제창자)
astronomer 천문학자
propose 제안하다
reluctant 마음 내키지 않는
belief 믿음, 의견, 생각
eventually 마침내, 결국
sensation 큰 이야기 거리, 대소동
controversial 물의를 일으키는
unfortunately 불행하게도
theory 이론

Review

A.

1. represent   2. audience

3. deceive   4. purpose
5. argue   6. ability
7. recover   8. utilize
9. increase   10. emerge
11. resource   12. threaten
13. defense   14. satellite
15. demand   16. launch
17. eventually   18. theory
19. propose   20. belief

B.

1. 다양한   2. 악마
3. 종교의   4. 행사, 경우
5. ~와 비교하다   6. 영구히
7. 언어의   8. ~하는 경향이 있다
9. 영향   10. 활동
11. 야생동물   12. 대륙
13. 공산주의자   14. 예산(안)
15. 10년(간)   16. 걱정하다
17. 천문학자   18. 마음 내키지 않는
19. 큰 이야기 거리   20. 물의를 일으키는

C.

1. ①   2. ④   3. ②

D.

1. 나는 책을 찾으러 도서관에 갔다.
2. 우리 가족은 내가 10살 때부터 이 아파트에 살았다.
3. The boss ordered him to finish the project by next week.
4. When I was young, my mother bought me this hat.

E.

1. ②   2. ①   3. ①

F.

1. various   2. recover   3. ability

CHAPTER 05

Preview

Word • Mini Quiz

1. introduce
2. unfair
3. public
4. deserve
5. reasonable
6. tendency
7. organic
8. tune
9. second thought
10. succeed

Grammar • Mini Quiz

1. ②
2. ③
3. ②

Unit 1

Answers

1. ④
2. (1) F (2) F (3) T

Word

wristwatch 손목시계
watchmaker 시계 제조업자
take a walk 산책하다
infant 유아
invention 발명
inspire 영감을 주다

Drill 1 • Grammar

1. 그녀는 얼굴이 빨개지는 것을 느꼈다.
2. 나는 몇 명의 아이들이 강에서 수영하는 것을 봤다.
3. People felt an earthquake shaking the ground beneath their feet.

Drill 2 • Translation

1. 첫 번째 손목시계는 1790년 스위스 제네바의 시계 제조업자에 의해 창안되었다.
2. 그는 젊은 여자가 양쪽 팔에 갓난아이를 안고 있는 것을 보았다.
3. 그녀는 손쉽게 시간을 확인하기 위해서 손목에 시계를 묶고 있었다.
4. 최초 손목시계의 발명은 똑똑한 젊은 엄마에 의해서 영감을 받았다.

Unit 2

Answers

1. ④
2. ⑤

Word

wage 임금, 급료
physically 육체적으로
deserve ~받을 만하다
for instance 예를 들어
invest 투자하다
medical 의학의
mention 언급하다
enormous 큰, 거대한
reasonable 합당한, 정당한
maid 가정부
janitor 수위, 관리인
suppose 가정하다

Drill 1 • Grammar

1. 그녀가 밤에 그렇게 늦게 집에 왔다는 것이 이상하다.
2. 사람이 죽음을 두려워하는 것은 이상하다, 왜냐하면 죽음은 필연적 종착역이고 올 때가 되면 오기 때문이다.
3. It is certain that people live longer than they did before.

Drill 2 • Translation

1. 당신은 더러운 일을 하는 사람들이 지금보다 더 높은 임금을 받아야 한다는 것에 동의하는가?
2. 공중화장실이나 다른 사람의 집, 사무실, 또는 거리를 청소하는 사람들이 높은 임금을 받지 못한다는 것은 불공평하다.
3. 예를 들어 의사가 되기까지 엄청난 노력을 기울여야 한다는 점은 말할 것도 없고 많은 돈과 시간을 투자해야 한다.
4. 그러면 그 일꾼들이 얼마나 중요하고 그들이 왜 높은 임금을 받아야 하는지 깨달을 것이다.

Unit 3

Answers

1. ④
2. ④

Word

tendency 경향
in terms of ~의 관점에서, 면에서
medical community 의료계
seriously 진지하게
play a role in ~에서 역할을 하다
illness 병, 질병
seek 찾다, 추구하다
research 연구, 연구하다
prove 증명하다
affect ~에 영향을 주다
a large portion of 아주 많은
organic 신체기관의
psychological 심리(학)적인

Drill 1 • Grammar

1. 음악을 영원히 바꿔놓은 비틀즈는 세계에서 가장 유명한 로큰롤 밴드였다.
2. John Pemberton은 코카콜라를 발명한 최초의 사람이었다.
3. 내가 어제 봤던 여자는 귀신이었다.
4. Mi-sun is the only girl that knows the secret.

Drill 2 • Translation

1. 수세기 동안 우리는 육체적인 신체의 관점에서만 건강을 생각하는 경향이 있었다.
2. 의료계는 우리의 마음이 질병과 치료에 중요한 역할을 할 수 있다는 가능성을 진지하게 보지 않았다.
3. 의료센터는 그들의 환자 중 더 많은 비중의 사람들이 신체 기관의 질병은 가지지 않았지만 심리적인 도움을 얻고자 하는 사람들이라고 보고했다.

Unit 4

Answers

1. ③   2. ①

Word

once 일단 ~하면
pass along 알리다, 전가하다
monk 수도(승)사
tune 곡, 가락
record 기록하다
simply 단순하게
dot 작은 점
composer 작곡가

Drill 1 • Grammar

1. 어떤 것을 할 때, 당신이 하고 있는 것에만 집중하시오.
2. 시는 우리에게 우리 자신의 삶에서 잃어가고 있는 것을 제공해 준다.
3. Kelly never forgets what she learns.

Drill 2 • Translation

1. 그 당시에 사람들이 불렀던 노래는 그들 자신이 만든 것이거나 다른 사람들에게서 배운 것이었다.
2. 일단 노래가 만들어지면 그것은 한 사람에게서 다른 사람에게로 전해졌다.
3. 하지만 약 900년 전에 몇몇의 이탈리아 수도승들이 가락이나 멜로디를 기록할 아이디어를 생각해냈다.
4. 그들은 음악의 소리를 단순히 선과 점만으로 기록하였다.

Unit 5

Answers

1. ②   2. ④   3. ⑤

Word

successful 성공적인
unless ~하지 않으면
negative 부정적인
decision 결정
accomplish 이루다, 성취하다
inspiration 영감
enjoyable 재미있는
especially 특히
make up ~을 결심하다
actually 사실은
no matter how 아무리 ~할지라도
moral 교훈
correspond 일치하다

Review

A.

1. infant
2. introduce
3. wrist
4. watchmaker
5. invest
6. medical
7. reasonable
8. enormous
9. seriously
10. prove
11. affect
12. seek

13. once
15. dot
17. negative
19. make up

14. tune
16. record
18. accomplish
20. inspiration

B.

1. 영감을 주다
3. ~하는 동안
5. 언급하다
7. ~받을 만하다
9. 의료계
11. 신체 기관의
13. 알리다, 전가하다
15. 작곡가
17. 재미있는
19. 일치하다

2. 발명
4. 묶다
6. 가정하다
8. 수위, 관리인
10. ~에서 역할을 하다
12. 심리(학)적인
14. 수도(승)사
16. 악기
18. 교훈
20. ~하지 않으면

C.

1. ③   2. ④   3. ①

D.

1. 나는 네가 내 이름을 부르는 것을 들었다.
2. 네가 취직했다는 것은 대단한 일이다.
3. He is the man that broke the promise.
4. What you are hearing now is my favorite song.

E.

1. ①   2. ①   3. ③   4. ③

F.

1. ②   2. ①   3. ④   4. ③

CHAPTER 06

Preview

Word • Mini Quiz

1. escape
3. memory
5. convenient
7. matter
9. indicate

2. origin
4. form
6. communicate
8. state
10. universal

Grammar • Mini Quiz

1. ③ will → would
2. ①
3. ④

Unit 1

Answers

1. ⑤   2. ②

Word

ancient 고대의

Egyptian 이집트(사람)의
symbolize 상징하다
everlasting 영원히 지속되는
marriage 결혼
take off 벗다
escape 달아나다, 사라지다
directly 곧장, 바로
origin 기원, 유래

Drill 1 • Grammar

1. 나의 형은 대학입시에 떨어졌기 때문에, 그는 재수해야 한다.
2. 그는 밤새 탐정 소설을 읽었기 때문에 하루 종일 잤다.
3. Since the bus was full, I had to walk home.

Drill 2 • Translation

1. 반지에는 끊어진 부분이 없기 때문에 그런 반지를 끼는 사람들은 영원히 행복하게 살 것이라고 믿었다.
2. 이집트인들은 반지가 끊어지면 불운이 찾아오고 결혼 생활이 끝날 것이라고 생각했다.
3. 그들은 또한 반지를 빼면 사랑이 사람의 마음에서 달아날 것이라고 믿었다.
4. 그들은 피가 사람의 심장으로부터 곧장 왼손의 네 번째 손가락으로 흐른다고 생각했다.

Unit 2

Answers

1. ②   2. ①

Word

past 과거
disease 질병
cause ~를 야기시키다
amnesia 기억상실증
serious 심각한
last 이어지다, 지속하다
permanent 영구적인
organic 조직의, 기관의
go on 계속하다, 지속하다
injury 손상, 부상
Alzheimer's 치매

Drill 1 • Grammar

1. 이명박은 한국에서 가장 위대한 리더 가운데 하나라고 생각되어진다.
2. 해리포터는 호그와트 학교 밖에서 마법을 사용하는 것이 허용되지 않았다.
3. My boyfriend is called a gorilla by everyone.

Drill 2 • Translation

1. 실제로 기억을 잃도록 만드는 병이 있다.
2. 그 중 하나는 기억상실증이라고 불린다.
3. 기억상실증에 걸린 어떤 사람은 이름이나 가족, 친구를 포함하여 자신에 관해 어떤 것도 기억하지 못할 수 있다.
4. 기억상실증뿐만 아니라 치매도 사람이 기억을 잃도록 만들 수 있다.

Unit 3

Answers

1. ③   2. ④

Word

challenge 문제, 난제
security 보안, 안전
on the rise 증가되고 있는
safety 안전
make sure 확신하다
take measures 조치를 취하다
protect 보호하다
method 방법

---

meet 대처하다

Drill 1 • Grammar

1. 어떻게 그녀가 갑자기 그렇게 바쁘게 되었는지가 모든 사람에게 수수께끼이다.
2. 어떻게 그가 큰 피자를 두 개나 먹고 여전히 배가 고픈지 놀랍다.
3. I wonder how he could solve the math problem.

Drill 2 • Translation

1. 인터넷의 사용이 매년 증가하고 있으며, 이것이 많은 문제를 일으키고 있다.
2. 예를 들어, 기업체들은 인터넷에 있는 자신들의 사이트가 사용자들에게 안전한지 확인할 필요가 있다.
3. 그들은 이메일 발송자들이 누구인지, 오고가는 정보가 정확한지를 알 필요가 있다.
4. 많은 회사들은 의사소통하기에 편리한 방법이기 때문에 이메일을 사용하지만, 회사들은 회사의 비밀이 보호되는 것을 확실하게 하기 위해서 조치를 취해야 한다.

Unit 4

Answers

1. ③   2. ⑤

Word

big bang theory 빅뱅이론(우주 폭발론)
theorize 이론(학설)을 세우다
expand 확장하다, 넓히다
current 현재의
state 상태, 형세
prior 이전의
approximately 대략
explosion 폭발
refer 언급하다, 관련되다
exactly 정확하게
particle 작은 조각(행성을 뜻함)

Drill 1 • Grammar

1. 사진에 웃고 있는 여자가 있다.
2. "디워"라는 영화는 한국에서 가장 흥미진진한 영화였다.
3. 그는 길에서 부서진 차를 나에게 보여 주었다.
4. I saw a strange woman in the locked car.

Drill 2 • Translation

1. 약 200억 년 전 거대한 폭발이 일어났을 때 우주가 이전 상태로부터

현재의 상태로 팽창했다는 이론을 세우고 있는데, 이것이 빅뱅이라고 불린다.

2. 비록 과학자들은 왜 그리고 정확히 어떻게 빅뱅이 일어났는지 아직 설명하지 못하지만, 그들은 이 폭발이 우주를 팽창하게 했다는 데는 대부분 동의한다.

3. 폭발하는 동안에 만들어진 물질이 차가워졌을 때, 그것이 우주에 있는 모든 것을 구성하는 행성들을 만든 것이다.

Unit 5

Answers

1. ②   2. ⑤   3. ③   4. ⑤

Word

foreign 외국의
communicate 의사소통하다
misunderstand 오해하다, 잘못 해석하다
index finger 집게손가락
thumb 엄지손가락
offer 제공(제안)하다
indicate ~의 표시이다, 표현하다
useless 쓸모없는, 무익한
universal 전 세계의
gesture 몸짓
verbally 말로, 구두로

Review

A.

1. directly   2. ancient
3. escape   4. marriage
5. past   6. disease
7. last   8. permanent
9. on the rise   10. protect
11. method   12. meet
13. theorize   14. state
15. prior   16. exactly
17. misunderstanding 18. express
19. language   20. useless

B.

1. 상징하다   2. 기원, 유래
3. 영원히 지속되는   4. 벗다

5. 조직의, 기관의   6. 손상, 부상
7. ~을 야기시키다   8. 기억상실증
9. 문제, 난제   10. 보안, 안전
11. 확신하다   12. 조치를 취하다
13. 대략   14. 폭발
15. 언급하다, 관련되다   16. 현재의
17. 교훈   18. 제공하다
19. 집게손가락   20. 엄지손가락

C.

1. ②   2. ①   3. ①

D.

1. 그는 일을 못 끝냈기 때문에 회사에 있어야 한다.
2. 우리 할아버지는 애국지사들 중에 하나로 생각되어졌다.
3. Getting better scores is how you make your parents happy.
4. Let's pick up fallen leaves in the garden.

E.

1. ④   2. ①   3. ③   4. ③

F.

1. last   2. express   3. security   4. current

CHAPTER 07

Preview

Word • Mini Quiz

1. proper	2. spare
3. order	4. defeats
5. professional	6. consider
7. determine	8. realize
9. admire	10. interact

Grammar • Mini Quiz

1. ① have done → had done
2. ②
3. ③ go → goes

Unit 1

Answers

1. ③   2. ④

Word

corporal punishment 체벌
means 수단, 방법
discipline ～을 벌하다, 징계하다, 훈련하다
spare 아끼다
rod 회초리
spoil 망치다
attention 주의, 주목
undisciplined 규율이 없는, 훈련을 받지 않은
severe 엄격한, 가혹한
violence 폭력
justify 정당화하다

Drill 1 • Grammar

1. 행운을 비는 제스처가 있다.
2. 그 음식을 요리할 유일한 사람이 윤선이다.
3. Practice is the only way to learn a foreign language.

Drill 2 • Translation

1. 집에서뿐 아니라 학교에서도 체벌은 때때로 아이를 훈련하는 최상의 방법이다.

2. 게다가 다른 모든 친구들이나 급우들뿐만 아니라, 벌을 받는 사람의 적절한 주의력을 이끌어낼 수 있다.
3. 체벌이 – 너무 가혹하지 않다면 – 그러한 아이들을 가르치고 교실에서 질서를 유지하는 효과적인 방법이 될 수 있다.
4. 체벌로부터 아이들이 배울 수 있는 유일한 것은 폭력이 정당화될 수 있다는 것뿐이다.

Unit 2

Answers

1. ⑤   2. ③

Word

take 데려가다
farm 농장, 농원
trip (짧은) 여행
backyard 뒤뜰
stream 시내, 개울
imported 수입된
speechless 말을 못하는
defeat 좌절시키다
purpose 목적, 의도

Drill 1 • Grammar

1. 그는 소리 지르는 채로 길을 달려 내려갔다.
2. 그는 하루 종일 만화책을 보는 채로 앉아 있었다.
3. The young boy lay sleeping on his bed when his father came into his room.

Drill 2 • Translation

1. 한 아버지가 사람들이 얼마나 가난할 수 있는지 보여 주기 위해 아들을 시골로 데리고 갔다.
2. 여행에서 집으로 돌아온 후 아버지가 아들에게 물었다. "사람들이 얼마나 가난할 수 있는지 보았니?"
3. 우리는 뒤뜰에 수영장이 있지만 그들은 끝없는 개울이 있어요.
4. 어린 소년의 말이 끝났을 때 그의 아버지는 할 말을 잃은 채로 앉아 있었다.

Unit 3

Answers

1. ④   2. ④

Word

renowned 유명한
guitarist 기타연주가
consider 생각하다, 간주하다
classical 클래식의
instrument 악기
suitable 알맞은, 적합한
even though ~에도 불구하고
composer 작곡가
play 연주하다, 공연하다
prove 증명하다, 보여 주다
performance 공연

Drill 1 • Grammar

1. 나는 그 핵폭탄이 지금까지 발명된 것 중에 가장 나쁜 발명이라고 믿는다.
2. 그 젊은이는 자신이 잘생기고 매력적이라고 생각했다.
3. All the students think him a fool.

Drill 2 • Translation

1. 안드레스 세고비아는 최초의 유명한 클래식 기타 연주자이다.
2. 대부분의 사람들은 기타가 단지 대중음악에나 어울린다고 생각했다.
3. 비록 몇몇 클래식 음악 작곡가들이 기타를 위한 곡을 썼지만 그것이 클래식 음악 콘서트에서 연주된 적은 한 번도 없었다.

Unit 4

Answers

1. ④   2. ②

Word

personality 성격
argue 논쟁하다
nature 본성
nurture 양육, 교육
scholar 학자
genetically 유전적인
determine 결정하다
experience 경험
affect 영향을 끼치다

relationship 관계
culture 문화
solely 혼자서, 단독으로
influence 영향을 끼치다
interactively (둘 다) 서로 작용하는

Drill 1 • Grammar

1. 비틀즈의 노래는 전 세계의 많은 사람들에 의해 사랑받아 왔다.
2. 축구는 브라질의 국민적 오락으로 일컬어져 왔다.
3. All the tickets have already been sold.

Drill 2 • Translation

1. 학자들은 수년 동안 사람의 성격이 어떻게 형성되는지에 대해 논쟁해 왔다.
2. 이 논쟁은 오랫동안 '본성 대 양육'으로 알려져 왔다.
3. 그들은 인간의 성격은 대부분 어렸을 때 부모와의 관계나 문화에 의해 영향을 받는다고 주장한다.
4. 그러나 오늘날 대부분의 학자들은 본성이나 양육 단 하나만이 인간의 성격에 영향을 미치는 것이 아니라는 데에 동의한다.

Unit 5

Answers

1. ⑤   2. ③   3. ②   4. ④

Word

Titanic 타이타닉 호
ocean liner 원양 정기선
luxurious 호화로운
maiden 미경험의, 처녀의
voyage 항해
construction 건설 작업
attention 관심, 주목
unfortunately 불행하게도
cruise 순항하다
enormous 거대한
rip 찢음, 상처
hull 껍질, 덮개
vessel (대형의) 배
approximately 대략의
capacity 수용력, 포용력
admiration 감탄
assistance 지원, 도움
salvation 구조
respond 응답하다, 대답하다
distress signal 조난 신호

eventually 마침내, 결국
disaster 재난
maritime 바다에 관한, 해상의

Review

A.

1. means
2. spoil
3. effective
4. maintain
5. farm
6. backyard
7. speechless
8. purpose
9. salvation
10. consider
11. instrument
12. performance
13. personality
14. argue
15. scholar
16. determine
17. luxurious
18. maiden
19. capacity
20. assistance

B.

1. 순항하다
2. 규율이 없는, 훈련을 받지 않은
3. 엄격한, 가혹한
4. 정당화(옳다고)하다
5. 시내, 개울
6. 수입하다

7. 좌절시키다
8. 데려가다
9. 기타 연주가
10. 알맞은, 적합한
11. 작곡가
12. ~로 밝혀지다
13. 교육, 양육
14. 유전적으로
15. 혼자서, 단독으로
16. 영향을 끼치다
17. 대략의
18. 감탄
19. 구조, 건축
20. 거대한

C.

1. ③
2. ①
3. ①

D.

1. 이 노래는 많은 사람들에 의해서 불려왔다.
2. 나는 바나나 한 송이를 든 채로 서있었다.
3. I am looking for a chair to sit on.
4. I think him a patriot.

E.

1. ②
2. ③
3. ②
4. ④

F.

1. violence
2. effective
3. performance
4. argument
5. construction
6. admiration

CHAPTER 08

Preview

Word • Mini Quiz

1. discouraged
2. occur
3. Knowledge
4. rush
5. progressive
6. solar
7. appreciate
8. investigate
9. scene
10. offend

Grammar • Mini Quiz

1. ④ will finish → finish
2. ② the way 삭제
3. is taking off

Unit 1

Answers

1. ⑤
2. ③

Word

proudly 자랑스럽게
announce 발표하다
trip 항해
spaceship 우주선
colony 식민지
beat 이기다, 무찌르다
straight 곧장 가는, 직진하는
laugh 비웃다

silly 어리석은, 바보 같은
melt 녹다

Drill 1 • Grammar

1. 학교가 끝난 다음에 무엇을 할 예정이니?
2. After she graduates from school, she will get a good job.
3. 영화를 본 후에 극장에 있는 모든 사람들은 굉장히 화가 났다.

Drill 2 • Translation

1. 그 로켓은 지구로 귀환하기 전까지 한 달 내내 거기에 머물렀죠.
2. "그건 아무것도 아닙니다."라고 여우가 말했다.
3. 로켓은 태양에 도착하기도 전에 녹아버릴 것입니다.
4. "우리는 그것을 밤에 보낼 것입니다."

Unit 2

Answers

1. ④   2. ⑤

Word

unexpectedly 예기치 못하게, 뜻밖에
among 사이에
expect 예상하다
forecast 일기예보
deliver 나르다, 배달하다
mainland 본토, 대륙
frighten 두려워하다, 겁에 질리다
turn over 뒤집다, 전복시키다
crew 선원
be about to 막 ~하려고 하다
horrify 무서워 떨게 하다
space 공간

Drill 1 • Grammar

1. 네가 더 열심히 공부할수록, 너는 더 좋은 성적을 받게 될 것이다.
2. The harder you study, the closer you get to your dream.
3. 그가 샤워하려고 더 오래 기다릴수록, 냄새는 더욱더 심해진다.

Drill 2 • Translation

1. 일기예보에서 날씨가 오후동안 맑을 것이라고 했기 때문에 정말 아무도 예상할 수 없었다.
2. 바다에는 본토에서 작은 섬으로 하루 두 번 관광객을 실어 나르는 나룻배가 있었다.

3. 파도가 커지면 커질수록 배에 있는 사람들은 더욱 더 두려워했다.
4. 그들 중에 엄마와 함께 막 보트에 타려고 했던 12세 소년 Tom이 있었다.

Unit 3

Answers

1. ③   2. ③

Word

eclipse (해, 달의) 식
solar eclipse 일식
block 막다, 차단하다
movement 움직임
completely 완전히, 완벽하게
persist 지속하다
several 몇몇의
appear 나타나다
spectacular 장관의, 장엄한
phenomenon 현상

Drill 1 • Grammar

1. 왜 그녀가 그 당시에 나를 떠나야만 했는지를 나는 모르겠다.
2. 이것이 왜 이명박이 한국의 대통령이 됐는지 이다.
3. I really wonder why he loved the strange woman.

Drill 2 • Translation

1. 일식은 태양의 빛이 지구에 차단될 때 일어난다.
2. 태양 빛이 왜 차단되는지 알고 있는가?
3. 이것은 달을 가운데에 둔 상태로 태양, 지구, 달이 일직선을 이루는 것을 의미한다.
4. 태양 빛이 완전히 가려질 때 지구는 어두워진다.

Unit 4

Answers

1. ②   2. ②

Word

pick 선택하다, 고르다
decision 결정
it seems that ~처럼 보이다
factor 요소, 요인

overheard 우연히 듣다
beholder 보는 사람
appearance 외모
reflect ~을 나타내다
quality 본질
make an effort 노력하다
disappoint 실망시키다
looks 외모
appreciation 감사, 진가, 존중
beyond (시각) ~을 넘어서

Drill 1 • Grammar

1. 그녀는 귀신과 얘기하는 것을 좋아하는 것처럼 보인다.
2. 한국에 있는 사람들은 햄버거나 피자를 정말로 좋아하는 것처럼 보인다.
3. It seems that he likes collecting stamps.

Drill 2 • Translation

1. 한국 사람들은 이것을 블라인드 데이트(소개팅 또는 미팅)라고 부르는데, 그것은 두 명 이상의 여자와 같은 수의 남자들이 함께 데이트 또는 "미팅"을 하는 것이다.
2. 어느 날 나는 한 대학생이 그의 데이트 파트너에 대해 이야기하는 것을 우연히 들었는데 나는 그가 오로지 관심이 있는 것이라고는 그녀의 외모와 그녀가 입고 있었던 것뿐이라는 것을 알게 되었다.
3. 하지만 나는 젊은 사람들에게 아름다움은 보는 사람에 따라 다른 것이고 외모는 인간의 좋은 본질을 전혀 반영하지 못한다는 것을 이해해야 한다고 충고하고 싶다.
4. 만일 그렇게 한다면 그들은 "신의 실패작"이라는 시각을 넘어서 고맙게 생각할 수 있을 것이다.

Unit 5

Answers

1. ④   2. ①   3. ③   4. ③

Word

fingerprint 지문
play an important role 중요한 역할을 하다
offender 범죄자
investigator 수사관, 조사자
dust (가루 등을) 뿌리다, 털다
latex gloves 라텍스 장갑
scene 현장, 장소
contaminate 더럽히다
valuable evidence 유용한 증거(물증)
a piece of cake 매우 쉬운 일 (누워서 떡 먹기)
database (컴퓨터의) 데이터베이스

ex-convict 전과자
unresolved 미해결된
case 사건, 소송

Review

A.

1. announce	2. trip
3. colony	4. melt
5. expect	6. forecast
7. deliver	8. crew
9. solar eclipse	10. block
11. persist	12. appear
13. factor	14. decision
15. overhear	16. quality
17. offender	18. investigator
19. scene	20. ex-convict

B.

1. 자랑스럽게	2. 이기다, 무찌르다
3. 곧장 가는, 직진하는	4. 어리석은, 바보 같은
5. 예기치 못하게	6. 본토, 대륙
7. 두려워하다	8. ~을 뒤집다
9. 장관의, 장엄한	10. 현상
11. 몇몇의	12. 움직임
13. 외모	14. 보는 사람
15. 노력하다	16. ~을 나타내다
17. 유용한 증거 (물증)	18. 먼지, (가루 등을) 뿌리다, 털다
19. 지문	20. 미해결된

C.

1. ④   2. ①   3. ②

D.

1. 날씨가 추워질수록, 너는 자신을 더 따뜻하게 유지해야 한다.
2. 너는 왜 그들이 파티에 안 왔는지 아니?
3. I will go out and play when it snows.
4. It seems that the child likes bread.

E.

1. ①   2. ④   3. ③   4. ①

F.

1. beat   2. appearances
3. valuable

CHAPTER 09

Preview

Word • Mini Quiz

1. promising	2. regular / basis
3. literally	4. enormous
5. method	6. sight
7. detail	8. urgent
9. vivid	10. unique

Grammar • Mini Quiz

1. ② like → 삭제　　2. ②　　　　　　3. cannot

Unit 1

Answers

1. ⑤　　　　　　2. (1) True　(2) False　(3) False

Word

at least 적어도, 최소한
probably 아마도
literally 글자 그대로, 정말로
trick 속임수, 기법, 트릭
decade 10년(간)
technology 과학기술
film 영화
pretend ~인 체하다
overlay ~을 (…위에) 놓다, 겹치다
complicated 복잡한

Drill 1 • Grammar

1. 나는 자원봉사 일을 하는 사람들을 존경한다.
2. 극장에서 내 앞에 앉아 있는(던) 남자가 코를 골고 있었다.
3. The woman holding a baby in her arms is waiting for the bus.

Drill 2 • Translation

1. 예를 들어 당신은 아마도 영화에서 하늘을 나는 슈퍼맨을 본 적이 있을 것이다.
2. 하지만 영화 제작자들은 그들이 나는 것처럼 보이게 만드는 속임수를 알고 있다.
3. 수십 년 전 지금처럼 기술이 발달하지 않았을 때 사람들은 영화에서 속임수를 사용했다.
4. 우선 그들은 구름이나 별이 아주 빠르게 움직이고 있는 하늘을 촬영했다.
5. 그래서 배우의 영상이 하늘의 영상 위에 겹치게 된다.

Unit 2

Answers

1. ⑤　　　　　　　　　　2. ②

Word

to begin with 우선, 먼저
House of Parliament 국회의사당
be located on ~에 위치해 있다
Thames River 템즈강 (런던 시내를 지나 북해로 흐름)
Big Ben 빅벤 (영국 국회 의사당의 시계탑)
weigh 무게가 나가다
Buckingham Palace 버킹검 궁전
royal family 왕실, 황족
notorious 악명 높은
criminal 범죄자
monument 기념비(탑)
Hyde Park 하이드파크 (런던의 공원)

Drill 1 • Grammar

1. 그는 그녀에게 연애편지를 보냈다, 그런데 그녀는 그것을 개봉하지 않은 채로 돌려보냈다.
2. 나는 물 한 병을 마셨다, 그런데 그것은 오줌인 것으로 밝혀졌다.
3. She gave me some advice, which I needed so much.

Drill 2 • Translation

1. 우선 국회의사당은 템즈강 북쪽에 위치해 있는데 그 강은 런던을 통과하여 흐른다.
2. 이것은 거대한 종으로 유명한데, 그것은 약 13.5톤 정도 무게가 나간다.
3. 당신은 또한 런던탑을 방문할 수 있는데, 그곳은 많은 악명 높은 범죄자들을 위한 교도소였다.
4. 런던은 또한 런던에서 가장 큰 공원인 하이드파크와 같이 많은 아름다운 공원들도 있다.

Unit 3

Answers

1. ⑤   2. ②

Word

distance 거리, 간격
autumn 가을 (=fall)
migrate 이동하다, 이주하다
Northern Hemisphere 북반구
Southern Hemisphere 남반구
fail to ~하는 데 실패하다
direction 방향
migratory 이동(이주)하는

Drill 1 • Grammar

1. 좋은 성적을 만드는 것은 열심히 공부하는 것을 요구한다.
2. 대학에 가고 싶다면 너는 TV 보는 것을 포기해야 한다.
3. She is proud of becoming a news anchorwoman for CNN.

Drill 2 • Translation

1. 어떤 종류의 새들은 매년 엄청난 거리를 날아간다.
2. 그들은 정확한 방향으로 날아가는 데에 절대 실패하지 않고, 매년 같은 장소로 항상 돌아오기 때문에 놀랄 만하다.
3. 과학자들은 새들이 어떻게 이렇게 할 수 있는지 확실히 이해하지 못하지만 그들은 철새들이 뇌에 매우 상세한 지도가 있는 것이 틀림없다고 믿는다.

Unit 4

Answers

1. ②   2. ③

Word

fog 안개
be lost 길을 잃다 (=lose one's way)
direct 길을 가르쳐 주다
elbow 팔꿈치
address 주소
stranger 낯선 사람
blind 시작 장애의
thick 짙은, 두꺼운
promising 가망 있는, 유망한

Drill 1 • Grammar

1. 노인은 눈이 감겨진 채로 빗소리를 듣고 있었다.
2. The actress sat on a chair with her legs crossed.
3. 우리는 손이 턱에 그리고 팔꿈치가 무릎에 있는 채로 벤치에 앉아 있는 한 귀신을 봤다.

Drill 2 • Translation

1. 어느 겨울 밤 나는 내가 안개 속에서 그리고 잘 알지 못하는 도시의 한 지역에서 길을 잃은 것을 알았다.
2. 그는 좋다고 했고 내 팔꿈치에 그의 손을 댄 채 우리는 함께 걸었다.
3. 내가 준 주소에 우리가 도착했을 때 나는 그에게 감사해 하면서 작별 인사를 했다.
4. 내가 악수를 하려고 뒤돌았을 때 나는 그가 내 손은 물론 우리가 왔던 길도 볼 수 없다는 것을 알게 되었다.

Unit 5

Answers

1. Fourteen countries participated (in the first World Cup).
2. ④   3. ④   4. ③

Word

federation 연합
association 협회, 단체
organization 조직체(단체, 협회 등), 기구
competition 경기, 시합
tournament 승자 진출전
hold 개최하다
celebrate 경축하다, 축하하다
independence 독립
host country 개최국
Jules Rimet Trophy 줄리메 컵 (FIFA 회장의 이름을 딴 상으로, 1930년부터 월드컵 우승 팀에게 주어짐)
celebrity 유명인사, 유명인
the English Channel 영국 해협
consecutive 연속적인

Review

A.

1. trick   2. pretend
3. complicated   4. technology

5. royal family
6. notorious
7. criminal
8. weigh
9. distance
10. autumn (= fall)
11. direction
12. fail to do
13. fog
14. be lost (= lose one's way)
15. thick
16. elbow
17. hold
18. celebrity
19. consecutive
20. celebrate

B.

1. 적어도
2. ~을 (…위에) 놓다, 겹치다
3. 글자 그대로, 정말로
4. 10년(간)
5. 우선, 먼저
6. ~에 위치해 있다
7. 거대한
8. 소유하다
9. 이동하다, 이주하다
10. 이동하는, 이주하는
11. 북반구
12. 세부사항
13. 길을 가르쳐 주다
14. 주소
15. 가망 있는, 유망한
16. 시각장애의, 장님의
17. 승자 진출전
18. 개최국
19. 독립
20. 경기, 시합, 경쟁

C.

1. ②
2. ③
3. ①

D.

1. 차 안에서 자고 있는 아기가 있다.
2. 그녀는 차가 두 대 있는데, 그 두 대는 Mercedes-Benz와 BMW이다.
3. Eating chocolate after meals is one of his habits.
4. The woman was sitting with a baby in her arms.

E.

1. ①
2. ①
3. ④
4. ②

F.

1. 거리를 유지하다
2. 잠시 기다리다
3. 잘못된 방향으로 가다

CHAPTER 10

Preview

Word • Mini Quiz

1. gifts
2. opinion
3. annoyed
4. advance
5. shock
6. risk
7. essentials
8. notice
9. tell
10. dismay

Grammar • Mini Quiz

1. ② glass → glasses
2. ④ will see → saw
3. much

Unit 1

Answers

1. ④
2. ④

Word

behavior 행동
behave 행동하다
false 잘못된, 틀린
belief 믿음, 확신
matador 투우사
sword 검, 칼
annoy 화나게 하다, 짜증나게 하다
tell 구별하다
instead 대신에
movement 움직임
no matter what ~이든 상관없이

Drill 1 • Grammar

1. 우리는 세상을 더 좋게 만들 수 있다.

2. 음식 냄새가 우리를 배고프게 만들었다.

3. Her smile always makes me happy.

Drill 2 • Translation

1. 당신은 동물들이 어떤 특정한 방법으로 행동하는 이유를 때로는 쉽게 이해하지 못할 수도 있다.

2. 하지만 그것이 동물의 행동에 대한 새로운 점을 배우는 것에 훨씬 더 흥미를 더해 준다.

3. 많은 사람들은 빨간색이 소를 화나게 만든다고 믿는다.

Unit 2

Answers

1. ③   2. ②

Word

advance 미리 하는

notice 통보, 예고

realize 깨닫다

announce 알리다

lecture 강의

panic 공포, 공황(상태)

screw 망치다, 틀리다

valuable 값진, 귀중한

assumption (증거 없이) 사실이라고 생각함, 가정

Drill 1 • Grammar

1. 시체는 피라미드 안에서 훨씬 더 오래 계속해서 신선하다.

2. 학생들은 캠프를 갈 때 날씨가 계속해서 맑기를 희망했다.

3. My nose keeps running.

Drill 2 • Translation

1. 모두들 Wilson 선생님이 결코 사전에 예고 없이 시험을 치르지 않을 선생님이라고 생각했다.

2. 모든 학생들이 앉았을 때, Wilson 선생님은 강의 전에 시험을 볼 것이라고 말씀하셨다.

3. 내가 오늘 배운 두 가지 값진 교훈은 다른 사람에 대해 함부로 추측하지 말아야 한다는 것과 항상 준비가 되어 있어야 한다는 것이다.

Unit 3

Answers

1. ②   2. ④

Word

country road 시골길

hare (야생) 산토끼

as soon as ~하자마자

thumping sound 쾅(우당탕)하는 소리

dismay 당황, 불안감

content 내용물

get puzzled 당황하다, 난처해하다

proudly 자랑스럽게

label 라벨, 꼬리표

restore 소생시키다, 회복시키다

Drill 1 • Grammar

1. 그는 아들이 한 명 있었는데, 그런데 그 아들이 훌륭한 변호사가 되었다.

2. 나는 나의 여자 친구를 사랑한다, 그런데(왜냐하면) 그 여자 친구는 항상 나에게 돈을 준다.

3. I passed the ball to Dennis, who missed it.

Drill 2 • Translation

1. 한 남자와 그의 어린 아들이 시골길을 따라 운전하고 있었다.

2. 어린 아들이 옆 좌석에 앉아 있었는데 차 밖으로 나와 죽은 산토끼를 보았다.

3. 남자가 당황하여 아들에게 물었다. "아들아, 뭐하는 거니?"

4. 그 통의 라벨에는 "헤어스프레이. 생기 없는 머리카락을 다시 살려 드립니다."라고 쓰여 있었다.

Unit 4

Answers

1. ①   2. ③

Word

adult 성인, 어른

Eskimo 에스키모인

igloo 이글루(에스키모인의 집)

polar bear 북극곰

challenging 도전적인

consider 간주하다

proof 증거

necessary 필요한, 없어서는 안 될

Drill 1 • Grammar

1. 열대우림은 지구 육지의 14%를 차지하고 있었다. 그러나 지금은 6% 이하밖에 안 된다.
2. 할로윈 때마다 아버지는 호박을 조각했고, 스파이더맨처럼 옷을 입곤 했었다.
3. I used to be crazy about American pop singers.

Drill 2 • Translation

1. 미국 사람들은 소년이 18세가 되면 성인이 된다고 생각하는데, 에스키모인들은 다르게 생각한다.
2. 그들 중 몇몇은 키가 9피트 이상이고 무게가 1,300파운드 이상 나간다.
3. 그러므로 혼자 힘으로 북극곰을 죽이는 것은 매우 도전적이고 위험하다.

Unit 5

Answers

1. ③   2. ⑤   3. ④   4. ④

Word

be good at ~을 잘하다
private 사설의
Arabic 아라비아 말의
anxious 불안한, 걱정하는
refuse 거부(거절)하다
insist 주장하다
the gifted 영재들
talent 재능, 소질
agree 동의하다

Review

A.

1. behavior	2. false
3. belief	4. sword
5. lecture	6. valuable
7. thought	8. panic
9. hare	10. dismay
11. proudly	12. label
13. adult	14. bravery
15. polar bear	16. proof
17. be good at	18. refuse

19. agree   20. anxious

B

1. 투우사	2. 구별하다
3. 대신에	4. 행동하다
5. 알리다	6. 망치다, 틀리다
7. 깨닫다	8. 가정, 가설
9. 만족한, 흡족한	10. 당황하다, 난처해하다
11. 쿵(우당탕)하는 소리	12. 소생시키다
13. 도전적인	14. 이글루(에스키모인 집)
15. 기회	16. 무게가 나가다
17. 주장하다	18. 재능, 재주
19. 재능, 소질	20. 아라비아 말의

C.

1. ①   2. ④   3. ②

D.

1. 이 음악은 나를 졸립게 만든다.
2. 그녀는 두 아들이 있다, 그런데 두 아들은 쌍둥이다.
3. The salad will stay fresh until he comes home.
4. I used to go for a walk to the park in the evening.

E.

1. ①   2. ②   3. ②   4. ③

F.

1. incorrect	2. irritate
3. announcement	4. essential

CHAPTER 11

Preview

Word • Mini Quiz

1. individual	2. alternative
3. mode	4. creature
5. review	6. suitable
7. predict	8. analyze
9. award	10. purposes

Grammar • Mini Quiz

1. ②
2. ③ which → where
3. were discovered

Unit 1

Answers

1. ①   2. ①

Word

scarcity 부족함, 희소성
involve 의미하다, 포함하다
individual 개인
tradeoff 거래, 교환
necessitate 필요케 하다, 수반하다
awareness 지각, 인지, 인식
consequence 결과, 중요성
alternative 양자택일
prohibit 금지하다
purchase 구매(하다)
impose 강요하다
merriment 즐거움

Drill 1 • Grammar

1. 나는 그녀에게 공공장소에서 담배 피지 말라고 경고했다.
2. 정부는 매년 사람들에게 세금을 지불하라고 강요했다.
3. The doctor warned my father to quit smoking.

Drill 2 • Translation

1. 희소성이 있다면, 개인들과 사회는 선택을 해야만 한다.
2. 이러한 선택은 '거래'를 포함하고, 그러한 거래 결과에 대한 인식을 필요로 한다.

3. 예를 들면, 당신이 쓸 돈 25달러를 가지고 있고, 양자택일권을 교과서 또는 데이트로 좁혔다고 가정하자.

Unit 2

Answers

1. ①   2. ③

Word

household 가구, 가계
consumer behavior 소비자 행동 양식
way 방법, 방식
seek 찾다, 구하다
content 만족한
mode 방식, 방법

Drill 1 • Grammar

1. 그는 빗소리를 들으면서 오랫동안 앉아 있었다.
2. Kelly는 아침식사를 하면서 신문을 읽었다.
3. My brother studied, listening to the MP3 player.

Drill 2 • Translation

1. 그들은 다른 즐거움을 추구하며, 다른 방식으로 돈을 소비한다.
2. 어떤 여자는 침실에 카펫을 깔기 위해 가계자금을 절약할 수도 있고, 반면에 그녀의 이웃은 중고차를 사기 위해 자금을 절약할 수도 있다.
3. 다른 유형의 소비자 행위, 즉 돈을 쓰는 다른 방식은 우리가 놀랄 일이 아니다.
4. 그러한 차이점이 삶을 재미있게 만든다는 것을 우리는 성장하며 믿게 됐다.

Unit 3

Answers

1. ④   2. (1) True   (2) False   (3) False

Word

wasp 말벌
buzz 윙윙 거리다

cricket 귀뚜라미
grasshopper 메뚜기
snap 탁(툭) 치다
belong （있어야 할[마땅한] 장소에) 있다
belly 배, 복부
creature 생물, 동물
evolution 진화
vocal sac 울음 주머니
inflate 부풀리다, 팽창시키다
nostril 콧구멍
deflate 공기를 빼다

Drill 1 • Grammar

1. 내가 어제 구입한 책들은 아주 재미있었다.
2. Jason이 내가 끼고 있는 이 반지를 사 주었다.
3. Is this the book (which) you were looking for the other day?

Drill 2 • Translation

1. 반면에 귀뚜라미와 메뚜기는 다리를 비비거나 날개를 툭툭 침으로써 소리를 낸다.
2. 곤충들이 이러한 소리를 내는 이유는 의사소통하기 위해서이다.
3. 종종 곤충의 귀는 그것들이 있어야 할 곳에 없는 것처럼 보인다.

Unit 4

Answers

1. ①   2. ③

Word

meteorologist 기상학자
analyze 분석하다
predict 예상하다
be affected by ～에 의해 영향을 받다
crop 농작물
ruin 망쳐놓다, 파괴하다
harvest season 수확 기간
go skiing 스키 타러 가다

Drill 1 • Grammar

1. 만약 네가 좋은 성적을 받길 원한다면, 너는 열심히 공부해야 한다.
2. 그들은 그들의 회사에서 일하게 되어 행복함에 틀림없다.
3. You must wear the uniform when you come to school.

Drill 2 • Translation

1. 날씨를 연구하는 과학자인 기상학자들은 공기, 바람, 비 등을 분석하고 가까운 미래의 날씨를 예측한다.
2. 품질이 좋은 농작물을 기르기 위해서 농부들은 햇빛과 충분한 양의 비가 필요하다.
3. 만약 아직 수확기가 되지 않았다면 이른 서리는 농작물 전부를 망칠 수 있다.
4. 짙은 안개는 자동차와 배의 사고를 일으킬 수 있다.

Unit 5

Answers

1. ③
2. It was invented for peaceful purposes but later it was used as a weapon in war.
3. ⑤   4. ④

Word

Nobel Prize 노벨상
Stockholm 스톡홀름(스웨덴의 수도)
award （상 등을) 수여하다, 상
field 분야, 영역
chemistry 화학
physics 물리학
physiology 생리학
economics 경제학
literature 문학, 문예
occasionally 때때로, 가끔
distinguished 뛰어난, 유명한
consist of ～로 이루어져 있다
certificate 증명서
establish 설립하다, 만들다
explosive 폭발물
purpose 목적, 의도
misuse 악용(하다)
sadden 슬프게 하다
income 수입
fortune 재산
be divided into ～로 나뉘다

Review

A.

1. awareness   2. impose

3. prohibit
4. merriment
5. household
6. be content with
7. way
8. seek
9. cricket
10. belong
11. evolution
12. belly
13. ruin
14. predict
15. analyze
16. crop
17. physics
18. certificate
19. purpose
20. establish

B.

1. 필요로 하다, 수반하다
2. 교환, 거래
3. 결과, 중요성
4. 부족함, 희소성
5. 소비자 행동 양식
6. 방식, 방법
7. 양탄자를 깔다, 카펫
8. 작은 별장
9. 생물, 동물
10. 울음 주머니
11. 콧구멍
12. 메뚜기
13. ~에 의해 영향을 받다
14. 수확 기간(시즌)
15. 기상학자
16. 항공기
17. 경제학
18. 뛰어난, 유명한
19. 약용(하다), 오용(하다)
20. 재산

C.

1. ①
2. ④
3. ③

D.

1. 전자사전은 내가 영어를 쉽게 공부할 수 있게 해 준다.
2. 여기 밖에 앉아 뭐하고 있어요?
3. Let's meet in front of the building which Alex talked about.
4. You must listen to your mom.

E.

1. ②
2. ③
3. ④
4. ②

F.

1. occasionally
2. misuse
3. ruin

CHAPTER 12

Preview

Word • Mini Quiz

1. Behave
2. transfer
3. granted
4. convinced
5. confident
6. anxious
7. expenses
8. outstanding
9. function
10. solar

Grammar • Mini Quiz

1. ② who → whose
2. ①
3. ④

Unit 1

Answers

1. ②

2. (d) since it had become a part
  → since it became a part

Word

invention 발명(품)
product 제품, 상품
influence 영향을 미치다
modern society 현대사회
behave 행동하다
transfer 옮기다, 전하다
means 방법
come up with 생각해내다, ~을 제안하다
electronically 전자적으로
transmit 전달(송신)하다
eventually 드디어, 마침내
grant 승인하다, 허가하다
patent 특허(권)

Drill 1 • Grammar

1. Smith씨는 시애틀로 이사 가기 전에 시카고에서 6년 동안 살았다.
2. 한 이상한 여자가 방안으로 걸어 들어왔다. 나는 그 여자를 전에 한 번도 본 적이 없었다.
3. 숙제를 끝내고 나서 나는 저녁을 먹으러 나갔다.
4. When I arrived at the party last night, Christine had already gone home.

Drill 2 • Translation

1. 브로드웨이 쇼 "Farnsworth Invention"은 성이 Farnsworth인 한 소년과 1930년에 그가 발명한 것에 관한 것이다.
2. 이것은 사람들의 생활의 일부가 된 이후로 단지 약 70년밖에 되지 않았지만 오늘날 이것이 없는 날을 상상하는 것은 불가능하다.
3. 1922년까지 과학자들은 그림을 소리와 함께 전달하는 방법을 찾으려고 시도했지만 그들은 가능한 방법을 생각해낼 수 없었다.

Unit 2

Answers

1. ④   2. ②

Word

audience 관중, 관객
imagine 상상하다, 생각하다
extremely 대단히, 지극히
self-conscious 자의식이 강한
unattractive 예쁘지 않은, 못생긴
convince 설득하다
pay attention to ~에 신경 쓰다
behavior 행동, 행위

Drill 1 • Grammar

1. 가난한 나는 차를 살 여유가 없다.
2. 컴퓨터로 인터넷 검색을 한(하면), 당신은 많은 정보를 얻을 것입니다.
3. Walking in the park, I happened to meet her.

Drill 2 • Translation

1. 다른 사람들이 그의 코에 전혀 신경 쓰지 않는다고 설득하는 것은 불가능하다.
2. 또한, 십대 소녀들이 친구들과 얘기를 할 때면, 그들은 과장되게 표현하거나 크게 웃고 얘기하며, 가상의 청중들이 있는 것처럼 행동한다.
3. 십대들의 행동은 다른 사람들이 자신들을 지켜보기에는 그들의 삶이 너무 바쁘다는 것을 깨달으면서 변하게 된다.

Unit 3

Answers

1. ⑤   2. ②

Word

indicate 나타내다, 보이다
associate 관련되다
college entrance exam 대학입학시험
be related to ~와 관련이 있다
psychological 심리적인
self-identity 자아 동일성
adolescent 청소년기의
mental disorder 정신 장애
anxious 걱정하는, 염려하는
assure 보장하다, 보증하다
sensitive 민감한, 예민한
pressure 압박(감)
excessive 지나친, 과도한
burdensome (견딜 수 없이) 부담이 되는

Drill 1 • Grammar

1. 교통사고로 다친(부상당한) 그 사람은 병원으로 보내졌다.
2. 나는 Bob이라고 불리는(이름 붙여진) 잘생긴 이탈리아 사람을 만났다.
3. The terrorist arrested by the police officer last week died in jail.

Drill 2 • Translation

1. 몇몇의 연구 결과는 대학입학시험과 관련된 스트레스가 심리적인 발달과 청소년기의 자아 동일성에 부정적으로 관련이 있고 심각한 경우에는 정신 장애의 위험을 증가시킬 수도 있다는 것을 보여 준다.
2. 한국 학생들이 시험에 대해 걱정하고 스트레스를 받는 많은 이유가 있다.
3. 많은 한국 사람들은 고등교육이 인생에서 성공을 보장해 준다고 생각한다.

Unit 4

Answers

1. ④   2. ④

Word

go abroad 외국에 나가다
foreign language 외국어
a number of 많은 (=many)

consider 고려하다
make a decision 결정하다
setting 환경
opportunity 기회
disadvantage 단점
cost 비용
outstanding 눈에 띄는
tuition 수업료

Drill 1 • Grammar

1. 내일 비가 온다면, 우리는 소풍을 가지 않을 것이다.
2. 죄송하지만, 예약을 하지 않으면 의사를 만날 수 없습니다.
3. The boss will be angry if Jason arrives at work late again.

Drill 2 • Translation

1. 만일 당신이 외국어를 공부하기 위해 해외에 가기를 원한다면 결정을 내리기 전에 고려해야 할 많은 것들이 있다.
2. 우선 당신은 어떤 나라로 가기를 원하는지 결정해야 한다.
3. 게다가 당신은 전 세계로부터 온 사람들을 만날 수 있고 그래서 하루 24시간 영어를 말하는 환경에 있게 된다.
4. 또한 당신은 다른 문화에 대해 배울 기회도 가질 수 있다.

Unit 5

Answers

1. ③   2. ③   3. ④

Word

greenhouse effect （지구 대기의）온실 효과
retain 계속 유지하다
continuously 끊임없이
outer space （대기권 밖의）우주(공간)
atmosphere 대기
escape 빠져나가다, 새나가다
average temperature 평균 기온
function 기능, 작용
refer to （～라고）말하다, 부르다
solar radiation 복사열
temperature 온도
radiate （빛, 열등을）방출하다, 퍼져 나가다
trap 막다, 붙잡다
elucidation 설명

Review

A.

1. invention	2. means
3. patent	4. product
5. audience	6. convince
7. behavior	8. pay attention to
9. research	10. assure
11. pressure	12. burdensome
13. opportunity	14. tuition
15. disadvantage	16. outstanding
17. retain	18. trap
19. atmosphere	20. temperature

B.

1. 옮기다, 전하다	2. 전달하다, 송신하다
3. 승인하다, 허가하다	4. 영향을 미치다
5. 예쁘지 않은, 못생긴	6. 대단히, 지극히
7. 자의식이 강한	8. 상상하다
9. ～와 관련되다	10. 정신 장애
11. 나타내다, 보이다	12. ～와 관련이 있다
13. 결정하다	14. 환경
15. 많은	16. 외국어
17. 기능, 작용	18. 복사열
19. 우주(공간)	20. 빠져나가다, 새나가다

C.

1. ③   2. ④   3. ①

D.

1. 오른쪽으로 돌면 너는 그 집을 찾을 것이다.
2. 그는 프랑스에서 막 돌아온 예술가이다.
3. Until yesterday, I had never heard about the rumor.
4. If you jog regularly, you will lose some weight.

E.

1. ③   2. ④   3. ②   4. ②

F.

1. products	2. means
3. sensitive	4. pressure
5. cost	6. function

CHAPTER 13

Preview

Word • Mini Quiz

1. force
2. react
3. conduct
4. potential
5. concern
6. factor
7. area
8. tradition
9. exist
10. trick

Grammar • Mini Quiz

1. ④ see → saw 2. ② 3. ④

Unit 1

Answers

1. ④
2. something irritates the nasal nerve

Word

sneeze 재채기하다
explosion of air 공기의 폭발 (파열)
lung 폐
irritate 자극하다
nasal nerve 코의 신경
force 억지로 밀어내다
in addition 게다가
germ 세균
courteous 예의 바른
hygienic 위생적인
spittle 침

Drill 1 • Grammar

1. 사람들은 당신을 당신의 행동에 의해서 뿐만 아니라 당신의 말에 의해서도 판단한다는 것을 명심해라.
2. 너뿐만 아니라 그녀도 회의에 참석해야 한다.
3. She as well as her husband can speak Spanish.
   〈as well as 이용〉
   Not only her husband but (also) she can speak Spanish. 〈not only, but (also) 이용〉

Drill 2 • Translation

1. 재채기는 폐에서 공기가 파열하면서 일어나는 것이다.
2. 어떤 것이 코 신경을 자극하게 되면, 두뇌에서 강제로 폐에 있는 공기를 코나 입을 통해 배출하라는 신호를 보내게 된다.
3. 그리고 여러분이 재채기하는 동안 폐는 공기를 흡수할 수 없게 되고 심장박동은 멈추게 된다.
4. 그래서 재채기하는 동안 손수건으로 입을 가리는 것이 위생적일 뿐만 아니라 예의바른 일이다.

Unit 2

Answers

1. ③
2. (d) touched plants → touching plants

Word

react 반응하다
environmental pressure 환경적 압력
in response to 명사 ~에 대응하여, 대답하여
rainfall 강우량
conduct 수행하다
be brought about ~이 야기되다
gene 유전자
actuation 발동 작용
finding 발견
indicate 지시하다, 나타내다
stimulation 자극
potential 잠재적인, 잠재력

Drill 1 • Grammar

1. 당신 앞에 있는 탁자에 손목시계를 놓거나 방 뒤에 걸려 있는 시계에 눈을 고정시키시오.
2. 그 구조대는 11시에 숲 속에서 길 잃은 등반객들을 찾아냈다.
3. The family in the next house wants to move out.

Drill 2 • Translation

1. 식물은 바람, 비, 그리고 심지어 인간의 손길과 같은 환경적 압력에 반응하는 것으로 알려져 있다.
2. 예를 들어 해안의 나무들은 강한 바람과 폭우에 반응하여 점점 작아지고 강해진다.
3. 스탠포드 대학에서 행해진 실험연구에서 하루에 두 번 식물을 만짐으

로써 식물 성장 형태에 같은 변화가 일어났다.

4. 연구원들은 또한 이 성장 변화가 유전자 발동 작용에서 기인한다는 것을 발견하였다.

Unit 3

Answers

1. ②   2. ⑤

Word

prefer A to B B보다 A를 좋아(선호)하다
curly 곱슬곱슬한
iron 다리미
a variety of 많은, 여러 가지
concern 관심
outlaw 금지하다, 비합법화하다
issue an order 명령을 내리다
trim 다듬다, 정돈하다
masculine 사내다운
ban 금지하다
crowning glory 최고의 미관, 백미
appearance 외모, 외관
nevertheless 그럼에도 불구하고
craze 대유행, 대인기

Drill 1 • Grammar

1. 얼마 안가 그 배는 바다 밑바닥에 가라앉았다.
2. 얼마 안가 큰 권투선수는 작은 권투선수를 때려 눕혔다. 심판은 열을 세었고 게임은 끝났다.
3. It was not long before the rain stopped.

Drill 2 • Translation

1. 고대에는 사람들이 곧은 머리보다는 곱슬머리를 선호했다.
2. 대신, 그는 남자들이 짧은 머리를 할 것과 수염을 기르고 다듬을 것, 그리고 콧수염을 곱실거리게 하도록 명령하였다.
3. 하지만 얼마 안가 제임스 1세가 1603년에 왕이 되었을 때 남자들은 다시 긴 머리 스타일을 가질 수 있도록 허용되었다.
4. 19세기에, 남자들은 짧은 머리가 긴 머리보다 더 남성적이라고 생각하기 시작했다.

Unit 4

Answers

1. ④   2. ③

Word

sense of smell 후각
various 다양한
area 분야
particular 특별한
manufacturer 제조업자(업체)
household goods 가정용품
aroma (달콤한) 향기
take advantage of ~을 이용하다
right 적절한
consumer 소비자
perceive 인식하다, 지각하다
survey 조사
detergent 세(정)제
scent 향기, 냄새
factor 요인, 요소

Drill 1 • Grammar

1. 언어는 사람들이 다른 사람과 의사소통하는 수단이다.
2. 신문은 일반 사람들이 세상에 대한 지식을 얻는 원천이다.
3. 그 교수님은 내가 관심이 있는 주제에 관해 강의했다.
4. This is the school from which I graduated.

Drill 2 • Translation

1. 냄새가 특별한 성과를 보이고 있는 한 분야는 마케팅이다.
2. 한 동안 제조업자들은 더 많은 가정용품들을 팔기 위해 우리의 후각을 이용해 왔다.
3. 그들은 향수가 소비자들이 브랜드를 인지하는 데 영향을 미친다고 믿기 때문에 알맞은 향기를 찾기 위해 수백만 달러를 쓴다.

Unit 5

Answers

1. ②   2. ③   3. ⑤   4. ③

Word

April Fools' Day 만우절
absurd 터무니없는, 어리석은
errand (잔)심부름
origin 기원

mock 가짜의
exist 존재하다
be passed 퍼지다, 전해지다
common 공통의, 흔한, 잘 알려진

Review

A.

1. sneeze
2. irritate
3. germ
4. courteous
5. react
6. rainfall
7. gene
8. stimulation
9. ancient
10. concern
11. masculine
12. appearance
13. manufacturer
14. various
15. survey
16. scent
17. absurd
18. origin
19. exist
20. order

B.

1. 위생적인
2. 코의 신경
3. 억지로 밀어내다
4. 폐

5. 수행하다
6. 발견
7. 잠재적인, 잠재력
8. 지시하다, 나타내다
9. 금지하다, 불법화하다
10. 다듬다, 정돈하다
11. 명령을 내리다
12. 그럼에도 불구하고
13. 특별한
14. 가정용품
15. 요인, 요소
16. ~을 이용하다
17. 가짜의
18. 퍼지다
19. 공통의, 흔한
20. (잔)심부름

C.

1. ②
2. ①
3. ④
4. ③

D.

1. 이 방에 있는 사람이 여러분의 사장님입니다.
2. 얼마 지나서야 그는 사실을 깨달을 것이다.
3. She as well as he ate a lot.
4. This is one of the music genres in which I am interested.

E.

1. ③
2. ①
3. ②
4. ②

F.

1. ③
2. ④
3. ②
4. ④

the difference

더 디퍼런스

더 좋은 책을 만들기 위한 남다른 열정